# Race the Sun

## Down the Road in Oklahoma

**Jay C. Grelen**

*december 2000*

*To Dorothy DeBock —*

*Happy trails —*

*Jay C. Grelen*

*John 3:16*

Illustration by B.W. Sandli

D0898771

Bigfoot Books
P.O. Box 30165
Coffee Creek Station
Edmond, Oklahoma 73003

Race the Sun: Down the Road in Oklahoma By Jay C. Grelen. ©2000 by Bigfoot Books.
Cover photos ©2000 by Jay C. Grelen.
Printed by Heritage Press in El Reno, Oklahoma.
Perfect binding by Printers Bindery of Oklahoma City. No part of this book
may be used or reproduced in any manner whatsoever without written
permission except for brief quotations used in articles and reviews.

The work in this book originally appeared between July 1999 and March 2000
in The Daily Oklahoman and The Sunday Oklahoman, a copyrighted newspaper
publication of The Oklahoma Publishing Company in Oklahoma City, Oklahoma.
Used with permission, which Bigfoot Books gratefully acknowledges.

Book cover layout by Chris Schoelen, artist, The Daily Oklahoman.

Title page illustration by Billy Sandlin, art director, The Daily Oklahoman.
The illustration originally appeared with Jay Grelen's "Down the Road"
columns in The Daily Oklahoman

Back page illustration by Glen Zimmer (aka Zen Glimmer) of Perry, Oklahoma.

First Edition, July 2000

ISBN 0-9702362-0-4

Cover photographs: The pickup truck in the photographs is a 1953 Chevrolet
with a five-window deluxe cab. The author drove the truck, provided by the
Oklahoma Publishing Company, for much of his tour of Oklahoma's seventy-seven
counties. The photograph on the front cover is a composite of two photographs,
which were taken at the same place on different days. The building in the back-
cover photograph is the Rock Cafe, which stands on the south side of Route 66
in Stroud, Oklahoma. The billboard on the back cover - including the photograph
of the author - was produced for The Oklahoma Publishing Company by
Ackerman McQueen.

# For ...

My parents, Harold and Janie
Grelen, who taught me
the language.

Marie Shipp, my journalism
teacher at Pineville High, who
saw something in the shaggy-
haired kid worth salvaging.

Wiley Hilburn, Jim Butler and
Lynn Stewart, editors and friends,
who taught me to write
and set my course
in newspapers.

The people of Oklahoma
who trusted me
to write their stories.

Stan Tiner,
who turned me
loose to write.

*And especially ...*
... My wife Cindi, who for more
than half of my life
has loved me, studied me, taught
me, read my stories,
prayed for me,
and still turns me
loose to dream.

# Road Map

# Love Letters To Oklahoma

NOT many people make the Grand Tour of Oklahoma like Jay Grelen and Frank and I have. You can live here for forty, fifty, even seventy-five years and never get to Buffalo out in the Panhandle, or Idabel down in McCurtain County. The far southwest escapes a lot of Oklahomans, and so do some of the counties up along the Kansas and Missouri borders. For most folks, if it's not right on the interstate, or fairly close to home, it's Way Out There.

That's hardly surprising. Oklahoma is a big place. With 69,903 square miles, we're larger than twelve European countries. Oklahoma is almost two-and-a-half times as big as Ireland, twice as large as Portugal or Hungary, about two-thirds the size of the entire United Kingdom. Eighteen American states are bigger, but only a few range as far from north to south or east to west. You could fit all of Maine, Massachusetts, New Hampshire, Rhode Island, Vermont and Connecticut inside our borders and still have room left over for a good rodeo and a cattle drive.

I went to all those places as First Lady of Oklahoma. You go places in the "first lady business" — lots of places, and I have loved it. I think Jay has, too.

Jay Grelen came to Oklahoma as a reporter and columnist. His self-appointed task was to explore, to interview, to listen — and to write about our state and its people. I suspect he was a little intimidated on those first excursions, but I also know he gloried in it. There's something adventurous about setting out for a new destination. Rolling out east, west, north or south around dawn, getting off the interstate onto one of those great tree-lined two-lane highways, you see the morning mist — that "bright golden haze on the meadow" — slowly lifting over cattle in the fields. Off on the horizon an oil pumper bobs up and down like a slow-moving bird. The first

thing you see of most Oklahoma towns is the grain
elevator, or if it's night, the red glow of the radio
station antenna. Coming into town, there's a highway
interchange, maybe a Wal-Mart, and always that wonderful
old café where the sign says "Family Style Cookin,'" and
it means it. Drop an experienced Oklahoma sojourner into
any community, and you'll hear a good guess about where
you are: Over east, the main street architecture is stone
and old brick. Out west the houses all seem to have low
picket fences, and some of them are still white-washed.
Everywhere you go the biscuits and gravy and hospitality
are pure Oklahoma, and that's as good as it gets.

You can also tell a lot by the accents and the
smiles. Jay has been listening to those accents and
absorbing the smiles, and he's been taking notes on what
people have to say. That's really his mission, to get to
know the people and to help us know them too. These
columns all deal, one way or another, with Oklahomans.
There's one column from each of our seventy-seven far-
flung counties, plus a wonderfully moving account of one
of our state's saddest days, the memories recaptured from
long ago. They all have one thing in common — they are
about us. Fact is, we're an interesting group of folks,
all 3.3 million of us.

Jay has become Oklahoma's newest "King of the
Road," in the apt words of the late Roger Miller, another
Oklahoman who went places. One of Jay's first discoveries
was the most obvious one — this is an interesting state.
We all know the famous names that sprouted from our soil —
Will Rogers, Vince Gill, Tom Stafford, N. Scott Momaday,
Carl Albert. But Jay has also discovered Oklahomans who
may not be known at all outside their home communities,
but who are just as interesting as an astronaut or a
national leader. He's found places that fascinate; there
are little gems of historical museums and parks and
historic main streets and old pioneer homes scattered all
across our state. Jay now knows "the reason God made
Oklahoma." I suspect he thinks we're doin' fine!

Sometimes, Frank and I receive letters from people
who have visited Oklahoma, or from newcomers who have
recently moved here. They inevitably comment on the
terrific people who live here. Their letters use terms
like "such friendly people" and "I never felt so welcome."
They have discovered a unique and special place, filled
with unique and special people, and you have a feeling
that they don't write letters to every governor or first
lady in the country. We treasure those letters and answer

X

them all.

Jay Grelen has written seventy-seven letters to his adopted state, and I don't think it would be an exaggeration — or violate his reporter's obligations to detachment — to call them love letters.

We love you, too, Jay. And I suspect that after reading this book, a lot of Oklahomans are going to set out right behind you. We'll see you on the road!

Cathy Keating,
First Lady of Oklahoma

# In the beginning ...

FROM the moment I learned about Ernie Pyle, I wanted to do what he did — travel and write. Mamadee, my El Paso grandmother, introduced me to Pyle's work when I was sixteen. She gave me her copy of *Home Country*, a collection of Pyle's writing about his wanderings. The dream was born.

For nine months, I lived my "Ernie Pyle" dream. My first project after joining *The Daily Oklahoman* was to travel to every county in Oklahoma and write a column from each. My goal was to include in each column at least one fact or story that most Oklahomans didn't already know.

I set out for the Panhandle in June 1999 and finished in March 2000. *Race the Sun* contains all seventy-seven columns plus a few.

"Down the Road" appeared on the front page of *The Daily Oklahoman* three days a week. I chased stories with neither rhyme nor reason to my itinerary. So in that spirit, I offer the columns here in the same order in which they appeared in the newspaper.

As the first draft of history, daily newspaper stories aren't always as polished as we would like. I have, therefore, edited and rewritten in the hope that *Race the Sun* will be a worthy addition to Oklahoma's library. I don't pretend that this collection is anything more than it is: Stories about Oklahomans that one story lover picked up along his way.

One of the funniest stories I heard is about Charlie Soap, husband of Wilma Mankiller, the Cherokee chief. Seems Wilma wanted Charlie to say a few words to an audience. Charlie, whose first language is Cherokee, was reluctant. The Cherokee put their adjectives last instead of first, and he feared he would mangle his modifiers if he spoke in English. But Wilma prevailed — she is chief, after all — and Charlie prepared brief comments.

When Charlie finished his speech, the applause was warm and prolonged. But, in the words of the person who told me this story, Charlie "couldn't leave well enough alone." He spoke again. "I thank you," he said, "from the heart of my bottom."

So here is my book. And from the heart, ahem, from the bottom of my Ernie Pyle heart, I hope you learn some things about Oklahoma that you didn't already know.

Jay C. Grelen
Edmond, Oklahoma

# Race the Sun

Ihave an appointment with the sun, and I'm running late. It's my first week to work in Oklahoma, and my aim is to view my first Panhandle sunset from the highest spot in the state. By my reckoning, by leaving Oklahoma City at noon, I have time enough and change to keep my date, but the wheat trucks, a cheese factory and a wedge of coconut meringue pie between here and there slow my progress.

In Kingfisher, it's the City Cafe, where the burger is cheap and the coconut pie hits the table five minutes before the burger. Yes, I eat dessert (but only a bite) first.

In Watonga, I follow a load of wheat to the scales, where Austin Lafferty gives me a quick lesson in sampling the grain: He pokes around in the truck-load of wheat with a long, brass probe, which looks like a fancy curtain rod. Then he shows me the machine that measures moisture in the wheat and the conveyor belt that elevates it to the correct bin.

Austin gives me directions to the famed Watonga Cheese Factory. When I tell him I plan to watch the sunset at Black Mesa, he checks his watch and expresses doubt that I'll make it. At the cheese factory, I stand in line behind members of a classic car club who are taking shelter from the sun in the cool store. The cashier explains the difference between finished cheese and curd, and offers me a sample of curd. (Stick to the cheese.)

Then I drive down the road steady, riding into the sun and toward the first of the seventy-seven counties on my itinerary. I check the progress of the sun against the clock on the dash of my car. I think I can beat the sun.

Inever have been on State Highway 3, but it is familiar to me. I have been on many roads like it.

My grandparents started in Gainesville, Texas, and settled in El Paso. I grew up traveling the desert beyond Dallas.

I tell people I was raised Southern but that — with parents from Texas — I am genetically Texan. I have had the best of both worlds.

But it is more than Texas in my genes. I have learned that it is more accurate (and in Oklahoma, safer) to say that I am genetically Western.

Our Southern friends couldn't understand why in the name of Will Rogers we would move to a bleak place like Oklahoma. They don't understand because they haven't traveled the geographic and emotional roads I have.

They haven't played the windmill game. When I was a kid traveling west with my parents, we played the windmill game. The rules were simple. Every time one of us three kids saw a windmill, we kissed Mama.

Our friends didn't — when they were six years old — stand in Mamadee and Papadee's back yard in the wind at night and smell the air. All these years later, when I breathe in the dry air, tinged with sage or creosote bush, no matter where I am, I'm at home. This is my grandparents' West Texas, or this is Colorado, where we lived for five years and welcomed our first-born daughter.

I remember these things as I rush west toward Kenton, all the windows down and the wind beating at the maps and books and plastic bags in the back seat.

As I near Guymon, I concede defeat. I won't make Black Mesa in time. The sun has won.

I back off the gas and absorb the landscape, which in the light of the descending, victorious sun, has become a gallery of silhouettes and long shadows.

Dandelion puffs, lit from behind, look like frizzy light bulbs. Even as the sun drops out the right side of my windshield, the nearly full moon ascends over my left shoulder. Wheat bins are the skyscrapers of the range. For a moment, the sun is positioned right behind a silo, outlining it in orange. Low, slow-flying clouds sift the light into individual slanting beams, slides for the angels.

At 9:05 p.m., by the car's clock, the bottom edge of the sun has dipped below the horizon. By 9:08, it has disappeared, leaving a glow that appears to be the edge of Earth afire.

I miss my appointment by ninety miles, so instead I enjoy the phenomenon of seeing the lights of Boise City in the distance, a full fifteen miles before I arrive in town, where I'm further delayed by the burrito plate at LaMesa.

By midnight, I'm finally in Kenton, population hardly any and every one of them already in bed, including a cowboy named Rob asleep in his bedroll in the lot next to the Baptist preacher's house. Pastor Grice has reserved a good guest bed inside, but Rob prefers the wide open.

The wind is up and rattling the weeds as I explore the Kenton cemetery by moonlight. The grave stones cast dim shadows in the mystic light. The wind is another reason I love the West, and the harder and the more it blows, the more I like it.

Before my first week in Oklahoma is up, I will have made a dozen new friends and heard three times as many new stories. Everybody has at least one story worth telling, if you listen long enough.

I will have drunk my first real milk (straight from the udder) and my first real water (straight from a windmill pipe on a ranch) and real beef (straight from the hoof to the freezer to the grill to the plate, leaving the ranch only long enough for a visit to the butcher).

Before I return to my new home in the city, I will have stored up enough windmill kisses to stay busy a whole day. I will have seen two tornadoes forming north in Kansas and will have helped hold a motel door closed in seventy-mile-per-hour winds in Texhoma.

But late on this windy Saturday night, I can see from the cemetery down the road to the rest of Oklahoma, and I know only this: When I stand here and breathe in the air, something deep inside connects. I am standing in a brand-new place that is as old and familiar as my childhood and my grandparents, the wind tousling my hair as if it has been waiting all this time for me to return.

## Cimarron County: Kenton

OF the two dogs, Jane Apple thought Cowboy would be the one to remain by Clint's side. But here comes Clint's faithful border collie, alone and dripping river water.

An hour since anybody has seen the four-year-old, and his soaking-wet dog comes up out of the Cimarron River without the boy. Clinton Apple, Jane Apple's grandson, is not prone to wander; his absence, then, is all the more ominous. To say they are near panic would not be an overstatement.

Word of his disappearance spreads fast. Thirty-five miles east in Boise City, the news makes the rounds of the tables at LaMesa's Mexican restaurant. At Camp Billie Joe, an Alcoholics Anonymous meeting adjourns so the members can join the search. The guests at the Black Mesa Bed and Breakfast head to the river with their hosts.

By the time Cowboy returns, the area teems with people. Seventy-five, maybe a hundred rescuers already have fanned out to search along the river bank.

They search on horseback and on four-wheelers. Some who saw Cowboy return immediately fear the worst. But not Anje Apple, Clint's mother, the one whose two phone calls set in motion this massive hunt.

After her initial panic and prayers, she has steadied. She stays close to the house as friends and strangers scour the sage and cactus within view of the Black Mesa summit, the highest point in Oklahoma.

Upon Cowboy's return, Anje doesn't flinch. She believes her son is okay, if only she knew where to find him.

On many days, Anje and her husband, Leon, can find Clint in the saddle. He is cowboy through and through, Anje will tell you, and loves to ride. He never leaves the house unless he's wearing his cowboy boots — brown at the bottom with a green bootleg. Some days he wears a cowboy hat, some days a baseball cap.

But on the day before Father's Day 1999, when he is wearing a T-shirt and cap, they can't find him, in the saddle or anywhere else.

LEON Apple is spending the day before Father's Day working at Lake Etling, where he is maintenance chief. That's his job, but his love is running his cattle. The day after Father's Day is branding. On Monday, they'll herd the stock toward the house, build the fire, heat the Apple brand.

While Leon tends things at the lake, Anje is at home on the range, caring for their two sons, Clint and his younger brother, two-year-old Dillon. Anje is a city girl from Amarillo, who as a child dreamed of working as a ticket agent for American Airlines. Then she met Leon. Two months after their engagement, American offered her a job.

"I met Leon," she tells people, "and all that didn't seem to matter anymore."

She learned to rope and has dragged her share of calves to the branding fire. Now, however, Anje limits her ranch duties so that she can devote herself to her family. She makes the choice without apology. That is her place for now.

Mid-afternoon is Dillon's nap time, so Anje lies

down on the sofa to comfort him to sleep. Clint goes outside, but Anje doesn't worry. He knows to stay in the
yard. The Cimarron River is half a mile from the house,
and it's more a creek than a river this time of year.

After fifteen minutes, Dillon is still awake and
squirming. Anje steps outside to check on Clint. She can't
see him.

"Clint," she calls.

"CLINT!"

She strides toward the cattle-gap, calling for him,
when aggravation turns to fear. Clint, she realizes, isn't
here.

"That's when," she would say later, "my heart
sank."

She calls Leon at the lake, and while he starts
home, Anje puts Dillon in the pickup, and she rides the
river, checking water and land for Clint.

She returns home, calls the lake again and asks park
ranger Deon Perkins and his wife, Julie, to help look. She
telephones her mother-in-law, but Jane Apple is cleaning
the family's bed-and-breakfast and doesn't hear the telephone. Bob, Anje's father-in-law, is entertaining a group
of inner-city kids from Oklahoma City on the ranch for the
day. So Anje places one more call, the call that sets off
a massive and immediate search.

Anje Apple calls Kenton Mercantile, the news, infor-
mation and gathering center in this tiny Panhandle town,
the only town in Oklahoma that is in the Mountain Time
Zone. Allan Griggs, who owns the store, isn't there, but
Marcia Gary, who really runs the place anyway, answers
Anje's call.

Within minutes, Marcia finds Allan, who goes to the
Apples' with Joe Bud Layton. Marcia dashes to the Hitching
Post to tell Jane Apple. By the time Marcia finishes her
telephone calls, everyone from Cimarron County Sheriff
Kenny Miller to the rescue crew from Boise City to the
sheriff from Baca County, Colorado, is en route. Someone
calls Bob Apple up on the ranch.

Lee Ross arrives on horseback. Members of the Keyes
Fire Department, fifty miles away, also are on the way.

As the searchers spread out, a storm is making to
the west. Jane Apple is confident yet numb. Two different
women pull Anje aside for prayer. She, too, is confident.
"All right, Lord," she prays, "I know he's all right, but
I want him now."

Three minutes later, they tell her the news.

UNTIL this moment, the search has been a frantic exercise of hither and yon. Sheriff Miller decides the volunteers had best regroup and organize. The call goes out over the radio that everyone should report back to the Apple home for instructions.

Monty Joe Roberts, aboard his four-wheeler, runs up on Ranger Perkins.

"What's the plan?" Monty asks.

"Sheriff wants us to regroup," Deon says.

Cows on the other side of the river catch Monty's eye, and he motors across the shallow Cimarron. And there he finds the missing cowkid. Clint, wet from the waist down, looks at Monty with a big grin. Pepper, the Apples' blue-heeler/border collie mix, is right beside him.

"Whatcha doing, Clint?"

"I'm driving some cows for Dad," says the four-year-old cowpoke.

"Well," Monty says, "your mama wants to see you."

Clint, simply driving the cows to the house for Monday's branding, is oblivious to the trauma he has triggered. He jumps aboard Monty Joe's four-wheeler for yet another adventure.

Back at the house, a radio crackles with the news that someone has found Clint. Leon and Anje jump in a truck and meet Monty Joe halfway across their pasture. There's Clint, grinning wide as the sky above him. Anje and Leon cover him in hugs and kisses, Anje hardly able to talk for her tears of joy.

ANJE Apple told me this story a month after it happened. She knew help would come, she said, but the experience reaffirmed her faith that in time of crisis, her far-flung neighbors are not bound by city limits or police jurisdictions or even state lines. She needed her neighbors, and they came. Even as Monty Joe found Clint, a Cimarron County pilot was cranking up his small airplane to join the search.

Allan Griggs, who owns the Mercantile, says that when he returned to the Apples' home, he saw his first traffic jam in the wide open. "Even after they knew he was all right, people still came," Anje says. "I really live in a good community. Everybody pulls together."

Jane Apple, whose in-laws have ranched here for generations, was overwhelmed at the spontaneous rescue effort. "This is what needs to make the news," she says. "This kind of spirit can be contagious. There are not words to say how moving that was."

ಬಂಧ   ಬಂಧ   ಬಂಧ

**H**IS dog-leg right wrist is not the first thing you notice about Monty Joe Roberts, the man who found young Clint Apple. If you weren't looking for Monty Joe, in fact, you might not notice him at all. He's tall. Doesn't say much. Here in No Man's Land, he blends into the cholla, dust, cottonwoods and barbed wire strung along crooked posts made of juniper. His handlebar mustache makes a complete loop on the left, a loop-and-a-half on the right. His cowboy hat — a "Jesus First" pin stuck on the front — covers a head gone slick on the top and cropped skin-tight everywhere else.

His arthritic-looking wrist doesn't come into the conversation until I'm standing atop the platform of one of the windmills on Monty's 7,500 acres. Monty looks up at me and says: "That's about thirty foot. That could be fatal. Almost killed me once."

**I**F anybody knows windmills, it's Monty Joe Roberts. He has been climbing them for most of his sixty-one years. He has built a few himself, and since he was forty-one, he has repaired windmills all over the county.

He built a windmill right outside the back door of his house, which stands east of Kenton proper.

Monty Joe and his wife, Vicki, are ranchers. But with the uncertainty inherent in ranching, they have worked other jobs to support their vocation. Monty grades roads ten hours a day in Cimarron County. For the last eighteen years, Vicki has delivered the U.S. mail from her pickup.

And for a few years now, the Roberts have run the Black Mesa Bed and Breakfast. Many of their guests come to see Black Mesa, which — with a summit of 4,793 feet — is the highest point in Oklahoma. Kenton, with Allan Griggs' Mercantile, three churches and one pay telephone, is the western-most county in the state and the only county in the United States that shares borders with four states — Texas, New Mexico, Colorado and Kansas.

Monty was born to ranching in this place. His mother's family homesteaded land here in 1917. His parents, both eighty-eight when I met them, still live on a homestead they bought in the 1940s.

Vicki, who stands six feet tall, is a rancher by marriage, a city girl transplanted to Oklahoma from Lubbock, Texas. Her parents originally are from Boise City, thirty miles east of Kenton. Her father owned a soda shop called the Oasis, and that is where Vicki's father met her mother. They moved to Texas to raise their family.

Vicki has milked cows, birthed their calves and

helped Monty Joe repair windmills. And she nursed him back to life fifteen years ago when a windmill repair job nearly killed him.

IN No Man's Land, windmills aren't simply romantic remnants of the cowboy days. "Windmills are still the cheapest way to pump water," Monty Joe says. "We have a lot of wind. The windmill is still a necessity of life for the cow man."

So when the rancher called for Monty's help fifteen years ago, he didn't hesitate to travel east toward Boise City to fix the windmill.   The call came a month into the calving season, when Monty Joe crawls out of bed every three hours to keep a watch on his laboring cows.

He was exhausted that afternoon as he began the repair job with the help of the rancher's fourteen-year-old son. To fix it, Monty had to pull the pump, which required pulleys and cable at the top of the windmill.

Monty never felt it coming. He passed out with exhaustion and fell backwards off the ladder. "I went to sleep," he says. "I woke up hurting."

He fell from the windmill onto a pile of concrete, lumber and sheep manure. The back of his head hit a cedar stob and a three-inch splinter sliced into his scalp. "It was," he says, "as big around as your finger."

He broke his back, and when his rescuers lifted his right arm, his hand flopped backwards. His wrist was broken in two, bones sticking out of his skin. Doctors thought they would have to amputate it because the manure had so fouled the wound.

Monty Joe spent eighteen days in the hospital at Amarillo. Vicki never left his side.

SO I'm standing atop one of Monty Joe's ten windmills, and he's talking about near-fatal falls, and you can bet I am careful when I climb down his windmill. That night, after we ate beef stroganoff that once had wandered their ranch, Monty Joe and Vicki recounted the story of how Monty's wrist came to be so crooked.

"I still don't know why that happened," he says. "I still don't know all the plan. But things happen to people sometimes to get their attention. God just give me the body to do so much. I was just trying to help people out. But I was too busy. Life gets too busy. You just leave God out. Now I start my days, 'Good morning, Lord. What we going to do today?'"

# Texas County: Hooker

SAM Toole's stare is unflinching. His eyes warn you not to cross that line, and he won't have to tell many people twice. Don't let his appearance lull you.

He doesn't look like a gunslinger who was so fast that Wyatt Earp wouldn't draw against him. He doesn't look like a real-life bounty hunter, though by his estimate there are thirty notches on his six-shooter. Yes, that's what those notches mean.

When I walk up, Sam is settled in a chair at the front of his long, narrow antiques store, his arms at rest by his side, broadcasting anything but speed and danger. On the counter, by his cash register, an antique General Electric fan oscillates, its cord frazzled to bare copper at the plug. Flies, which he ignores, swarm about him.

He sends his son-in-law home for a scrapbook, in which Sam has catalogued the newspaper clippings and photographs that tell the story of his life, at least the public part. (He is guarded about his work as a bounty hunter.)

But even without the published evidence, if he ever turned his eye on you — let alone his gun - you'd likely do whatever he said, even if he was sitting drowsily in his chair with an old GE fan evaporating his sweat. You would do what he said, even if you thought you could outshoot him, because when you look into his eyes, you can't be absolutely sure that you can.

"Don't ever," he says, "underestimate me because I'm short, fat and old. I can still beat you."

Sam Toole learned to shoot in his hometown of Montgomery, Alabama, where, at the age of nine, he went to work at Pruitt's Shooting Gallery. Many of the customers were soldiers showing off their marksmanship.

His reputation as a hot shot bloomed when he challenged his boss in front of customers. "I told him I thought I could beat him. He said, 'I'll bet you your paycheck against double your paycheck you can't.'"

Mr. Pruitt, he says, paid him double that week.

At fifteen, Sam lied his way into the U.S. Navy for the tail end of World War II. Afterward, he went into the gun business, buying and selling. For ten years, he owned a gun store on West Colfax in Denver, and for fifteen years, he owned a store on Southeast 29th Street in Oklahoma City.

During Sam's time in Denver, Red Fenwick — a

legendary columnist at *The Denver Post* — adopted Sam as
his pet gunslinger, writing a fusillade of words about
him, occasionally setting up duels. Fenwick liked to make
note — and sport — of the tough guys who refused to
compete.

Sam performed at places like Magic City in Denver
and at shows in Dodge City. With his right hand, he could
drop a coin from belt high, then draw his gun and fire
before the coin fell to the bottom of his holster. In
matches, Sam would wait until a challenger's gun had
cleared the holster before he drew his own gun, and he
still would beat him to the trigger. The stories are all
there in yellowed newsprint.

He once beat actor Jim Arness, who played Marshal
Matt Dillon on the television series "Gunsmoke." (Sam had
a part in one episode of the show.) "I was faster with my
left hand," Sam says, "than he was with his right."

Sam Toole retired his hired gun thirty-five years
ago, and went into the antiques business with his wife.
But from the time he was nine, he says, until he quit the
business when he was thirty-five, Sam was in demand for
everything from acting jobs to repossessions to bounty
hunts.

"I wore out probably ninety pairs of boots," he
says. "I weighed 142 pounds and was tougher than a boot."

He tells about the time he tracked two men who had
stolen a prize bull worth 15,000 dollars. (He told me —
but wouldn't let me print — the name of the person who
hired him. You would recognize the name.) He found the
rustlers' tracks, he says, and followed them south for
three days. When he heard them ahead of him, he rushed
around south and waited. They walked into his ambush.

"I told them they had to take the bull back to
Utah," he says. "They killed the bull." Then they
threatened to kill him. "I let them carry out their
threats. Then I called the authorities and told them where
their bodies were at."

In one way or another, Sam Toole has lived his life
by the gun. It is fitting that he has settled in the north
part of Texas County, one third of Oklahoma's No-Man's
Land, where outlaws and libertarians once roamed. Folks up
here still don't much like the government telling them
what to do.

On the subject of government gun control, for
instance, Sam bristles. The only gun control this country
needs, he says, is for parents to control their children
and to teach them gun safety.

"I've owned 5,000 or 6,000 guns," he says. "I've

never hurt a man that didn't need hurting."

He hasn't done any shooting since he wrecked his shoulder in an automobile accident several years ago. But that doesn't mean he wouldn't consider an assignment. "If the pay was good," he says, "and the person was mean enough, I'd go after him."

ಬೂಲ  ಬೂಲ  ಬೂಲ

DOWN south of Hooker there stands a town with one name but two addresses. "This town is so big, it took two states to hold us," brags Dean Thrasher, whose house straddles the state line in Texhoma.

Dean and his wife, Kay, grew up here. Kay's father, W.O. "Slats" Chrismon, owned the Ritz theater and Chrismon Drug. She jerked sodas at the drug store and popped corn at the theater, both of which were on the Oklahoma side of town.

Nowadays, the Panhandle town is without either a theater or a pharmacy. The residents of Texhoma in Texas County have to drive to Guymon for their medicine.

In the earlier days, the Oklahoma side had most of the business, and Texas grew the biggest boys, Kay says. "They had the best athletes. They beat us at basketball, whatever," she says. Dean played football for the high school in Oklahoma.

In those days, the Oklahoma high school teams were the Red Devils. The Texas teams were the Bulldogs. Eventually they consolidated, and they all became Red Devils.

In the early days, both sides of town had a police department but one couldn't police for the other. So if you ran afoul of the law in Texhoma, Oklahoma, (not to be confused with Lake Texoma, which has no "H",) you could speed across the state line into Texhoma, Texas.

That's a gambit of the past. Now, the Texhoma, Oklahoma, police department is allowed into Texas.

The Texas side, in fact, no longer has a police department, but each town still has its own government. Bob Berry is mayor in Oklahoma. Garland Dahl is mayor in Texas.

As for the Thrashes' house, straddling the state line as it does, there are some complications. Their back yard and their recreation room are in Texas. Their pool table is in two states. When their two sons, now grown, would have overnight guests, they liked to sleep half in Texas, half in Oklahoma.

The Thrashes pay their household taxes to Oklahoma,

but they pay property taxes to both states. Everything but their recreation room is in Oklahoma; their telephone number, however, has a Texas area code.

The residents of Texhoma share a town name, but never call an Oklahoman a Texan. At least while one is still breathing. In the end, though, even the most chauvinistic of the Oklahomans move south of the border. "Us die-hard Oklahomans will finally give it up," Kay Thrasher says, "'cause we're all buried in Texas."

## Beaver County: Beaver

FANNIE Judy knows this dusty range the way only a rancher can. She has observed it from the back of a horse, the days of her youth spent "riding hither and yon," as she tells it.

In her ninety-four years, she has seen it from the seat of a wagon and the cab of a pickup. She survived the winter of 1911-1912, the worst she can remember. As a child, she saw the Cimarron River leave its banks, form a rolling wall of water and, in a flash, flood their land, trapping her cousin Fred atop her family's chicken coop. As a mother, she taped her windows and doors against the clouds of dust that blew into every crack of their home in '35.

She has lived her entire life within twenty-five miles of the place where she was born in the four-room house her daddy built. For her entire life, she has made her living off this wind-bitten land. She raised two children here, and then she and her husband, Tom, moved into Beaver in 1985.

She's not the least bit sentimental or nostalgic about any of it. "I guess I'm too old or too tired," she says. "I grew up with it."

You can't argue with the *old* part — anyone who makes it into their tenth decade can wear their age as a crown — but if Fannie Judy is tired, she isn't showing it. She sure didn't exhibit fatigue the day I took her to the place where she started this life. ·

I went in search of her because Ned and Darlene Kygar, owners of Ned and Darlene's Cafe, said Fannie was the woman in Beaver County with all the stories. They can keep track of her because she drives herself to lunch at their café every day.

I found Fannie, as Ned predicted, at the town's museum, fresh from her weekly visit to Jan Bennett at the beauty parlor. Fannie and Jean Long, curator of the Jones and Plummer Museum, were going through a packet of writings that had just arrived from a woman in Forgan.

Fannie didn't hesitate when I asked if she would show me her home place, which is north of the Cimarron River, nearly to Kansas.

FROM the start of our three-hour trip until the finish, she supplied a running narrative. Nothing escaped the sweep of her gaze. We stopped at the crumbling home where the Eubank family used one room of their two-story house as the local post office. When she was as young as six, Fannie would ride her horse the three miles here to check for mail.

Two wooden railway cars, bleached and falling apart, remind her that her husband had wanted one of those, "but Eubank got them both."

We picked sandhill plums, which as a child she picked and canned. We passed the spot where her mother's parents settled and planted a cedar tree from Fort Supply for each of their children. "Only one is still alive," she says, pointing to it. "It's more than a hundred years old."

She's not real happy with the cattle she sees in the pastures, a mix of who-knows-what breeds. "We always had Hereford cattle, whitefaces. We always tried to keep improving the herd. I don't know what these are."

We stopped at the house where she and Tom first took up housekeeping. A wind charger supplied the power for their thirty-two-volt iron, toaster and sweeper.

At our destination, the house where she was born, the first door she tried was latched. She gained entrance through the second door to discover that the house has become a storage shed.

She stopped in the kitchen. "We didn't have a fireplace. We had a stove." We moved aside old furniture. She pointed out her room. "The good bed was in the corner," she says. That was reserved for company. Even in her own room, she slept on a cot.

In her parents' room, we paused again. This is the place where she was born, the very spot on this Earth where — nearly a century ago — she drew her first breath. She has survived the century in far better shape than the house.

I waited for some emotion from her, a heart-tugging sentiment about the moment, a word of wisdom to sum up her life or life in general.

But Fannie Judy wasn't going for that. "Lordy Pete,"

was all she said. "I'm glad my sister can't see this."

## Blaine County: Watonga

IN the winter, the kitchen at the Watonga Cheese
Factory is a steamy refuge from the cold. But on
one of Oklahoma's rather warm summer days, it's hot enough
to curdle milk or melt a man.

Thing is, however, there aren't many men working
back here now to melt. Now it's mostly women who are
making the cheese in what was for the longest time an all-
man factory. In those days, the women worked out front.

Jo Lana Farris, whose title used to be simply office
manager, is one of those women. In the spring of 1999, she
added "cheese maker" to her job description.

"The work in back is hard," says Jo Lana, a Watonga
native who grew up on a farm and knows something about
hard work. "I've built fences, drove a tractor, harvested
wheat. Making cheese is some of the hardest work I've ever
done. It's difficult to find people who will come in and
do the work. On a hundred-five-degree day, it's pretty
warm back there."

Air conditioning would interfere with the cheese
making, so an exhaust fan provides the only relief. The
heat comes from the steam baths used in making cheese.

The process begins with the milk tanks, each of
which holds about fifteen tons of milk. They run two vats
a day. Each vat holds 14,500 pounds of milk and yields
only 1,400 pounds of cheese.

"Milk is ninety percent water," Jo Lana says.
"That's why cheese is so expensive."

The milk travels by pipe to the pasteurizer, which
kills all the bacteria so the cultures can be added. Then
the milk flows to the vats. They make four cheeses:
cheddar, colby, Monterey jack and cojack.

THE cheese factory is a squat, cinder-block
building painted cheddar-cheese orange. It opened
in 1940. The Knudsen family, which owned the factory,
bought milk from as many as 400 farmers, many of whom
would deliver the milk in old-fashioned milk cans.

Now the milk is delivered in tanker trucks.

Jo Lana, Marsha Romack and Cleveland Hartfield — the
outnumbered man at the factory — are learning to make
cheese from Gomer Sledd, who retired from the factory
about 1993. He comes in every couple of weeks, when they

need another batch of cheese.

While the work force has changed, the process hasn't. The Watonga Cheese Factory is one of the few places left that still does everything the old way.

The factory, in the shadow of the Watonga water tower and courthouse (if it were tall enough to cast a long shadow), is an institution in town that isn't always fully appreciated, Jo Lana says.

"Ninety percent of my customers who walk in are from out of town. A lot of locals have earned a living here. Watonga cheese," she says, "is important to Watonga."

&#x10C;&#x10D;&#x10C;  &#x10C;&#x10D;&#x10C;  &#x10C;&#x10D;&#x10C;

JIM Sinclair whittles with chain saws. While lesser whittlers pull out a Barlow or maybe a Bowie, Jim Sinclair gasses up a sixteen-inch, neon-green chain saw, yanks the cord and goes to cutting.

Other whittlers, of course, whittle on sticks, so a folding knife is sufficient. Jim Sinclair carves his art from 200-pound tree trunks. He needs a bigger blade.

Jim, whose wife, Naomi, says he's always been something of an artist, took up chain-saw whittling in the fall of '98 after they saw the work of a fellow in Montana. The man had carved bears that Jim and Naomi liked, but his prices scared them off. "I said, 'I could do that,'" Jim recalls. "I've always looked at things as, 'If you can do it, I can do it. It might not be as good, but I can do it.'"

So that day he studied the man's work, and when he came home, he pulled out his chain saw. Now, people stop to look at *his* bears, cowboys and Indians standing guard on his porch.

If he has one to spare, he'll sell it. Mostly, he sells only enough to earn enough money to pay for his equipment.

Long before he took up his chain saws, Jim Sinclair was already well-known in these parts. He worked twenty-six years with the Blaine County Sheriff's Department, the last half of that as sheriff.

He retired in '88, and he and Naomi spend much of their time traveling. It was during a stay in Gunnison, Colorado, in 1995 that Jim learned to whittle faces into tree bark and chunks of aspen.

Now, with his new-found skill with power tools, any piece of wood holds possibilities. He whittles anything from wall hangings to bottle stoppers to walking sticks.

And thanks to Jim, I still have my twenty-five-pound

chunk of the Dan'l Boone elm. This unwieldy wedge of wood came from Kentucky, and for seven years, I have hauled it around with me. For a long time, it served as a primitive, if historic, foot rest. Recently, it has occupied a spot in the garage.

My chunk of wood is a piece of a 200-year-old elm that — until 1992 — stood at the creek-side site where Dan'l Boone first settled in what was to become Lexington. For a reason that escapes me, someone cut down the tree.

Do the math, and you can figure that Dan'l himself might well have leaned against this tree when it was a sapling. Surely, he at least touched it, or gazed upon it.

Well, when we learned that a tree under which ol' Dan'l once slept (the story enlarges with each telling) had been cut, a couple of friends obtained permission to salvage pieces of the tree. When I asked them to bring me a chunk, I was thinking something the size of a, say, pencil holder. But my friends think big. That's how I came by my twenty-five pound Dan'l Boone foot rest.

In my ongoing and ever-futile effort to unclutter, I was on the verge of chunking my chunk of history at about the same time I learned about Jim.

So before I headed for Watonga, I put the wood in the back of the truck. After Jim, Naomi and I had visited awhile, I asked if he would demonstrate with his chain saw. I had, I told him, brought my own wood. In forty minutes, my chunk of wood became a work of art, which I dubbed "Dan'l Boone Bear."

He admits, with a chuckle, that his first effort at a bear was a little rough. "The first lady that came by said, 'Oh, what a pretty little pig.' I just agreed with her."

## Logan County: Guthrie

ON my second lap of downtown, I noticed it, all bright and brassy and beckoning. I had been straining my neck, gawking at the antique buildings in this pretty little land-run town, all the while weaving dangerously close to parked cars and possibly pedestrians. (I say "possibly," because I can't be sure. I was looking up. My wife hates to ride with me in the mountains.)

My plan had been only to pass through Guthrie for a look-see, and to return another day.

But when I saw the brass fire pole gleaming from inside the ninety-six-year-old fire station, I had to stop. I found a parking spot right in front of the world's largest cigarette lighter museum. (There's irony for you: The fire-fighting station is next door to a museum honoring the cigarette lighter, a device complicit in more house fires and forest fires than any other invention.)

I never harbored the boyhood dream of becoming a firefighter, but I have always wanted to slide down a firehouse pole. The dream has not diminished with the years. And now it was within my reach, if I could persuade the fire fighters to let me do it.

It may not sound like much, but it is a little difficult for a grown man to walk into a strange firehouse and ask of a firefighter – a total stranger — permission to slide down the fire pole. I stammered about a bit and finally uttered my request.

Of all the people I could have asked, Bill Martin, a thirteen-year veteran of the department, could understand the attraction. He grew up in Guthrie, and as a kid, he slid down this pole a few times, never knowing that someday he would be paid to slide down it. Bill, however, couldn't give me permission. I'd have to find someone higher up the fire-fighting ladder.

That's when Captain Mark Smedes walked out of the back office.

I hemmed and hawed again. But my reluctance was unfounded. As soon as he heard my request, his mustachioed mouth turned up into a grin as bright as boyhood. He understood. "You want to slide down the pole? No problem. Follow me."

So I followed him up the stairs, where he showed me the bunk house, the television room and the windows where in winter the snow blew on their beds before they covered the broken panes.

This place holds some history. The Guthrie fire-fighting company occupied a couple of stations around town between 1889 and 1903 until this one was built at 111 South Second. Records show that the company began as the Heim and Waite hose company in 1890, and the next year became a hook and ladder company.

A wooden hose tower behind the station, possibly the last still standing in the state, is historic, too. This is where the firefighters hung their canvas hoses to dry after battling a fire.

The site on South Second originally was home to a restaurant called Frink and Lowe Cafe. It was renamed Frink by Hisself by owner Andy Frink after he and his partner, W.M. Lowe, dissolved their partnership.

All that is history, however. The brass pole is now,

and there it stood: Bottom of the first floor rising nearly to the ceiling of the second. Captain Smedes, who has slid down this pole a few times in his twenty-year career, gave me a detailed and highly technical lesson in the skill of pole-sliding.

"Hold onto the pole, wrap your legs around it and go until you hit bottom," he says. "Don't let go. Make sure you're out of the way when you hit bottom 'cause the next guy's down on your head. In winter, you've got your long sleeves on. Phoof. You're down."

The captain went first. Phoof. He was down.

Then it was my turn. Your fearless correspondent did as he was told: I held onto the pole, wrapped my legs around it, didn't let go, and phoof, I hit bottom.

The years of anticipation, the dreams of danger and thrills, and phoof. We made one more run, the captain and I, and my grand adventure was over.

But that wasn't the end of my day. Bill Martin and another firefighter, Erin Jones, were down below, and we visited a bit. Erin's a pretty chipper firefighter, considering one of her less-than-perfect days on the job. She was working a car fire one night when a passing driver ran over her. Broke her foot and nose, gave her a concussion and banged up her knee: "I come plum out of my boots."

Somehow during our conversation it came up that while any ol' body could slide down a fire pole, Bill could go up it. And so Bill, the forty-eight-year-old who fights fires for a living so he can indulge his hobby of farming, did just that. Without a bit of help from his legs, Bill shimmied hand-over-hand up the pole, the veins of his Popeye-like forearms a-bulging.

Then he invited me to try, to which I replied, no thank you, that trick's for Bill by hisself.

# Roger Mills County: Berlin

GLENA Belle Crane's husband wrote the book, literally, on the graveyards of Roger Mills County, and even she doesn't know why John J. Puryear is buried catawampus.

A theory or two persists, but no one seems to know exactly why Puryear's grave is crossways to all the others in this cemetery on the western Oklahoma plains.

It's certain, however, that Puryear and his wife, Mary, lie north and south while every other person buried at the Berlin Cemetery lies east and west.

Little is known of Puryear, even before his death in 1901 at the of age sixty years, six months and seventeen days. Lorene Mikles notes that every Memorial Day, when Confederate flags are placed on about twenty of the graves here, one is stuck at Puryear's plot. So someone has reason to believe he was a soldier for the South in that most uncivil of wars.

It is the Christian tradition that the deceased be laid to rest with their toes pointed east and their heads to the west so that they are facing east, ready for the return of Christ.

Puryear, however, lies perpendicular to tradition.

Of the ruminations that Lorene has heard on the subject, the first is that Puryear was an atheist and asked to be buried that way.

The second theory implies Mr. Puryear had no say in his eternal repose. To quote Lorene, who was quoting a friend: "This man lived crosswise to the world, and he was buried crosswise to the world."

Or, as someone told Glena Belle: "He always voted 'no' when he should have voted 'yes.'"

AFTER Lorene showed me Mr. Puryear's grave, she took me to the Ivy Rose Cottage Bed & Breakfast in Cheyenne, where we were the guests of Glena Belle, Lorena Males (Glena Belle's older sister) and Judy Tracy.

For two hours, the stories flew across the elegant lunch table. Toward the end of lunch, Glena Belle pulled out the tome about cemeteries that her husband compiled. Glen Crane's book lists every cemetery in the county, and to the best he knew, it listed the name of every person buried in each cemetery.

John J. Puryear is there all right, but other than his dates of birth (April 28, 1841) and death (November 17, 1901), all the book says is: "Buried crosswise."

But we had plenty more than the mysterious Puryear to discuss over our fried chicken salad, like family history. The sisters' father made the Cheyenne land run of 1892, and while living in a dugout, opened a mercantile in the town of Hammon.

Lorena and Glena Belle recall the Indians of Hammon, where they lived as children. When the Indian girls started school, Lorena said, they weren't allowed to wear their shawls, or anything else too "Indian," to school. The girls would leave their shawls at their father's store during the school day.

They also told of another Roger Mills man of

mystery, Joe Muhlbacher. He was an immigrant from Russia who apparently didn't adapt well to his new country. He was rather reclusive, although he welcomed visitors to his ranch. He played the accordion and was known for playing music while his neighbors danced on the flat roof of his house.

His eccentricities included sculpting, and a few of the townsfolk took exception to some of his work, which was rather anatomically lifelike, in a classical sort of way. In at least one case, his statuary was rather liberal for the times.

According to a poem that Glen Crane wrote about Muhlbacher, he had sculpted a statue of a pregnant woman that demanded: "Women's suffrage now."

Glen Crane's poem noted that a well-meaning, if misguided, group of townfolk stormed Joe's ranch and destroyed the offending statues.

Glena Belle shook her head over the memory. "Shameful what they did to him," she said, "and on his own property."

But while Joe brought shame, he also brought Roger Mills County a measure of fame. In 1941, he went to New York to appear on the "We the People" radio show and then was filmed in a documentary that was shown at the local Rook Theatre.

After the documentary, Joe played his accordion on stage.

"He made Cheyenne famous, really — and we had never been famous for anything," teacher Oweita Calvert once told a reporter for *The Daily Oklahoman*.

Talk then turned to Judy Tracy, whom the sisters contend is the most useful woman in the county. It was through Tracy's leadership that the one-room schoolhouse from Roll was moved to Cheyenne, renovated and now is used to teach children about the school days of old.

Judy dresses the part and starts her day at nine-thirty a.m. with a Scripture reading. At nine-fifty a.m., her scholars go to penmanship, and at a quarter-past ten, they undertake orthography. (If you had been a scholar in 1910, you would know what that word means.)

Judy, who is quick to give all the credit to the Lord, and to the work and generosity of others, says her initial motivation was to teach school kids that, even in 1999, they can pray and read the Bible in public school so long as students — not teachers — lead.

"I haven't heard from the ACLU," she said, "but I expect to."

THE wind has picked up since morning, when I first viewed the final resting place of John J. Puryear. Grass burrs stick to my shoelaces and pants legs as I cross the sandy road to his grave.

I kneel in the sparse vegetation, viewfinder of my camera to my eye. Stickers puncture my skin through my jeans. I wiggle to a spot where I can photograph both Puryear's headstone and one behind it, to illustrate that his is, indeed, turned sideways.

As I look into the camera, the name of the headstone behind Mr. Puryear's appears to hang right over his gravestone. In my viewfinder, they merge almost as if they are one stone. If you look at the gravestones from my angle, the family name on the far stone combines with his name and reads like this:

Poor

Puryear

Regardless of the reason he was buried crosswise, we can hardly begrudge Puryear the sentiment, seeing as how he's not here to defend himself.

## Lincoln County: Stroud

ED Smalley wasn't the only man ever to meet his future wife at Rock Cafe, but he was the only one who went on to buy the little joint on Route 66.

The Rock, according to Ed, was *the* place in Stroud. Roy Rives built it entirely of stone that was excavated for construction of Route 66. Mamie Mayfield, one of its early proprietors, would drag the jukebox to the window so teenagers could dance in the parking lot. But by town ordinance, the juke box had to be turned off at ten p.m.

Long before he met Aleta, Ed was intimately familiar with the Rock. After it opened July 4, 1939, he spent a year working there, earning a buck a night washing dishes from six p.m. until six a.m.

The Rock was a gathering place that also served as a Greyhound bus stop, which explains how this love story began.

Ed had been off to World War II, and he came home on the Greyhound. When he stepped off the bus at the Rock, he saw Aleta sitting in a booth.

He knew she was the girl he would marry. He was twenty-one. She was sixteen.

That was April 4, 1946.

He remembers buying Aleta a Coke. She doesn't

remember that. "I just thought he was pretty cute," she says now, fifty-three years later. "I asked who he was. He was in his uniform. He was telling his cousin when I was working at the Rock that he was going to marry me. My mother had a fit."

Their courtship was fairly long, hindered as it was by her mother's misgivings about this man of the world. Aleta's mother had a good perch from which to observe him. When Ed first came home from the Army, he ran a little joint called The Coney, and Aleta's mother worked for him.

"We would have to slip around," he says. "Her mother thought I was too old for her. When we wanted to go out, I'd make sure her mother was working."

Several months later, Ed leased the Rock from Roy Rives. Ed's partner, Woodrow "Doc" Sosbee, ran a taxi service out of the cafe. (Doc, Ed adds, also ran a little whiskey between cab fares.)

Ed's marriage to Aleta was another nine years in the making. She went off to college. He, meanwhile, gave up his lease on the Rock and went into the oil business. But he never lost track of Aleta, and they tied the knot in Clayton, New Mexico, on May 11, 1955.

Forty-four years later, they are still married, and Ed turned out okay. He and Aleta are members at the Baptist church, and in 1978, he was Stroud's Citizen of the Year. And the Rock, where it all began, continued to be a part of their lives.

In 1983, after he ran another restaurant for a while, they bought the Rock lock, stock and hamburger grill. Their son ran it, but eventually they closed it. Then in 1993, they sold the business to Dawn Longacre Herr and her husband, Christian, whose plans at that time did not include working in Stroud.

Dawn, a former captain of the girls' track team at Yukon High School, met Christian while she was working on a cruise ship. After they married, they wanted to open a restaurant in Costa Rica and bought the Rock's kitchen equipment. When Ed offered to lease the building to them for 200 dollars a month, they opted for some on-the-job training in Stroud.

"When we opened the doors to this restaurant, neither Christian nor I could flip an egg," Dawn says. "The day before we opened, we were in the mall buying cookbooks."

The stress of running a restaurant together was too much for their marriage, and they divorced. Now the restaurant is a daughter-mother-granddaughter outfit. Dawn's mother, Linda, and Dawn's four-year-old daughter,

Alexis, now run the Rock. When a diner enters the door, Alexis grabs menus and escorts them to their seat.

Many an interesting character stops for a buffalo burger, the brisket they smoke themselves or a dish of peach cobbler; Dawn inherited the secret recipe from her great-great-grandmother. One man who stopped was riding his bicycle around the world. "He ate eight pancakes and smoked cigarettes the whole time," Dawn says.

Another interesting diner was a sixty-six-year-old woman who was walking from Los Angeles to Chicago, a dream trip she never made with her husband before he died.

On another day, TV news star Bryant Gumbel and his crew strayed in. He sent the crew on to their motel and stayed the whole evening. He played in the rain with Alexis and helped clean up the kitchen at closing.

At my request, Dawn, her mother and Alexis, gathered in the Rock's tiny kitchen with Ed and Aleta Smalley for a photograph. As seventy-five-year-old Ed leaned against the sink where he scrubbed dishes as a teenager, they talked about all the stories they've heard of romance that started at the Rock.

The Rock relationships, Linda says, must be as solid as the restaurant where they started. "I've never heard anyone say, 'I met my former wife here.'"

# Harmon County: Hollis

TWO men. Two stories. Different but the same. One, the late N.W. Warren, was the mayor and a farmer. The other, Bill Dill, is a city councilman and a farmer. When Mr. Warren became mayor in 1958, Bill Dill was still working on his daddy's farm in Harmon County.

Mayor Warren kept a store in town. Bill Dill's parents traded there.

Their stories are the same in ways that embody the courage and generosity that define this place. In their own ways, they both looked out for the little guy. Mayor Warren died seven years ago at the age of eighty-seven. Bill Dill continues to help his neighbors.

BILL Dill: Everyone in Harmon County knows how to find Bill Dill's four acres of black-eyed peas, where the cute little legumes are free for the picking.

By Mr. Dill's estimation, fifty families stock their freezers for the winter, and another hundred or so live off his peas all summer. Not to mention the organizers of the Black-Eyed Pea Festival, who depend on his peas to raise money.

Bill's banker grows produce on the other side of Bill's peas. On some days, the banker can't go to his irrigation pump for all the pea-picking cars parked on the road.

Some days, Bill himself will stop at the patch and ask someone: "Who gave you permission to pick these peas?"

"Invariably," he says, grinning, "it's somebody from Amarillo or from some other state. You can usually trace it back to somebody you know."

Bill Dill knows something about growing up poor. There were times his family might not have survived without the help of a neighbor.

So Bill perpetuates this patch to help others who might not make it. Sometimes, he throws in some of the cantaloupes or watermelons he has raised. "This right here is a necessity for a lot of people," he says.

Bill Dill could be occupied at any number of other professions with a steady, guaranteed paycheck every week. His college degrees are in sociology and history. He worked as a counselor at the state pen in McAlester. He was there when the inmates burned it. He has received invitations to work in big towns.

But the soil called him, his wife and his two sons back to Harmon County. To make it through the lean '80s, he worked the night shift as a police officer in Hollis. They made him chief. But prices improved. Now he farms and serves on the city council.

In Hollis, his peas are important for more reasons than the nutrition they provide his neighbors. He began farming the four acres twelve years ago and word spread. That is how out-of-staters know about the patch.

In Hollis, he is the Black-eyed Pea Man. For it is Bill Dill's four acres that supply the bounty — without cost to the city — for the tiny town's annual Black-Eyed Pea Festival. The entertainment includes their own version of "Hee-Haw," and a western show at Jackrabbit Junction, a stage set that Odel Lemons built just for this.

Sylvia Hudson, one of the many volunteers who runs the festival, points out that black-eye peas — cooked with ham and cornbread — are the perfect nutritional meal: protein, grain, dairy (if you put on plenty of butter) and vegetables.

The festival raises money for the town's museum, whose treasures include the four dressing gowns that belonged to the Keys quadruplets and the wedding dress that each of them wore.

The organizers of the festival have made it clear they depend on Bill and his peas. "One year, I didn't raise them," he says, "and I spent hours on the telephone explaining to the ladies why I didn't."

NAY Winford Warren: Mike Warren holds up the old sign, which his late father lettered by hand. The message on the brittle poster board is plain: "Notice! Positively No Eggs for Sale or Offered For Sale in This Store!" There is more to the sign, but that would rush the story.

The story, Mike says, unfolded like this: N.W. Warren was a farmer in Harmon County. In 1930, after he married Maudie, they opened Warren's Grocery and Market. In those days, many a farmer would trade eggs with Mr. Warren in exchange for groceries.

For years, Mr. Warren graded and candled the eggs himself. In 1958, however, the state government stepped in to "help" with new regulations that required all retailers to purchase their eggs from wholesale producers.

Mr. Warren, knowing how much some of his customers depended on eggs for barter, respectfully thumbed his nose at the state's help. That's when he proclaimed his new egg policy on the sign: "Notice! Positively No Eggs for Sale or Offered For Sale in This Store! Purchase the container. Eggs are free!"

Now he could continue to buy the eggs, and his neighbors could continue to eat. His salute to the state, however, stuck in the state's craw like a chicken bone. The state took him to court. Mr. Warren, newly elected mayor, was certain his cause was just and asked for a jury trial in his home county. The jury exonerated him, saying customers had the right to buy egg cartons, full or empty.

Now Mayor Warren *really* had ruffled the government's feathers, and while the court of civil appeals considered the case, the agriculture police tried to catch the mayor in the act of illegally selling eggs.

Mr. Warren had warned his employee, Arthur Kirby, to walk on eggshells should anyone suspicious show up wanting to buy eggs.

One day, when Mr. Warren was gone, two men in suits and ties entered the store eager to buy eggs. They brought a carton of eggs to the counter. *We would like to purchase these eggs*, one of them said.

*Not for sale*, Kirby informed them. *The eggs are free. But I can sell you a carton to take them home in.*

*Not a problem*, the agents said, *just give us the eggs*. Kirby obliged and attempted to load them into their arms.

The men, their government credentials notwithstanding, couldn't carry all the eggs. So they asked for a sack, which Kirby provided.

As they were leaving, however, Kirby stopped them and said they owed him money. The government men, thinking they had made their case, balked. *We thought the eggs were free*, one said.

*They are*, Kirby replied. *But the sack is the same price as the carton.*

THE appeals court confirmed the jury's verdict, and the Oklahoma Supreme Court, in the *State v. Warren*, refused to reverse the original verdict.

"That cost him 300 dollars," says Mike, who is an associate district judge. "That was big money back then. He didn't benefit from it personally. He was a little guy, too. He farmed, ranched and bought the store. He did this for the farmers. Dad told me principle is important but it can be expensive."

# Muskogee County: Haskell

A piece of J. Paul Getty is stuck to the bottom of my shoe — in a sludgy, metaphysical sort of way. This extraordinary event came to pass in a rather ordinary manner on what had been a perfectly ordinary day.

My day in Haskell began at the Bashara home, where eighty-eight-year-old Marguerite Bashara still presides. She and her ten siblings grew up in this house, and as the oldest of the eleven, she was — and still is — in charge. I learned the history of this family over a Lebanese lunch, which Marguerite made from scratch.

Their mother died in a car crash when their father fell asleep at the wheel of their two-seat Ford roadster. Marguerite was eighteen then, so much of the raising was left to Marguerite, who never married or had children of her own.

Their story begins in Lebanon, where her mother's father served as an alderman in Beirut in the late 1800s.

Tony, Marguerite's father, left Lebanon at sixteen, bound for the United States. He docked in New York and traveled to Scranton, Pennsylvania, where for six months he bought and then peddled notions. Using his earnings, he traveled to St. Louis, where he restocked his supplies.

Then the young man walked the railroad tracks from

St. Louis to Oklahoma, where he first stopped in Wagoner. To survive his journey, he skewered chunks of meat on green limbs and cooked it over chunks of coal he gathered on the tracks.

He spoke the language of the Creek Indians before he learned English. His children tell of the night he became lost in the mountains and bunked with seemingly friendly folk. In the night, he heard them plotting to rob him, so he slipped out. Later he learned he had been sleeping with Belle Starr's band of outlaws.

He married a young woman from the Bristow area, who bore their daughter but within two years died of the "quick consumption," as Marguerite describes it, leaving Tony with their only daughter.

When Tony learned of plans for settling Haskell (named for the first governor of Oklahoma), he wandered over, set up a tent by the surveyor's shack and opened Haskell's first business. The tent, however, blew away in a tornado. Tony then erected a wooden building and opened for business. He later built Haskell's first stone building, which still stands.

Nine years later, he returned to Beirut, where he met and married his second wife, the mother of Marguerite and her ten brothers and sisters.

Marguerite remembers the cold November night she and her siblings stood at the front window of their house and watched fully costumed members of the Ku Klux Klan march to the Methodist church, where they burned a cross. (Years later, she says, when one of Haskell's early buildings was torn down, workers found a collection of KKK gear.)

She remembers that the nineteen-year-old son of the Methodist minister was the first person in Haskell to die in the influenza epidemic of 1918.

Her father once was thrown in jail when he confronted a pastor preaching on the street. "It was one of your good Baptist preachers talking about the nuns and priests," said Marguerite, whose family is Catholic. "Papa calls him a liar. They arrested him for disturbing the peace."

A local banker posted his bond, and several of the bank's customers pulled out their money in protest of the man's support for a Catholic.

The Bashara house is a collector's paradise. Marguerite has figurines from all over the world, most of which were gifts but some that she bought herself in her world travels.

Knickknacks, soup tureens and antique clocks fill the walls and shelves. In a small chest, they have stored their mother's wedding dress, a yellowing wonder of pleats and lace and silk and taffeta that still rustles.

IN the midst of all the storytelling about their family and Muskogee County, Marguerite mentions that J. Paul Getty's first oil well is down the road from Haskell.

Well, that's all I need to hear. We drive down to the family's flower shop, which they operate out of a building their father and uncle built in 1915. There, Toni Haney, the baby of the family, takes over the tour.

With Toni navigating, we turn off the pavement and travel a sandy road until she says stop. "There it is," she says, and gives me the okay to cross the barbed wire to take a close look. "We know everybody around here," she assures me.

Nothing here denotes this as a spot of any significance, although it is on the Oklahoma register of historic places as the place where Mr. Getty's oil fortune was born. Weeds and sticker vines carpet the ground around the large wooden reservoir, its antique planks held tight with four bands of steel. Seventy years have taken their toll, but a rap of the knuckles shows the wood remains solid. The wooden platform that holds the barrel off the ground appears to be as solid as it must have been when Mr. Getty was climbing around on it. Discarded pipe and a steel tank litter the area.

Right below the tank, the ground is covered in a black sticky substance, which a couple of folks later tell me is a bit of oil and paraffin that have oozed out.

After a half-hour of looking at Getty's ghost of an enterprise from every angle, I make one more circle around the tank.

My right foot slips, and I nearly fall. When I pick up my right foot, the bottom of my shoe is loaded with the black sticky substance that Mr. Getty first discovered here seventy years ago.

So now I have my own link to the past of our nation and of Oklahoma. I am leaving my own sticky tracks in time and history — and, I am sorry to report, on the carpeted floorboard of my tour guide's car.

## Pontotoc County: Ada

Pete Cantrell, owner of Bedre Candy Company, flips a few switches on the "chip-dipper" and a river of warm chocolate flows from a pipe. Squint, breathe deeply, and you're in Willie Wonka's chocolate factory.

Pete doesn't allow swimming or slurping, but otherwise he is generous with his chocolate. "Everyone," says his wife, Melissa, "can eat as much chocolate as they want at work."

Lou Harris, Debbie Walker, Ruby Wesley and eleven-year-chocolate-factory veteran Faye Miller will tell you that may not be as much fun as it sounds.

The four women are the production, packing and shipping crew at Bedre Candy Company, which makes its home in the old Homer Elementary School just outside the city limits of this Pontotoc County town.

They spend their days drizzling heavy coats of chocolate on everything from peanuts and pecans to pretzels, potato chips and Oreo cookies. All day long, they smell chocolate. Several times a day, they must sample chocolate to ensure quality.

After a few weeks of constant exposure, Melissa says, even the most avid aficionado will beg for mercy.

Bedre Candy Company, which has been in business for fourteen years, began as a supplier of gourmet nuts for the Kron chocolate company, which Pete bought with several other investors. The New York company was near bankruptcy when Pete and Melissa took it over and saved it. "In the process," he says, "we learned to love making chocolate."

After he left the company, he experimented with his own concoctions, deciding he could do better than Kron. Thus the name of his company, Bedre, which is Norwegian for "better."

Now they sell their inspirations all over the world, specializing in private-label candy for stores in places like New York City and Honolulu.

Neither risk nor failure frightens Pete Cantrell, who was born in 1929. At sixteen, he followed his father into the oil business.

He wasn't sure that was the right choice because he wanted to be a writer. An English teacher, however, told him that considering his grammar skills, he had better find another profession. He made his final decision after learning he earned more money in the oil field than he could teaching. He went from roughneck to driller to entrepreneur.

"I thought I was going to retire at thirty. At twenty-six, we lost everything," he says of the company he formed with his father and brother.

But he was working with the right equipment. "The drilling rig," he says, "is the only tool you can dig yourself out of a hole with."

Not all voids, of course, are physical. Pete's first wife, Frances, lost a breast to cancer early in their marriage; the cancer recurred, and in their thirty-ninth year of marriage, she died. Six months after her death, Pete married Melissa, a single mother of three who had recently returned to Ada to recover from a divorce and the death of a child.

"A lot of my friends and relatives were astonished when I remarried," he wrote in his self-published book, *Yea, Tho I Walk Thru the Oil Patch*. "I was astonished that they were astonished. ... My new family not only filled the vacuum in my life, but has caused me to grow spiritually and mentally."

He has learned much, he says, mostly that without a personal relationship with Jesus Christ, life has no meaning. Every day, he says, he asks God for directions. "Then if I drill a dry hole, I can say, 'Me and God drilled a dry hole.'"

PETE had seen chocolate-covered potato chips, but they were coated on one side only. "They looked awful," he says. The key was to find a way to cover both sides without having to dip each chip in chocolate. That meant finding a way to coat both sides on a conveyor belt. "I tried flipping them with air and with springs."

Eventually, he solved the problem. When he turns on the machine, he adjusts it so that it creates two "waterfalls" of liquid chocolate. He turns on the conveyor belt and loads it with ridged potato chips; the chips pass under the first chocolate waterfall so that one side is coated. Then the machine flips the chips, which pass under the second chocolate fall.

While most of their sales are by mail to big companies, they also sell to individuals. They call their chocolate chips "High Dollar Chips" for a reason. The chocolate they make is European-style, without preservatives or a drip of the paraffin often found in commercial American chocolate.

"I love this business," Pete says. "It gives you an avenue to let your creative juices flow."

## Pottawatomie County: Pink

WE were searching, my daughters and I, for Pink when we happened upon Robin Hood. Pink is a place in Pottawatomie County, although little of it remains except for the highway signs telling you that you are there.

Blink, and you miss Pink.

South of State Highway 9, you can find the Pink town hall and the Pink senior citizens center, neither of which, by the way, is pink. Back on the highway to Cleveland County, we did see one pink mailbox, but the mail is delivered from somewhere other than Pink: Their post office closed on Valentine's Day 1906.

I wanted to visit Pink for that noblest of journalistic causes: I thought Pink would look catchy in the dateline, that little line at the start of a story that tells readers to which city you ventured to bring them the news. I collect datelines the way gunslingers collect notches. I have had datelines from Burnt Corn and Possum Trot in Alabama. My goal is to write from Toad Suck, Arkansas.

While I found just enough of Pink to justify notching my typewriter, I did find Chris Giles, an eighteen-year-old archer who has done something remarkable.

CHRIS Giles was a senior at Bethel High School when I met him. He began shooting in October 1998, and when Roland Chaffin and David Mount opened an archery store and shooting range near his home, Chris was there every afternoon. He was determined to shoot a Robin Hood, which is the hole-in-one of archery. That is when you split an arrow in a target with a second arrow. Aim must be perfect. Even a hair off square, and the second arrow will glance off the first.

On Friday the thirteenth, 1999, he declared he wasn't leaving until he Robin Hooded.

By his eighth shot of the afternoon, he had scored. Roland and David have hung his Robin Hood on the wall.

I, of course, have never shot a Robin Hood. So I called Chris and asked him to shoot for me. I told him I'd replace his arrows if he shot one.

He arrived at the range with his parents, Rick and Paula, his thirteen-year-old brother Case, and his twelve-year-old sister, Lauren. We watched for about an hour. I didn't have to buy Chris any new arrows, but at least four times, he punched two arrows so close to each other on the target that their feathers touched. Once, the shafts of the arrows were less than a quarter-inch apart.

Robin Hood or no, that's pretty good shooting for a young man who grew up so close to a place called Pink.

# Cleveland County: Norman

DON'T mess with Battieste Norman. His kid sister'll whup you. She whupped me on a fine Friday afternoon, but not because I was picking on Battieste, which I wouldn't do anyway. At six feet and 350 pounds, Mr. Norman's physique speaks for itself.

No, Dionne whupped me because I flat-out asked for it.

Here's the deal: Battieste and Dionne want to be champion arm wrestlers.

So to see how strong they are, I arm wrestled each of them on the counter between the telephone and the cash register at Herring's Tire and Auto, where Battieste works.

Their grip, when you lock thumbs, is like a vise. Their wrists are reinforced steel. Suffice it to say, both of my matches ended quickly.

Battieste has been arm wrestling off and on for several years. The last time anybody beat him, he said, was ten years ago in Purcell when a forty-seven-year-old roughneck pinned him. But it took the fellow three minutes to put his wrist to the table. "He was stacked," the thirty-year-old Battieste said of the man's muscles.

The brother and sister are following the path of Cynthia Yerby, a national champion from Seminole County who represented the United States in Russia in 1998.

Battieste said he stays strong tossing tires on the job, but he and Dionne also work out together at his house. "We're close," she said. "We're around each other all the time."

I wasn't the only person they beat that Friday. Bill Spores, who owns a muffler shop across the street, gamely agreed to put his manhood on the line. They both beat him, too.

"I'm working on my stamina," said Dionne, who is a year younger than her brother. "Bat wants me to get up there and slam 'em. I don't think it's going to be that easy. ... I think we were born strong."

Batiste stays sharp by challenging anybody with big biceps to a match. Once, a customer at the tire store challenged Batiste. "He said, 'I'll give you my pack of cigarettes against your dollar that I can beat you.'"

J.L. Herring, Battieste's boss, laughs at the memory of that short match. "He was a little ol' wimp like me," he said. "He sounded like a woman in labor."

## McClain County: Newcastle

SOME day, Roberta Hale says, when she has fewer doctors' appointments, she'll sit down, and we'll talk. Then she'll tell me her story. Roberta is Newcastle's miracle lady, the woman no one thought would survive the tornado that ran roughshod over Oklahoma City on May 3, 1999. When rescuers found her, 250 yards from her home, she was bleeding and in bad shape.

But Roberta is back. We met at Peanuts Antique Mall, where she had joined three friends for lunch at the store's old-time soda fountain. Marie Bales, Jean Garrett, Leona Matthews and Roberta — all members at Woodland Hills Baptist Church — bowed their heads and asked God's blessing on their meal. This was Roberta's first trip to Peanuts since the storm. The friends, you sense, are grateful for more than their sandwiches.

The owners, Holly and Larry Chambers, hugged Roberta on her miraculous return to their shop. Roberta joked about her new short hairstyle, necessitated by the head wounds she suffered when the tornado knocked down her house and tossed her the length of two-and-a-half football fields.

Peanuts is that sort of place, a Mayberry kind of stop where conversations turn easily from miracles to menus and the customers feel free to pray. With the antiques in the front of the store and the kitchen at the back, it's like a visit to your grandmother's house.

The Chambers opened their store in February, after their house could no longer hold all their antiques. Their original plan was to rent a booth, but that wasn't enough for Larry. "My husband doesn't do anything a little bit," Holly says, so they opened a store and rented booths to others.

So many things reminded here me of my grandparents' homes. Grandma, in Bryan, Texas, had floors that shook when we walked through the house. We had to walk very softly in the early mornings or when she was baking a cake.

Mamadee and Papadee in El Paso built their thousand-square-foot stucco house in 1930 and lived there until they died. The hand-cranked White Mountain ice cream freezer in one of the Peanuts' booths reminded me of back-yard nights in El Paso, with Papadee at the crank.

The soda fountain dining room is as comfortable as home. People like Sandy Jones, an insurance agent, take lunch here. Jamie Burke and Tony Nelson spent their lunch break here too, pausing from their furniture-making jobs at Troy Wesnidge Inc. These guys make high-priced furniture for hotels in Paris and Las Vegas, but they eat their lunch at Peanuts. Twila Middick and her three-year-old Austen stopped for lunch after the rush and had the soda counter and Holly and Angela to themselves.

Holly is a Missouri woman, having grown up and escaped from the small town of Ava, near Branson. "I came here when the oil boom was going on," she says. "I had a lot of friends already here. That was about the time the boom went bust. Everybody moved back to Missouri except me."

Now she is back in a small town like Ava, which had its own drug store and soda fountain. "We'd leave high school and go up there for lunch almost every day," she says. "That's where I got most of the ideas for ours."

Angela Row, a night-shift nurse, works at Peanuts for fun. She moved to Newcastle in the fifth grade, and except for the addition of two traffic lights, little has changed. Joe Cox, principal of Newcastle's high school, was principal when she graduated in 1983. Cindy Stanley, principal of the middle school, was one of Angela's classmates.

Whatever the news in the Tri-Cities area, you eventually can learn all about it at Peanuts. (That's one thing I learned: The city leaders of Newcastle, Blanchard and Tuttle — thinking grandly — have dubbed that little corner of Oklahoma the Tri-Cities.) Eventually, the stories that are making the rounds of the four other official gossip stops make it to Peanuts.

And it's not only the locals who do the talking. Strangers who wander in, memories prompted by the antiques, share their lives. "Everybody," Holly said, "has a story."

# McCurtain County: Broken Bow

MOST people don't know it, but Smokey Bear has a baby brother who was born right here in the southeast corner of Oklahoma. While Smokey is an icon in a realm with Mickey Mouse and Charlie Brown, Smokey's little brother, Tree Bear, is just embarking on his national career.

Most people don't know this, either, but the father of Smokey and Tree Bear has played an important, artistic role in preserving the history of McCurtain County.

Harry Rossoll is a Yankee artist who lived in the South while doing the most significant work of his career for the Forest Heritage Center in McCurtain County.

"It was," he told me in 1996 when I met him in Atlanta, "the highlight of my life."

Harry was a slight fellow who looked a bit like a skinny Colonel Sanders, a skinny chewed cigar always in his mouth and several others nearby. Harry looked like an artist.

The first time I met Harry, I was two years old. He came to our house in Brewton, Alabama, when Daddy was stationed there with the U.S. Forest Service. Harry was a Forest Service artist.

He drew a picture of Smokey that said, "Hi, Jay, Help me prevent forest fires." He signed it, "To Jay, From Smokey Bear/Harry Rossoll."

In 1996, my wife, daughters and I caught up with Harry in his studio in Atlanta. He had endured some hard times since I last had seen him more than thirty years before. His daughter, a missionary, died in a car wreck in El Paso, Texas, when she was twenty-five. Three years later, his twenty-nine-year-old son died in a boating accident. Now his wife was dead. "I'm all alone," he said then. "I'm the last of the Rossolls."

HARRY is a first-rate story teller. He was eighty-seven when we visited him, and he remembered in great detail the story of Smokey's birth.

His loneliness had not slowed his work or his creativity. During our visit, as he told about Tree Bear, he also told us that the birth of Smokey had not been nearly as easy as the birth of Tree Bear.

In his effort to help the Forest Service teach Americans to prevent forest fires, Harry first created Ranger Jim, dapper and trim, with a neatly tied necktie and a pipe. "He was," Harry said, "a flop."

Next, Harry created the Forest Fire Devil, a horned creature made of wood that would have an instinctive aversion to forest fires. Another flop.

Then Harry trotted out the creation he thought for sure would be a hit: A beaver that could flap out fires with his tail. The flapper was flopper Number 3.

"So, H.M. Sears, one of my forest service friends, said, 'How about a bear?'"

He took H.M.'s advice, but that path, too, had its

bumps. His first attempts at Smokey weren't successful.

The first Smokey had a pointed snoot with a bulb nose (by Harry's own description, he looked more like a possum in dungarees) and a World War II helmet. "He was," Harry says, "scraggly."

Tree Bear was an Oklahoman because of Harry's friendship with Quintus Herron. Mr. Herron, a famous forester in McCurtain County, was looking for a positive approach to counter environmentalists' message that to cut a tree is a sin. Good things come from trees, Mr. Herron believes, and like corn or wheat, a crop of trees is a renewable resource. He talked it over with Harry, and Tree Bear came to life.

But Harry's relationship goes back further than that. In the 1970s, after McCurtain County foresters had built the Heritage Forest Center at Beavers Bend State Park, they decided their museum needed something special.

So Lee Clymer, the first director of the center, suggested they talk to Harry. Harry traveled to Oklahoma, looked at the center and accepted their commission. "He thought he could do it in a couple of years," says Michelle Finch-Walker, director of the forest center.

Twelve years later, in 1990, he finished the last of fourteen murals, which traced the life of the forest from the days of the dinosaur.

Harry painted the 7-foot-by-21-foot dioramas in his studio in Atlanta, rolled them up and mailed them to Broken Bow, where Director John Bain would glue them up. Harry then would come to Broken Bow to paint the foregrounds.

Harry's passion for the work was clear as he told us about it during our visit to Atlanta. After our trip, he and I talked on the phone once in a while. He sent me a rough sketch of a Tree Bear comic book he was drawing and asked for my critique. I haven't, I'm sorry to report, written him back. And until recently, I had forgotten all about the most important work of his career.

O N the advice of many Oklahomans, my family and I made the trip to Broken Bow. It was on the morning after our first night in a cabin that I recalled the Oklahoma chapter of Harry's life.

I was loitering in the Heritage Center when a headline on the front page of the *Hochatown Tourist* startled me: "Creator of ... Smokey Bear Dies." I grabbed the paper and sure enough, there was a picture of Harry Rossoll. Somehow, I had missed the news of his death in February.

It was appropriate, though, that I learned of his death here at the Forest Heritage Center, home to his best work.

I learned more of his story from Mrs. Finch-Walker, her husband, Terry Walker, and Doug Zook, all of whom spoke with affection of their resident artist, and of his sense of humor and creativity. The three of them traveled to Atlanta in the summer of 1996 and set up a Tree Bear booth at Centennial Plaza at the 1996 Summer Olympics. Their booth opened the same day as the bombing at the Olympics, and that was the end of Tree Bear's debut.

Recently, Doug was cleaning the front case of one diorama and discovered one of Harry's half-smoked, half-chewed cigars. Michelle pulled it from a shelf in her office to show me. "It was eerie," she said. "It was like Harry was still with us."

HARRY Rossoll has left much of himself behind: Smokey, Tree Bear, his dioramas, his half-smoked cigar and his stories, like this one he told me:

Harry grew up in Connecticut, where his father wanted him to stay and raise chickens. Instead, he followed the art that was in his heart and took a job as an illustrator for the *New York Herald Tribune*. He also went to art school.

To earn a living, however, he and his wife, Olga, moved to Mississippi, where his odd jobs included painting polka dots on women's high heels to make them stylish. It was while he was working for the Works Progress Administration that he enjoyed a rather abrupt introduction to the South.

One day in Jackson, a driving rainstorm caught Harry without protection. He asked an elderly woman, who was swinging on her porch, if he might take refuge from the rain.

The woman, who appeared to be in her eighties, talked along pleasantly enough and soon asked him: "Where are you from?"

Harry sensed from her tone that he might be in trouble.

He dodged the question.

She asked again.

He evaded again.

When she persisted a third time, he finally confessed.

"I'm from Norwich, Connecticut," he answered.

"You're a Yankee," she said.

"Lady," he replied, "I was born there. I can't help

where I was born."

"My brother was killed in the Civil War."

"The war has been over for years."

"You're a Yankee," she said. "You're a (blankety-blank) Yankee. Get off my porch."

HARRY Rossoll wasn't the only artist to help birth Smokey Bear. Rudolph Wendelin was the artist to refine and soften Harry's original concepts, and Rudy often receives acclaim as Smokey's creator. Harry acknowledged that and lived with it, but sometimes his irritation showed.

His irritation, however, didn't evolve into bitterness. Harry continued to work. For years, Harry drew the "Smokey Says" comic that appeared in hundreds of newspapers. And even late in his life when many others are looking to retire, Harry took on the biggest project of his life, the history of the forest, and that is his gift to Oklahoma, his and his alone.

## LeFlore County: Poteau

FOR the record, I have done dumber things than try to ride my bicycle up the World's Highest Hill in 102-degree August heat, but at the moment I'm hard pressed to name one.

Anyway, here I am on my twenty-four-speed mountain bike, and the sun-boiled asphalt pops beneath my wheels like plastic bubble wrap.

This bicycle thing, I can't help myself. Maybe it's hanging onto childhood, to something my daddy taught me to do on the junior high parking lot. Certainly, bicycling is one of the best ways to see the world.

Whatever the cause of this obsession, however, I am obsessed. Hills don't scare me. I often take my bicycle with me on my travels, just in case I encounter a hill that needs conquering.

So from the moment I heard about Cavanal Hill, this ride was inevitable.

I start near the high school, which is on Highway 59, and the first mile isn't too bad.

Halfway into the second mile, however, I feel like the weeds along the road look: Rain is in short supply here in LeFlore County, and the vegetation is drooping.

I, too, am drooping and pooping out. The water in my water bottles is as hot as the air; it wets my whistle but doesn't cool it.

Now I'm off my bicycle, my jelly legs quivering as I pace in the sparse shade of a cedar and pour my hot water on my over-heated head.

The road before me shows no signs of relenting. That's okay. I'll show the road who is boss.

If I had talked to F.L. Holton before I started my ride, I might have begun early in the morning or waited until autumn.

Mr. Holton first ascended the hill as a ten-year-old kid, riding to the top on his Shetland pony. Or *sometimes* riding: "You had to pull your horse about halfway up the mountain," he says.

From the bottom of Cavanal Hill to the top, you gain 2,000 feet in six miles. The road to the top of Pike's Peak in Colorado gains 6,000 feet in eighteen miles. The rate of incline is the same.

And no less an authority than "National Geographic" has declared that Cavanal Hill is the world's highest hill, Mr. Holton says. The people who decide these sorts of things say a mountain must rise at least 2,000 feet above the local terrain.

Anything shorter than that is a hill.

Well, while Cavanal Hill's official height is 2,479 feet above sea level, it rises only 1,999 feet above the Poteau terrain. Poteau's leaders measure from city hall, with an elevation of 480 feet, leaving Cavanal twelve inches shy of mountainhood.

Sam Sorrels, a Poteau man, bought land at the top of the mountain and was the first to build a road to the top, which still is the basic route.

Don "Diamond Don, Jewel of the Airwaves" Barnes, a local radio personality, was a member of the Jaycees class that helped raise money to improve the road. In 1991, Diamond Don was elected mayor of Poteau and had the city place a huge granite marker next to the pavilion at the hill's top.

Through the years, folks have envisioned grand things for their hill, but beyond coal production, little has come to fruition.

Among landowners on Cavanal, the late Senator Robert S. Kerr may be the best known. After he purchased his acreage on high, Senator Harry Byrd from Virginia gave him apple trees to plant. The orchard failed.

In the last decade, a company spent several million dollars in search of natural gas, but hit nothing.

There's also naturally sweet water beneath the hill, Mr. Holton says.

Diamond Don still has hopes for tourism on the hill. "I am," he says, "trying to generate some interest in an annual all-terrain vehicle race to the top of the world's highest hill."

AT three miles up the hill, I'm halfway there, but I'm doubting I'll make it. At four miles up the hill, having averaged about six miles per hour, I say "uncle." Cavanal Hill has won.

I rest a minute, drink more of my hot water and ride back down the hill.

I hang my bike on the rack and drive up the hill. The road folds back on itself several times. I know this: My decision to drive was the right choice.

But this I also know: No little strip of switch-backing blacktop is going to whip me, even if it does wind. to the top of the World's Highest Hill. I'll be back.

In November.

# Choctaw County: Hugo

MORE than most gravestones in a cemetery, these tell a story. "Frank Whalen, 1908-1967, Showman to the End." "Zefta Loyal, Queen of the Bareback Riders, Original Loyal Repensky Troupe." "Ikirt, Boss Elephant Man for Carson & Barnes Circus."

"Charles Fuller, June 24, 1950 — April 3, 1967. Drowned in a swimming accident while with Carson & Barnes Circus. Erected by John Carroll's fund."

What the headstones don't tell, your imagination fills in. Charles Fuller: seventeen when he drowned. Had he run away from home to join the circus? His headstone was paid for from an endowment left by another showman. Was there no mother or father to pay for Fuller's tombstone? Did they even know he had died?

There is a special poignancy to this part of Mount Olivet Cemetery, known as Showman's Rest, the plots where the circus people are laid to rest. These are the people for whom the circus was life.

Eight, nine months out of the year, seven days a week, circus performers drive miles for smiles under the big top. Away from the applause, the silence of the cemetery seems even louder.

Even in death, the circus is their life. Their tombstones are unlike any other, cut to look like the big tent that was their work place, or etched with a sketch to illustrate their talent, like walking the tightrope or riding bareback.

Ted Bowman's grave is the freshest one here, so new that the dirt is still mounded up and his gravestone doesn't show the date of his death. He died in his bed early on July 30, 1999, a Friday.

Only two days before, on Wednesday, Ted had granted an interview to a reporter for the Hugo newspaper. Cindy Clark, who was with him at the interview, says the story never was published. "We're all still in shock," she says. "Our town historian has died."

Ted, originally from Tulsa, joined the circus in 1949. When he retired in 1993, he moved to Hugo, winter home of the five-ring Carson & Barnes Circus. His knowledge of circus history was unparalleled, Cindy says, at least in these parts.

He was known as Mr. Route for his collection of circus route cards, which list a circus' itinerary. When he couldn't find a route card, he went into newspaper offices along the routes, read the ads from years gone by and reconstructed the routes.

"Ted had the best collection of circus routes in the world," says Doyle Milson, general agent for Carson & Barnes and a pallbearer at Ted's funeral. "He was really quite a historian."

Ted's tombstone is a wheel from a circus wagon, called a "sunburst wheel," Doyle says. The wheel derives its name from its orange paint. "That's the way they painted the wagon wheels in the old days," Doyle says.

Ted's grave is next to a tombstone etched with a picture of a big-top tent and a performing elephant: "A tribute to all showmen under God's big top," it says.

Ted, who never married nor had any children, worked his way up to general manager of the circus. He was taking tickets at the front gate when he retired. His epitaph is among the most bittersweet.

"There's nothing left but empty popcorn sacks and wagon tracks," it says. "The circus is gone."

But the show has never stopped. Showman's Rest is on many a tour bus route. Says Cindy Clark, whose husband is caretaker at Mount Olivet: "We're probably the only cemetery to have bus route signs."

## *The Circus is Over*

*After my first visit to Hugo, I had planned to*

*return to meet D.R. Miller, who ran the Carson & Barnes Circus. But he died on the road with his circus, less than two weeks after I visited his adopted home town. Instead of an interview with Mr. Miller, I covered his funeral for The Daily Oklahoman. This is the story I wrote for the November 11, 1999, newspaper.*

THEY turned D.R. Miller's funeral into a circus. Which, of course, is exactly how he planned it. "He wanted the publicity for the circus," his daughter Barbara Miller Byrd said after the funeral.

On Tuesday, a crew of men and Miller's beloved circus elephants erected a big-top tent. On Wednesday, they held his funeral in the tent, complete with bleachers, spotlights and a band.

A parade of circus animals led the procession to Mount Olivet Cemetery. Miller's body, which has been in storage in Denver since his death September 8, arrived in a horse-drawn hearse built in 1872.

Most everything the Millers and the circus do makes headlines in this town. In September, when Isa the elephant gave birth, the top headline in Hugo's newspaper was, "It's a girl."

D.R. Miller's funeral was no exception. They closed school for the day, and some businesses closed. The Upper Crust Bakery, which usually has sold all its Bavarian cream pastries by nine in the morning, still had a counter full, and the shop was empty.

"This is a true D.R. Miller production," his nephew Kevin Murray said. "It's guaranteed to be at least one hour and forty-five minutes long, and there will be no intermission."

THE lighting crew provided one set of spotlights for Mr. Miller's funeral, and the sun provided the other. As his granddaughter Kristin, his nephew Kevin, friends and the Reverend Steve Goughnour each took a turn at the microphone, the sun beamed into the tent through the pole holes in the top.

As the morning and the service progressed, the beams of light moved ever so slightly through center ring, where Mr. Miller's casket rested atop two bull tubs, the stands on which elephants perform.

Behind the speaker's stand, one beam moved across a miniature circus wagon, lighting up the artificial greenery and the tiger inside the cage. The cage was in the spotlight.

The funeral directors slid the flowers to the foot

of his casket and opened the lid. As hundreds filed past
for a look at Mr. Miller, in his red elephant tie and a
Carson & Barnes hat nestled at his elbow, the sun spot
moved off the tiger's cage and onto the grass.

As Jon Paul Bozeman wiped the fingerprints off the
shiny red paint that coated D.R.'s solid copper casket,
the sun spot moved onto a wreath of artificial flowers.
The wreath encircled the words, spelled out on poster
board: "D.R. Miller. King of the Showmen."

As Mrs. Byrd tucked a red handkerchief in the top
pocket of her father's suit coat, the sun lit the yellow
flowers and the top of the sign. Miller was in the
spotlight again.

As the seven pallbearers, circus men all, hoisted
his coffin and walked out of the big top, the sun moved
off the wreath and shined to the ground behind. The
spotlight was off. The show was over.

ON the last day of his life, a Saturday in
September, the circus was in McCook, Nebraska.
Dores Richard Miller wasn't feeling well, and after he
fainted, his family took him to the hospital. The doctors
said he was okay.

Mrs. Byrd was driving him back to the circus grounds
and they lost their way. "You know," he told his daughter,
"I saw my first circus here." He had never told her that.

The year was 1924, and he was eight years old.

On September 8, 1999, after he returned to his
trailer, he rested while his daughter checked on the show.
When she returned, her father was in his golf cart.

"Dad, what are you doing?"

"I want some chicken soup."

She found some. He ate it. Then he wanted to see a
photograph a fan had given him. The photo showed his wife
in the early days. His maid tried to find the picture.
Miller collapsed.

Mrs. Byrd was walking toward the midway when she
heard shouts of: "Call 911!"

But her father was gone. He saw his last circus in
the town where he saw his first one.

D. R. Miller and his circus have been in Hugo
since 1942, when Vernon Pratt visited their
winter home in Mena, Arkansas, and lured them to Hugo with
free rent and utilities. In return, the Millers showed
their animals on Sundays.

In the years since, more than a dozen circuses have
wintered in Hugo. The cemetery has a special plot,

Showman's Rest, where only circus people are buried. On the day of his funeral, Showman's Rest was the eighty-three-year-old showman's destination.

Cindi Cavallini led the procession on Chopin, a black Friesian horse. Behind her, Gizmo and Bert, the camels, followed. Then the llamas Lucky and Sam. Three more Friesians. Then Susie, a forty-eight-year-old elephant that was one of the first five Miller bought.

Then the band wagon, on loan from the International Circus Hall of Fame in Peru, Indiana, followed. A brass band and a clown named Peanut were aboard.

The 130-year-old funeral coach was last, its sides of oval glass giving the hundreds who lined Fifth Street a view of Miller's fancy casket.

Goughnour said words of comfort while gold leaves of the sweetgum rode the breeze to the ground, the same breeze on which yellow butterflies flittered in the sun.

THEN it was over. They put Dorey, as his friends called him, in the 3,000-pound copper vault over the grave that Glenn Clark had dug.

Then Leonard Massey turned the crank that lowered Dorey into the ground. Clinkety, clinkety, clinkety, the strain on the cables evident in the sound of the crank.

Clackety, clackety clack. The sound of the crank as the coffin settled in the 5-1/2-foot-deep hole. Then the cables went slack.

Two months after he died, three hours since the start of his funeral, Miller's body was at its rest. Back at the big top, the tent lay flat on the ground. The crew rolled up the flame-retardant vinyl.

Around the perimeter of the tent, a trainer prodded Nina, one of Dorey's elephants. "Nina! Head down."

He wrapped a massive chain around one of the stakes that had held the tent in place. The other end of the chain was connected to Nina's leg.

"Nina! Pull up."

Stake by stake, Nina took down Miller's big top.

Back at Mount Olivet, friends continued to arrive to see the fresh mound of dirt atop Dorey. Sweetgum leaves rode the wind. Yellow butterflies flittered and mingled among the mourners.

Tent down.

Grave covered.

Spotlight dim.

Show over.

Nina!

Head down.

# Grady County: In Three Parts

NEAR RUSH SPRINGS — Night has fallen, too dark to tell the difference between a twenty-dollar bill and a ten, but eighty-year-old Ruby West is still at her melon stand on U.S. 81 north of Rush Springs. Been there since seven a.m.

"You can't catch me till eight, nine o'clock in the eve'nin'," she says. "'Bout a month ago, the doctor told me I had a good, strong heart. High blood pressure is all that's wrong with me, that and old age. Never been in the hospital except to have my second child. Had my first one in the house. Sixty-one years ago, the doctor came to the house to deliver my first one."

Her tone is one of incredulity when I ask if she still works in her melon patches. "What else am I going to do? I was out there hoeing, wasn't I, Joe?" She is inquiring of her hired hand for her alibi. "I think exercise is what keeps you going. I get used to the heat. I don't stay under air conditioning. I don't like air conditioning."

She's been selling melons at this spot for fifty-nine years, working in melons for longer than that. She and her husband, Ray, raised melons and cattle. She first worked in a melon patch when she was a teen-ager. "Used to, if we could get a quarter apiece, three for a dollar, we thought we were making the money," she says.

In September 1999, her melons are selling for four bucks apiece, five apiece for the black diamonds. Cantaloupes are a dollar apiece.

In the early dark, Ruby looks seventy, or maybe even sixty-five. She says whatever comes to her mind. Mention a competitor who is selling watermelons for two bucks apiece, and she erupts: "He ought to be horsewhipped."

Her husband died ten years ago. She just buried her older son, who was sixty-one when he lost a long fight with cancer. Now her younger son, forty-seven-year-old Bobby, is helping her keep track of the melons, their black Angus cattle, and their oil and gas wells.

"It's hard work," she says. "You better believe it's hard work."

ᔕᘓᏻ  ᔕᘓᏻ  ᔕᘓᏻ

MIDDLEBURG — This is a moment of outdoor worship, conducted by four men in boots and work clothes soiled with red dirt. Jeff Courtney washes down the newly poured cement sidewalks. Ernie Sheltry moves dirt with a shovel. Les Courtney, too, wields a shovel. Steve Grodecki checks progress.

"A project like this is, in its own way, an act of worship," Les says. "Swinging a hammer is like singing or teaching a Sunday school class. We are working to a high standard."

Ernie, owner of Rose Ridge Ranch, puts it like this: "Swinging a hammer and doing it to the best of our ability is a form of praise."

Middleburg Baptist Church, then, was built mostly with the praise of its members, all the way back to its start in 1959, when they broke ground.

Bill Baxter, who now lives one county over in Lindsay, was the bivocational pastor of the church then. The church sits on the original site of a Baptist church that was built in 1907 and closed in the 1920s.

A group of men formed a board of trustees and the church building became the Community Church, open to any denomination for services. The church was used most often for summertime revivals, Bill says.

In the 1950s, after First Baptist Church in Chickasha held a revival there, the church members decided Middleburg needed its own church. That's when they asked Bill Baxter to be its pastor. When it came time to construct a new church building, First Church of Chickasha offered free lumber to Middleburg. All they had to do to claim it was to tear down a two-story house on the First Church property.

On Labor Day 1958, the men of the Middleburg church took down the house in one day and stacked the lumber in a member's yard. During the week, the women and girls of the church pulled nails from the timber.

At a church business meeting, the church voted to borrow only 2,500 dollars with which to build. "That was as deep in debt as we wanted to go," Bill says. "With material out of the house and 2,500 dollars, we would build until we ran out of resources. We never stopped building."

When it came time to finish the outside, they decided to use natural rock rather than brick. With a borrowed pickup, Bill and Mike Whinery, a teen-ager, made trips to several quarries to haul back the rock.

Their mason was a seventy-nine-year-old man, last name Pulis, who lived with Baxter and his family during the week. Once a man stopped and offered to pay Pulis double what the church was paying him. "I don't know," Pulis replied. "I'm doing this work for the Lord. I don't know if you can double that."

One Sunday evening when Bill went to pick up Mr. Pulis for the week, his wife told Bill she hated to see the job come to an end. "My husband is an alcoholic," she said. "He hasn't had a drink since this job started."

The mason never would tell the church what to pay him. "Sleep me and feed me," he said. When he was finished, this is all he asked: Put a wooden box with a hole in the top at the back of the church. Padlock it and tell people what it's for. Leave it there for thirty days. After thirty days, he said, he'd take the box home and that would be his wage. "I never did know what he got paid," Bill said.

Last fall, church members remodeled the inside of the sanctuary. Now they are laying a sidewalk and building a new vestibule, which they gave up last year to enlarge the auditorium. "There's the obvious fellowship," Ernie says of the benefit of working together instead of hiring the work done.

And, says Les: "The church becomes yours in a way it doesn't if you just go there."

ಜೋಲ ಜೋಲ ಜೋಲ

RUSH SPRINGS — Sharon Fleener unconsciously rubs her crew cut hair and then says, almost as an afterthought: "You can tell I've had cancer." Later she jokes: "I don't have to worry about my hair. It doesn't blow in the wind."

She is sitting at a table in her diner, which she closes at half past one in the afternoon. Now, it's almost seven. She has just returned from her supply run, which ended across the street at Teel Grocery & Market with the purchase of tortillas for burritos and enchiladas.

Sharon's diner is in the building that was called T.C.'s when she was growing up. She opens at six-thirty for breakfast. She works the front. Her sister, Linda, runs the kitchen and cooks biscuits, burgers, Mexican food, chicken fried steak and everything else — except the breakfast gravy — from scratch. "We were so busy during the watermelon festival, that I bought frozen french fries," she confesses. "Everybody kept asking when we were going to have good potatoes."

Sharon has five sisters and six brothers. She was one of the triplets born to her mother on March 3, 1957. "Three is my lucky number," she says. "Born March 3 - 3/3. And a triplet. I was the last of the triplets born." That also makes her the last of the twelve children.

She talks freely about her cancer and believes she is going to lick it. On Labor Day 1998, as Sharon was doctoring a sunburn, she found a tiny lump in her right breast. By the time of her surgery in early 1999, cancer had spread into her lymph system.

But she doesn't talk about fear or loneliness. She talks about the comfort and strength she derives from her seven-year-old son, Jimmy. "So many times a day, he tells me he loves me. That is the best medicine." And the members of her church, who pray endlessly for her, give her strength. "I feel like I'm going to be all right," she says. "With the good Lord's help, I'm going to be okay."

She talks about the many people in Rush Springs who always ask how she's feeling, of classmates from grade school who come to the diner to hug her.

A mile or so east, at Jeff Davis Park, quart-size football players are butting heads on the practice field. Two at a time, they lie on the ground, one holding a football. A coach whistles. They roll to their feet. The one with the ball charges, the other tackles him. Upon impact, their plastic helmets and shoulder pads crack like the muffled report of a twenty-two-caliber rifle.

The sun, a bit of autumn hue mixed into its slanting rays, lights half the field, the rest of which lies in the shade of the cottonwoods. The temperature is in the low eighties, and the breeze makes the air feel even cooler.

Downtown is empty; nearly everyone has gone home for supper or to the park for practice. The last of the customers leave John Teel's grocery. From her seat in the diner, Sharon can see the corner where Kay's Dairy Queen once stood. This is Rush Springs, watermelon capital.

This is what she came back for, life in a small town where almost everyone knows her well enough to hug her. When she was bald, she didn't wear a wig. And she won't wear a prosthesis. "Everyone in town knew I had breast cancer," she says. "I decided I would go natural."

She tried living away from Rush Springs but came home, in part, to simplify her life. Now she's trying to simplify again. She wants to sell the diner, which she opened in 1994, before the divorce. "I feel like it's time," she says, "to spend more time with my son."

She lived in Corpus Christi and San Antonio and even in Oklahoma City. But home is where her heart is. "It is nice," she says, "to be back to the four-way stop."

# Canadian County: Calumet

THIS story sounds like he made it up, Alvin Moberly admits, but Buddy, his low-riding spitz, really did help him dig a grave at Canadian Valley cemetery.

Make no mistake, Alvin Moberly is a story a minute, and most of his stories do *sound* like stories. But when you've done some things in your life, your tales have that element of intrigue. And Alvin has the scars, the Purple Heart and the photographs to back up his stories. So you can take his story about Buddy for true.

One day, Alvin was digging a 3-foot-by-3-foot grave. (Alvin, by the way, knew that a 3-by-3 wasn't going to be big enough for the deceased. "What are you going to do, double him over?" Alvin asked. The man's body, it turns out, had been cremated.)

The rain-softened soil wasn't cooperating as Alvin tried to square off the corners, so he tossed Buddy into the grave and showed the dog where to dig.

After the funeral, Alvin stayed behind with the undertaker and another fellow. The man threw in a few shovels full of dirt and Alvin said, "Let's let the dog do it." So he placed Buddy on the mound of dirt and said, "Dig." Buddy kicked the dirt behind him into the square grave. "Them guys, I thought they'd laugh themselves to death," Alvin says.

I found Alvin Moberly out front of his store, washing down his Ford Jubilee '53 tractor, which he uses to — among other things — mow the Canadian Valley cemetery.

The store isn't exactly his any more, but it's still in the family, and his house is still attached. Alvin and Alma bought the place in 1953 but retired in 1998 when they decided not to spend the money to bring their gas tanks up to the new EPA standards.

They turned the store over to their son, Jimmy, and his wife, Earlene, who now sell antiques and marbles from the rock-wall building. Jimmy has been buying, selling and trading marbles for about seven years, and he's selling marbles worth thousands of dollars each.

In its heyday, the Moberlys' store was the place to buy cream and eggs, but state regulations put them out of that business. They also butchered beef until rules, again, interfered.

Alvin, who is seventy-six, remembers the store from his days as a kid when a Mr. Breeze owned it. "On

Saturdays, he would toss pennies to the kids," he says "It was the biggest scramble you've ever seen." He bought the shop from Mrs. Sam Griesel, who leased it to Doug Wall. Alvin traded twenty-three head of cattle to Doug for inventory and equipment inside the store.

He has lived his entire life here, except for the Army years. He still owns a piece of a farm that his grandfather, Caleb, homesteaded in the run of 1889. Caleb had come out with two brothers, who brought along a woman. Caleb was the only one of the three brothers to obtain his land, so the other two set off for the Northwest and said they would be back for the woman. But they never returned. "That's where my grandmother came from," he says.

Alvin, his wife, Alma, and both of their children graduated from Calumet's high school.

Two pictures of Alvin on two different horses stand high on an old freezer case in the store. These pictures were taken during his F Troop days with the U.S. Army's last mounted Cavalry unit.

In one of his first horseback postings, he patrolled the border between the United States and Mexico, but he wasn't looking for illegal immigrants. He was patrolling for Germans and Japanese, whom the U.S. government feared would invade the United States through Mexico.

Then his unit was shipped out to help open the Burma Road. He lost a number of friends and comrades in that campaign, especially on February 2, 1945, the day they took a hill at the cost of a couple hundred lives.

He still bears two scars from that tour, one on his left hand, one on his left leg. He burned his hand on the barrel of his Browning automatic, still hot from shooting at Japanese soldiers. Shrapnel tore up the thigh on his left leg, but the doctor stitched him up in the field. "I didn't miss a day of combat," he says.

Life is slower now, less exciting. The Moberlys are retired from gas and groceries, but they still give away air and water out front, and Alvin still inflates bicycle tires for children. They have reduced the number of gas pumps out front from six to one, and that pump is for sale.

The rock store — Alvin did much of the rocking himself — remains a refuge from the heat and the world, a place to tell his stories. The store served its purpose for them. They raised their children, earned a living. "It was time," Alma says, "to retire."

They haven't quit life. They keep up with the F Troopers and attend most of the reunions. And every time a car stops out front, Alvin jumps, as if he still is running a service station. It's such a habit, it's instinctive. "Alma, Jimmy and I, washed a million windshields."

## Kingfisher County: Loyal

BOX 4 at the Loyal post office doesn't see any mail these days. Roy Gill died a few months back, and postmaster Elaine Kadavy forwards the mail to one of his children out on the rural route. Roy's contract doesn't expire until October, however, so Elaine keeps the box open for him.

"He knew everybody," Elaine says. "Anybody needed information, that's where you sent them."

Elaine has worked at this post office for twenty-six years, the last seventeen of them as postmaster. Often as not, she knows who is sick and who is celebrating. "Generally, I do know if a bunch of cards come when it's somebody's birthday or anniversary. You generally find out who's in the hospital, if you haven't already heard. You know when it's bill-paying time."

The post office is a good source of information, she allows, but a better source is across the street at Turner's Café, where Coraletha Turner has no regular opening time. "It opens when the first guy who wants coffee gets down here," she says. Several of her regular customers have a key to the cafe. First one in starts the coffee. "We've done that for years," she says. "You couldn't do that in most places."

Coraletha came here more than forty years ago. She was a divorced, twenty-seven-year-old mother of three who married a forty-year-old loyal bachelor from Loyal. When she came, the cafe was more of a recreation hall with card games and dominoes. Now it's the place where the farmers talk and watch the sky refuse to rain.

"They are probably down at the elevator now," she says as the clock creeps toward three. Many will return for their afternoon coffee at four. "They are waiting for a rain so they can start sowing wheat."

LOYAL hasn't always been Loyal. Bob York, one of the old-timers, writes in a brief history of the town that originally it was named for the town of Kiel in Germany. Doctor Paul Friedman came here, took possession of a small tract of land, built a home and opened his medical office. On June 15, 1892, Doctor Friedman applied for a post office permit and opened it in his doctor's office. He apparently named the town when he applied for the postal permit.

In its early days, Kiel had a blacksmith shop, a feed lot, a drugstore, a lumberyard and a mercantile store. The first school was built of sod. Jennie Bunch, the first teacher, earned twenty dollars per month. Rain was scarce the first couple of years, Mr. York writes, but those who held on for the third year made a good crop.

The theft of horses became a problem, and the town quickly organized the Anti-Horse-Thief Association, with Henry Callison as its president. They learned the horse thieves were hiding about ten miles southeast of Kiel.

"The Association made up a posse, went to the place, turned the horses loose and ordered the family ... from their home and burned the house," Mr. York writes.

Kiel became Loyal on October 1, 1918, the town's way of showing its loyalty to the United States.

WHOEVER would have that Elaine Kadavy would wind up as postmaster here, in charge of everybody's mail? Elaine Kadavy could have been an outcast here in Loyal, a town in a county where basketball is — and always has been — a big deal.

Talk to her long enough and you learn that she was a member of the 1954 women's state championship basketball team. But for the wrong team. Elaine, who was at Schaberg in her basketball days, was a guard for Big Four High School, the team that beat Loyal for the crown that year.

Except for basketball, life is pretty slow in Loyal. Elaine sees most of her thirty box holders at least once a day in this nearly hundred-year-old building that once was a bank. Across the street, Coraletha sits behind her counter in the afternoon and reads the Enid newspaper, waiting for the farmers to return for their afternoon coffee. Elaine likes her post office, Coraletha her cafe.

"It is," Coraletha says, "just a little place in a little bitty town."

# Caddo County: Hydro

THEY are so young to have suffered this, these two brave sisters. But youth is their anesthetic. They lie there in the dark, as often they do, behind their rock-wall house, lie there on the blanket, their eyes on the heavens. Out here, the dark is darker than in the city. The stars are bigger.

The song they sing is one of their favorites. Young as they are, they understand the part about the broken heart.

> *There once was an Indian maid*
> *A shy little Indian maid*
> *Who sang all day, her love song gay*
> *As on the plain she would while away the day.*

Their mother, as she often does, comes out. Sometimes she joins the song. She likes the song about Red Wing, but really she prefers hymns. The hymns sustain her as she endures the grief. Sometimes she sings, sometimes she only listens — listens for the other voice, the voice of that third little girl who ought to be harmonizing with these two.

Sometimes, in the dark, when they have paused in their music, Myrtle will speak to Jackie and Rita. "Honey," she'll say, and they understand she is speaking to both of them, "you see that bright star up there? That's Shirley."

SHIRLEY was the first of the three daughters born to Cody and Myrtle Thomas, delivered by Doctor Joseph Henke right there in that one-room house set back from the sandy road. She always was older than her age, reading right through the primers her parents sold at the family's drugstore in downtown Hydro.

Eighteen months after Shirley's arrival, Jackie came, and in another eighteen months, Rita arrived. Even at three and four years old, Shirley mothered her baby sisters, rescuing them from danger the way she did the day Jackie stepped in the bed of red ants.

Their daddy was one of the pharmacists in town, proprietor of North Side Drugs (not that there really was a north side of town, but the store sat on the north side of the street). Cody Thomas sold more veterinary supplies than medicine for his human customers, and often he helped administer the drugs to the animals. He delivered prescriptions and would open at any hour for someone in need of medicine.

Their human customers drank to their health at the soda fountain, where the Thomas children chipped ice from hundred-pound blocks for the soft drinks. Their daddy bought milk for milkshakes from Fred Stange, even after the bureaucrats over in Oklahoma City made up new rules that said he couldn't. Cody believed that homogenized milk caused cancer. "Nobody," he declared, "has milk any cleaner than Fred Stange."

Some Saturday nights, he didn't close until after midnight when the last of the weekend shoppers finally left for their farms. He sold Pangburn's chocolates, and when age or heat marred their beauty, Cody Thomas took the candies home to his wife and daughters.

Hydro, which takes its name from its wealth of fine well water, was surrounded by fields of wheat. When the Thomas children weren't at the drugstore chipping ice or playing in the old cosmetics their mother left in a drawer for them, they were around the corner at their house, playing at the edge of the wheat fields, sitting on the steps of the Methodist church next door to their house, building castles in the sand that was their road and their front yard.

They made the castles by piling sand on a hand, slowly pulling out the hand and adorning the mold of the hand with flowers. For the privilege of viewing their castles, they collected a one-cent fee from Lon Flansburg, their mailman and next-door neighbor.

Sometimes they had chewing gum, not often though. Grain plucked from the head of the wheat served as a good substitute.

On a day in September 1932, shortly after Rita's first birthday, Shirley, Jackie and their friend Lornell Blakley sat on the steps of the Methodist church, chewing wheat for gum. Neither they nor anyone in town could have known that within seventy-two hours, one of the little girls would be dead. In three days, Shirley's star would slip from their home in Hydro to the dark sky above.

J ACKIE Thomas Long is sixty-nine now; Rita Thomas Russell is sixty-eight. Jackie clearly remembers Shirley. But for Rita, Shirley is only a story — the big sister for whom their mother often cried.

The sisters grew up as good friends in a house where their parents expected them to respect one another. Their father sometimes drank to excess but quit the day that his surviving daughters found him drunk and told their mother. Myrtle ordered him to leave the house, informing him she could raise the girls fine without him. He promised to quit, and as far as anyone knows, Cody Thomas never drank again.

On their way to adulthood, the sisters lived a good life. They remember the times in fall when their mother would call ahead to the Skirvin Hotel in Oklahoma City and reserve a room for the two of them and two friends. The foursome would catch the Greyhound bus at the drugstore, where their father was the Greyhound agent, and spend two or three days at the state fair, watching their friends show their livestock.

They both played basketball for Hydro High School, and were on the team the year coach Garvin Isaacs took them to the state championship tournament.

It was March 1948. The team and their families drove to Oklahoma City on a Wednesday as the worst blizzard of the season shut down travel. The Thomases' car was the last one allowed through on Route 66.

Supper their first night in town was at Beverly's Chicken-in-the-Rough, famous for its chicken in a basket and apple-honey ice cream. Their coach and parents promised them a banquet in the upstairs room if they won the championship, which wasn't likely since they were playing against schools much bigger than Hydro, in the days before the tournaments were broken down by class.

Jackie, on offense, had a lethal hook shot almost impossible to defend. Rita stayed at the other end of the court on defense.

On Thursday night, the Hydro Bobcats beat Amorita, 38-24. Friday night, the Bobcats beat Lexington, 34-31. But Saturday night, with one quarter left to play, their energy and their optimism were fading as McLish High ran them ragged. This is how *The Oklahoman* reported the game in its March 14, 1948, edition:

"Hydro was down 7-15 at the close of the canto, in the hole 20-29 at the half and lagged 29-36 at the three-quarter mark while Tiny (Jacqueline) Thomas was sinking most of her 10 fielders and 10 charities. ...

"But when (Linda) Delaplain was pulled during the second period, little Thomas, with her almost blind hook shots ... plus Jo Ann Moore's fielders from the outside, pulled Hydro from the 7-15 mark to a 20-20 deadlock.

"Doolittle and McElroy had catapulted McLish into the lead at 34-20 just after the opening of the third quarter, but Jacqueline Thomas, hitting seven points in succession, and Moore pulled Hydro to the 29-36 level at the three-quarter mark.

"From there, their own backcourt defenders Rita Thomas, Marylin Phipps, Donna Raetz and Eileen Niehues caught some of the McLish fire to set the stage for the telling Hydro advance.

"With Delaplain still out of the fray, Hydro leaped to a tieing (sic) 38-38 tally. From that point, the lead changed hands four times and the count was deadlocked on three occasions.

"Hydro's Edith Scott shot her team into the lead at 41-40 with two-and-a-half minutes to go. At 45 seconds the score was tied again at 43-43, but Thomas and Moore clinched the battle with setups.

"Little Jacqueline Thomas, who probably doesn't scale over 95 pounds, sparked Hydro's two uphill drives with 30 points as the Hydro girls captured the state high school basketball crown 47-43 over McLish Saturday afternoon.

"The victory ... was totally unforeseen."

They had their celebration banquet, but not upstairs at Chicken-in-the-Rough. The champions were forced to eat shrimp cocktail at the Biltmore. They returned to Hydro as heroes. The week of their conquest, the blizzard was back-page news. The Lady Bobcats were the top story in that week's *Hydro Review*.

As the sisters approach their seventieth birthdays, they still live in Hydro and still see each other often, usually every day. "I don't know how we could be any closer," Jackie says. They speak gently to each other, call each other "honey." Their husbands are the best of friends. Jackie and Rita, like their father, became pharmacists. Rita and her husband Bob, who also became a pharmacist, took over her father's store.

The families also opened a hardware store, a dry goods store, a skating rink and a movie theater. (The sisters were so concerned about wholesome entertainment for the children of Hydro that once they made the projectionist stop a movie in the middle because it was not appropriate. "We just told him to shut it off, refunded their money and sent them home to their parents," Jackie says.)

A few years back, Jackie was awarded the Jim Thorpe Award as one of the best athletes in Oklahoma history, but she refused to allow news of it into the local newspaper because Rita hadn't been similarly honored.

Shirley's death during their childhood wasn't the end of deep sorrow for Rita and Jackie. Her death was, in fact, the beginning of seemingly endless calamity to come. On March 19, 1983, one of Rita's two daughters was killed in a car crash on the way home to Hydro from a funeral. Her husband, in the car behind her, saw the crash that killed his wife.

Only five months ago, Rita's other daughter, Jalee Abbott, lost a teen-age son in an accident on a four-wheeler. It seems a curse, almost, the mothers in the family losing a child. First Myrtle. Then Rita. Then

Jalee. Generation by generation.

Rita, then, has lost a sister, a daughter and a grandson. Rita understands the sorrow of a mother. Jackie, as close as a sister can be, understands pretty well too. She has seen Rita and Jalee and her own mother. "I honestly think," Jackie says, "Mama had to sing church songs to make it through."

ON that day in September 1932, the girls were chewing wheat in the sunshine and freedom of a late-summer afternoon. But something was wrong. The girls stomachs cramped. They went home. Shirley and Jackie were violently ill. Jackie was throwing up.

Two days later, Jackie, who was two, had improved, but four-year-old Shirley hadn't. Cody and Myrtle took Shirley to the hospital in Elk City. She never recovered.

The grownups made an awful discovery. The girls had been chewing "poison wheat," wheat treated with strychnine to attract and kill mice and rats. The children had found it on the ground at the church and assumed it safe to chew.

Neither of their parents ever recovered from Shirley's death. Years later, at the supper table, their mother sometimes would grow quiet and say, "It feels like somebody is missing."

So, as they grew up without Shirley, the girls and their mother sang. Any songs. Mostly church songs. "Mother would put the blanket out back," Jackie says. "We'd lay out there and look at the stars and sing."

They were so young to have suffered so, to lose their sister, and really, to lose their mother and father. Jackie still recalls how sick she was after chewing the wheat. Jackie and Rita both well remember singing under the stars.

Now, they are grandmothers with experience aplenty. By any measure, they are adults who have lived lives with full measures of happiness and more than their share of grief.

But as they sit in Jackie's living room and recall Shirley, and recall those nights out back of their house and try to recall the words to their favorite song, their voices of experience become voices of shy little sisters singing with a strange man listening.

Halting and high, their voices summon the words of the song about their Indian maid:

*She loved an Indian brave*
*This shy little Indian maid*

> *Until one day*
> *He rode away*
> *And fell bravely in the fray*
> *Oh, the moon shines tonight*
> *On pretty Red Wing*
> *Her brave is sleeping*
> *While Red Wing's weeping*
> *Her heart away.*

They were so young to have suffered this, these two sisters. They suffered it, and survived it and tell of it still. It's as fresh in memory as their breakfast this morning. In their memories, they lie there in the dark, behind their rock-wall house, lie there on the blanket, their eyes on the heavens, singing to Shirley, the prairie wind swirling with their voices of innocence, carrying their song to the star, the brightest one, the one that has winked back at them these sixty-something years.

# Creek County: East of Bristow

I tried to ride my bicycle up Cavanal Hill in Poteau — the world's highest, you'll recall — and it beat me. Never one to shy away from danger, though, I accepted another challenge: To hazard a bicycle ride on one of the Dead Man's Curves on Route 66.

Obviously, I survived. Somehow, though, the thrill doesn't translate from a souped-up '56 Chevy to a trip on a bicycle, even one with a bunch of gears. The fastest speed I mustered was twenty-six miles per hour, hardly a hair-raising ride on a fat-wheeled mountain bike.

While I didn't exactly cheat death, I did find myself in a contemplative mood. So I sat down under the Shoe Tree to contemplate the meaning of a bunch of shoes and cowboys boots that hang high from an elm tree at the eastern end of Dead Man's Curve.

This strip of the Mother Road, which is two-tenths of a mile long, is no longer in service. The curve has been straightened. Dead Man's Curve cuts through property that Ken and LaVonne Plute now own.

The Shoe Tree is the creation of their four sons: Chris, Rusty, Ronnie and Tim, now all grown.

LaVonne can't say why they started the tradition, but one day about ten years ago, one of her sons threw a pair of his old cowboy boots in the tree. Another son followed with another pair of shoes.

Then one day, a weary traveler noticed the tree with shoes in it and threw his shoes into the tree.

Another traveler noticed, and then another, and then sacrificing shoes to the Shoe Tree became fashionable, and once a thing becomes fashionable, neither rhyme, reason nor rational thought can explain or stop the thing.

One pair of cowboy boots led to a pair of sneakers, which led to a pair of flip-flops, and soon, the Shoe Tree was sprouting shoe leather, shoe canvas, shoe plastic, shoe rubber and cotton shoelaces. One fellow threw ten or twelve pairs into the thirty-foot tree.

Based on my count (and remember, I'm in newspapers not accounting), at least forty-five pairs of shoes were hanging on the tree when I stopped to count. The collection included three pairs of boots, a pair of white Gitano sneakers, one pair of yellow, green, red and purple Famolare sandals, black high-tops by Sportific, and one white sneaker signed: "The Simon Jones, Oklahoma."

LaVonne's eight-year-old granddaughter, Amanda, mails her old shoes from Virginia. The most-traveled pair was a pair of Nike sneakers from New York City. The shoes were still in great shape. "He signed them and dated them," LaVonne says, "and in three weeks they were gone."

At least one day a week, usually a Friday or a Saturday, LaVonne sets up shop at the east end of Dead Man's Curve to sell garage-sale stuff, a recently acquired hobby. "If I'd'a garage saled for years," she says, "I'd be rich and Wal-Mart wouldn't."

The Shoe Tree, which now is official because LaVonne painted a sign for it, has made LaVonne famous. She has been interviewed by a TV reporter from Tulsa, and the tree has made the official Route 66 newsletter.

The Shoe Tree, if you have shoes to discard, is about 4.3 miles east of Stroud's Rock Cafe on Route 66. If you are traveling east, it will be on the south side of the highway. (Come to think of it, if you are traveling west, it still will be on the south side of the highway.)

Your landmark is a stop sign planted next to a steel highway barricade. "I'm having a blast," LaVonne says. "I'm meeting people from the community and out of state."

She envisions someday that the Shoe Tree, like the highway that runs beside it, will be legendary, a part of the pop culture consciousness.

"I thought it would be fun to have an annual shoe toss," she says, "to see who can get their shoe up the highest. I'll try, and the shoes might not even hit the tree. It's not as easy as it looks."

ഇൗരു  ഇൗരു  ഇൗരു

DOWN the road from the shoe tree, in the burg of Bristow, Wendy Anne Spendiff mistakenly believes that she sounds something like a native. "I'm so proud," she says, "that I'm beginning to sound Okie."

To the folks back home in the United Kingdom, the edge of Spendiff's south London accent may have dulled. To Oklahoma ears, however, she's certifiably British.

While her seven years here and her ownership of a landmark Route 66 restaurant qualify her as an Oklahoman in good standing, her accent still attracts attention the way her hamburgers draw diners. "People tell me not to lose it," she says. "They like to hear me talk."

Her arrival in Oklahoma is the remarkable climax of a lifelong mystery that began when Spendiff's teen-age mother gave her up for adoption shortly after World War II. At age forty-seven, Spendiff saw a photograph of her mother for the first time. Shortly thereafter, Spendiff and her family pulled up their British roots to live near her mother in Oklahoma.

It was a long search with a happy ending. "I had to be counseled whether searching for my mother would be wise," she says. "The social worker said my situation was pretty hopeful because my mom had named me."

For her entire life, Spendiff had known her name was Wendy Anne. Now she knows why her mother named her that.

FROM the time she was five, Spendiff's adoptive parents had been honest with her about her adoption, telling her all they knew about her mother.

Her mother was a teenager in London who became pregnant by a soldier, most likely an American. Spendiff's grandfather said his daughter was too young to marry the man and go to the United States.

So when Spendiff was two months old, her mother put her in a church home. Seven months later, her mother gave her up for adoption. One of the mother's requests was that her child be given musical training. She also asked the adoptive parents that they tell their daughter about her. "Her last sight of me was in a little bonnet and a frilly dress," Spendiff says.

By the time she began her search, Spendiff was married to an actor. They had two sons with another on the way. Spendiff's first move was to send a letter to the address she found in the adoption papers. For a year, she didn't receive a response.

Then she received a letter from a Mrs. Lloyd, who

lived next door to her mother's childhood home and had been a friend of Spendiff's grandmother.

No one had responded sooner, Mrs. Lloyd wrote, because the new owner of the house, uncertain of how to respond, had placed the letter above the fireplace, where it sat for a year.

Mrs. Lloyd reported that Spendiff's grandmother had died recently and all that she knew of Spendiff's mother was that she had gone to the United States.

Spendiff and Mrs. Lloyd had been corresponding for several years when Mrs. Lloyd remembered that Spendiff's mother had a sister, who had a son named Trevor "who had something to do with the church."

So Spendiff contacted church officials, and after she had pestered them for several months, they gave her the name of a minister who remembered an intern named Trevor Marzetti.

"That sent me straight to the phone book," she recalls, where she found five T. Marzettis. On the third call, she found Trevor's home. When she reached him, she had asked him a couple of questions when he interrupted: "Suddenly, he said, 'You're June's baby!'"

ALL went as Spendiff had hoped. She soon learned that her mother lived in Oklahoma, and that she had eight half-siblings in the United States.

One of Spendiff's brothers flew with their mother, June, to London. Then Wendy Anne and her husband, Richard, went to Oklahoma.

Upon their return to England, Spendiff's stepfather Jim called and said: "There's no need for you to be in England anymore. You need to get your butt back here."

In 1993, they did.

Richard, the actor (his last movie was *Our Miss Fred*), also restored antiques, so he opened a shop in Bristow. Wendy Anne, a frequent stage performer, went to work in Le Cafe, her aunt's restaurant.

Now she and Richard own the restaurant, which Johnny Landrum opened as The Hamburger King seventy years ago and which was a favorite spot of entertainer Bob Wills. Mae West and Gene Autry also ate here, she says.

While Spendiff may overestimate her western drawl, to say that Oklahoma has been good for her is no exaggeration, she says. "It was a good decision. I've never looked back, never been back."

Of her mother's life, Spendiff learned that June left England two years after the adoption to live with relatives in New Jersey, where she met and married the man who brought her to Bristow.

Spendiff and her mother have marveled at their similarities in appearance, manner, speech and interests. And after all the years of separation, Spendiff learned her mother picked her name based on a book she was reading at the time. "Wendy Anne," Spendiff says in an accent that ain't Oklahoman, "rhymes with Peter Pan."

## Rogers County: Claremore

SOME of the displays at this world-class gun museum stop you quicker and hold you longer than others. And then there is the little space in the case that Walker Lee occupies. This one gripped me in a way that none of the thousands of guns could.

In the photographs of him, you see that Lee was a black man and that he shaved his head. The sign by Lee's picture doesn't tell you much about his life, except that he was accused of killing a woman. And in a rather solemn but graphic and gut-punching way, you learn exactly what happened to him.

THEY call this the biggest privately held collection of guns in the world, and whether or not that is accurate, I'm not inclined to disagree with folks who possess enough firepower to arm the population of Rogers County and have guns left over.

The gun that started it all is a small-gauge shotgun. The story goes that in 1894, after seven-year-old John Monroe Davis had bravely swallowed a dose of medicine, his father rewarded him with a muzzle-loading four-ten that set the family back a buck-fifty.

J.M. Davis' first gun is only one tiny firearm in a collection of more than 20,000 guns, swords and accessories that fill a 40,000-square-foot museum on Route 66 just north of downtown Claremore.

Will Rogers was from here, and his museum sits atop a hill. One of Claremore's main streets is named for Lynn Riggs, whose book, *Green Grow the Lilacs*, inspired the musical "Oklahoma!"

Singer Patti Page (whose real name was Clara Fowler) is known for songs such as "Tennessee Waltz." She, too, is from here and has a street named for her. Sam Walton's widow grew up in Claremore, which now has one of those round-the-clock, one-stop super-center Wal-Marts.

Like Rogers, Page and Riggs, J.M. Davis has a street

named for him. It's one block over from the old Route 66.

Among those who know about guns and collections, Davis is a famous fellow. Several collectors have made bids for the collection, and the Smithsonian has tried to acquire it, says Shirley Johnson, a twenty-six-year employee who now is the director of the J.M. Davis Arms and Historical Museum.

Davis grew up in Union County, Arkansas, and made his first money in timber. In 1916, according to a brochure, he traded 2,000 acres in Arkansas for the Mason Hotel in Claremore. In 1917, he moved into the Mason and took over its management.

By 1929, he owned ninety-nine guns and displayed them in the lobby. As his collection grew, it spread into the ballroom, the coffee shop and the upstairs hallways. He filled seven private rooms with the collection.

PHOTOGRAPHS of the three-story Hotel Mason show a sign advertising the "Greatest Collection of Guns in the World. Stop. See. Free." By the 1960s, Hotel Mason was bulging with guns and the other things Mr. Davis collected.

J.M. and Genevieve Davis had no children, and Mr. Davis wanted to ensure that his collection remained available for all to see. So he gave the collection to the state on the condition that it be forever housed in a museum on Block 82 in Claremore and that the museum be open for free. The state built the building. In 1969, all the guns were moved to the new building.

The oldest gun is a hand cannon made in 1350. Many guns from China, Saudi Arabia and other parts of the world are 200 years to 500 years old. They represent all the well-known gun makers and many obscure ones.

The Gallery of Outlaw Guns exhibit is my favorite. It includes Emmett Dalton's forty-five-caliber Colt, Pretty Boy Floyd's forty-one-caliber Colt and two thirty-eight-caliber Colts, and Cole Younger's Schofield Smith & Wesson.

On January 4, 1931, the display notes, George Hartness murdered his wife's parents with a thirty-eight-caliber Colt that hangs here.

THE display that has stuck in my imagination is an instrument of justice. On August 17, 1921, in Kansas City, Missouri, Walker Lee, the "Singing 8 Ball," was hanged. His picture hangs in a display case, right next to the black hood that covered his head at the moment of his execution.

And next to the hood, mounted neatly and in an understated fashion, is a seventy-eight-year-old piece of rope knotted in a familiar way.

Right there behind the glass is the noose, tied in the hangman's knot, that broke Walker Lee's neck as he made his final exit.

## Ottawa County: Miami

WILL Rogers was coming to the Coleman Theatre Beautiful, and the townsfolk were excited — so thrilled that everybody left the theater to meet him at the airport. But the day was foggy, and Mr. Rogers was unable to land at Miami, so he diverted south to nearby Narcissa and caught a ride to town in the back of a chicken truck.

The theater, of course, was empty when he arrived, because everybody was at the airport watching for him.

When his fans deduced that he wasn't going to arrive in Miami, they returned to town, where they found him across the street from the Coleman, pitching pennies with young Miamians.

That was 1931, only two years after the opening of the palatial theater. In the seventy years since its opening, weather, wear and age took chipped away at it — you had to know where *not* to sit during rainstorms — but it has remained open in some form or another. The floors are bare concrete, and the balcony is unusable, but the shows have gone on.

The city of Miami now owns the theater, a gift from the granddaughters of George L. Coleman Sr., who built it in 1929. For the last nine years, a group of locals has been raising the 5 million dollars needed to restore the Coleman to its gold-leaf grandeur.

Will Rogers was only one of many who entertained on the stage here. The stage has been host to Tom Mix and his horses, Sally Rand and her fans, and Bob Wills and the Texas Playboys performing with Leon McCauliff.

That's all according to Jerold Graham, an art teacher and sculptor who is leading the restoration program, a private-public project run by the Miami Downtown Redevelopment Authority. (That title is bigger than the name of the town. Speaking of which, you pronounce it "Mi-am-uh." I recently saw a story in *The Dallas Morning News* in which the free-lance writer spelled it like it's pronounced: Miama.)

Laura Downum, who still lives in Miami, saw Mr. Rogers' performance, and she also saw Tex Ritter. She recalls the majesty of the place, the opulence of the soft, plush carpets: "You didn't bother anything. You went in and sat and were really quiet." In 1989, when the planning and money raising began, the civic group, Friends of the Coleman, solicited memories about the theater and received forty-five letters.

Maxine Taylor was one of those who wrote: "I was a little girl the opening night. As my mother and I walked in, it looked like a castle to me, the red carpets and everything was so beautiful. The first movie at the Coleman was Clara Bow. ... Everyone enjoyed it and talked about it for months."

Mr. Coleman, who made his money in the zinc mines near Miami, was also part owner of both the Glory B and the Ottawa theaters. Neither, however, matched the splendor of the Coleman, which could seat 1,600. The carpets, woven especially for the Coleman, had the family's coat of arms, which included a pick and shovel to symbolize the source of Mr. Coleman's wealth. Mr. Graham has a piece of the original carpet, which will be reproduced as money arrives.

Lillie Mae Knight Welch felt much the same as Mrs. Taylor upon her first visit in 1932. "I was about six years old. My Grandma and Grandpa Knight and my Uncle Dewey took me there. I had never been to a theater, and I thought I was a queen walking into the prettiest palace I had ever seen."

Nellie Heistand's best memory of the Coleman was the "sing-along" nights, when the audience sang songs, following the ball that bounced along the lyrics on the screen. Juanita Goforth first went to the Coleman with her grandparents to hear "Alfalfa Bill" Murray, who was a candidate for governor.

Myrtle Sparkman Roberts was one of the contestants in the Bathing Beauty Spring Revue. The Hub Clothing Company sponsored her. "We didn't win," she wrote, "but we had a bang-up time." She thinks that Thelma Morton, representing Montgomery Ward, was the Bathing Beauty Queen. Her favorite memory, she said, was of the Master Morning of 1953, when all the Miami churches united for a worship service.

Buddy Hargis spent his birthday money for a trip to the theater: "On my 14th birthday, December 5th, 1938, one of the gifts I received was a quarter. I rode the bus from Commerce and returned for five cents each way. I went to the Coleman Theater for a dime, and had five cents left over for popcorn. On the stage was my western hero, Ken Maynard, and his horse Tarzan."

The Coleman helped at least one family during World War II, according to Lela Shaver's letter: "Some friends had not heard from their son for a long time. I took my 3-year-old son to the show. We stayed until the newsreel. ... Part of the news was of a USO (show) that was in the Far East. As they scanned the boys, there was my friend. I went home and told my mother. She talked to the boys' folks, they came to you and you were good enough to run the reel for them, and there he was, so for you taking time for these people, they found their son."

*Gone With the Wind* was a big night for Genevieve S. Craig: "Although going to the Coleman was always an event, there was an exceptionally titillating excitement in the gathering of the glittering crowd for this grandest of all opening nights. After the brilliant crystal chandeliers dimmed, Jane Griffin began the prelude of martial music on the magnificent pipe organ. ... So in love was I, and newly engaged to Henry ... it was a poignant drama in such a very special theater that even yet my insides glow when I remember. ... "

The Coleman sponsored a "gift night" or "bank night," depending on who is remembering, when they drew a number and gave away fifty dollars. If no one won, the money was added to the pot. One night in 1951, when the pot was 450 dollars, lovesick Frank Sanders told his girl that if he won the money, he would buy rings and they would marry. They called his number — and his bluff. "In his haste to claim the prize money, he sprained his ankle (chipped a bone), and had to limp across the stage," wrote Emalou Sanders, who was seventeen that night. "A night to remember."

Laura Downum remembers it as Bank Night. They drew the number at the Coleman, but announced the winning number at both the Coleman and the Glory B. Once Mary Crain, one of Laura's friends, won. "She left her coat and ran to the Coleman in five-degree temperature. She lost her coat, but won the money."

Laura, whose sister is Colleen Austin of Midwest City, says their mother never missed Bank Night. "The show was stopped, the curtains drawn, the organ was played until they were ready to give the money away, the curtains opened and a large drum held the numbers.

"We were never late for supper on Wednesday, because Momma cleared the table at five o'clock. If you got there late, you didn't get any supper," Laura told me. "Momma was going to Bank Night."

# Mayes County: Spavinaw

MAC Estep waits beyond a small bend of the highway, just inside the city limits at the spot where the speed limit drops to twenty-five miles per hour. His radar unit is calibrated and ready. Below him, in the valley next to a reservoir, two Spavinaw teen-agers throw a rubber basketball toward the goal, the ball thumping on the concrete in the last of the day's light.

Supper time in Spavinaw, and other than Mac and the teen-agers, few of the town's 465 inhabitants are about.

Unaware that the chief of Spavinaw's one-man police force is parked along my route, I buzz along oblivious, ever closer to Spavinaw. The windows of my Jeep are down. The air feels like autumn. Frogs and cicadas perform the soundtrack for my loop through Mayes County.

I entered Mayes from the west on State Highway 28; this was after I broke off Route 66 at Foyil in order to see the famed totem pole. As I drove east in the shadow of the totem pole, I topped a hill and suddenly Mayes County opened up in front of me like a valley lit with sun reflecting off gold.

I followed a few narrow roads into the countryside, passing through green pastures brightened with bouquets of yellow flowers like the ones I know as black-eyed Susans. I tried to follow the signs to a country Assembly of God church, where I hoped I might meet some of the neighbors, but missed a turn and followed a gravel road, where suddenly I was confronted all at once by a rooster, two angry, car-chasing dogs and a couple of seven-foot ostriches, who appeared out of nowhere in the middle of nowhere and ran beside me.

All the while, I'm nearing Mac Estep and his radar gun.

The road to Disney held the surprise of the Pensacola Dam, which you cross on a weathered concrete bridge lined with alternating U.S. and Oklahoma flags. On the left side of the bridge, the water looked close enough to touch. To the right, the land seemed to drop straight down like a canyon. Because I didn't expect the drop-off, the sight was unnerving.

Disney sprang up like a little mountain village. At Pistol Pete's, lit up with orange, yellow and blue neon, they were cooking in the barbecue pit, which is built to look like a train engine. The BBQ Express was beside the highway, and the aroma covered the town. Inside the little kitchen, which offered no place to sit — you order through a window — sliced potatoes bubbled in a deep vat of cooking oil. The menu offering burgers and barbecue was hand-lettered in English and in Cherokee.

Prayer meeting was in progress at the Baptist church of Disney, which was named for Wesley E. Disney, a Kansas Democrat elected to Congress from Oklahoma in March 1931. Four pickups, two vans and eleven cars were parked outside the church.

And just down the road, Mac Estep waits, patiently, like a spider in a web, for someone to fly by.

As I leave Langley on Highway 82, the road becomes a snake of asphalt. It's a mountain road. I am lost in thought, trying to pick out the walnut trees from the hickory, and occasionally spotting a pecan tree. The sky, what I can see through the trees, has turned sunset orange.

A pickup motors maddeningly close to my rear bumper, pushing me to hurry down the road. It is as I'm fretting over this pushy driver that I round the bend and come suddenly upon Spavinaw and its chief of police, waiting there for somebody like me.

But the story ends happily. Even in the aggravation of having someone push me from behind, I had seen the speed limit sign and pumped the brake pedal. I was traveling the limit as I passed Mac Estep, probably saving the truck driver a speeding ticket.

Mac Estep's arm hung out the window, and he gave a friendly wave as my bumper buddy and I passed through his town.

"People say we are a speed trap, but we're not," he says. "Most of the time, I just warn people. We have a lot of kids in this town, and they are riding their bicycles and crossing the street."

He issues about thirty tickets a month, more in the summer. Sometimes, he'll go three or four days without writing a ticket, and sometimes he'll write three or four in a day.

In his two years here, he has investigated one murder and had to shoot one man. But that's about all for big crime. "It's kind of boring, but you get to know most of the people," he says. "Even the bad people are nice most of the time. I get along even with the criminals, but they do know I'll take them in."

# Seminole County: Bowlegs

Two years in the sawmill business, and a lifetime before that in the oil patch, and all of Charlie Troglin's fingers are present and accounted for. If you ask, he'll shuck his leather gloves and show you.

The blade that's at the heart of Charlie's rough-cut little sawmill could, without doubt, remove a finger, a hand or a leg for that matter, but he has built in precautions to prevent the involuntary loss of a limb.

If, however, you are talking about the limbs or the trunk of a tree, they don't have a chance. Charlie's forty-six-inch blade is outfitted with carbide teeth that slice easily through the hard hearts of oak, cedar and any other hardwood you poke at it.

Charlie Troglin is no John Walton, although Charlie works just as hard as the television woodsman. A dark caterpillar of a mustache hangs beneath Charlie's nose, and he smokes a cigarette or two between cuts.

But Pa Walton would be comfortable here in Charlie's mill, where on cold mornings you can find Charlie and his crew (and sometimes neighbors) drinking coffee at the iron, wood-burning stove at the north end of the shop. (Fuel for the fire is always in great supply.)

Charlie grew up here among these hills, which as far as you can see are green with the crowns of hickory, oak, elm and cedar. He has ridden horseback through these trees, hunting deer, turkey and squirrels.

For nearly ten years, Charlie flew between Oklahoma and Alaska, where he rousted about in the northern oil fields. Two years ago, after adding several chunks of land to his father's original fifty acres, he decided to stay home. "I was," he says, "always climbing onto a plane or off of one.".

He bought a sawmill rig from a sawyer in Tyler, Texas, moved the outfit to his ancestral acreage and set up Troglin Timber.

The man in Tyler powered the mill with a four-speed Chevy engine. When he needed to speed up production, he shifted into a higher gear. Charlie has converted to a 50-horse electric motor that races at 560 revolutions per minute.

Word of mouth is attracting more business than he can shake a stick at. Charlie, Steve Roberson and Jason Brauning trim the bark off the trunks, cut them into boards, edge them on another saw and stack them for delivery. Customers who are putting up a building will leave a blueprint at the mill, and Charlie and his crew cut the timber to order. "A lot of people like to watch you cut their wood," he says. (And a lot of people buy the scraps for firewood.)

Troglin's Timber recently cut enough timber for a man at Keystone Lake to build a two-story board house that looks like a barn, complete with a wooden silo for an entrance. "Southern Living" magazine is planning to include pictures of it in a future issue. Now Charlie is cutting timber for an Oklahoma City veterinarian.

He is picky, Charlie says, about the origin of his lumber. Trees that are harvested along fence lines often will have nails or barbed wire hidden inside the wood, which is bad news for saw teeth. He prefers to buy trees that grew in creek bottoms.

Charlie doesn't spend all his time trimming trees. He hunts and rides his horse on weekends; Tuesday nights are for recreational roping at a nearby arena, calves provided. "Pay ten dollars," he says, "and rope all you want."

Bowlegs is close to Maud and between Seminole and Wewoka, which is home of the Whipping Tree. The community, whose high school football team is the Bowlegs Bisons, lies southwest of Cromwell, where frontier lawman Bill Tilghman was killed.

It's home to Charlie and Steve, who knew each other growing up, and to eighteen-year-old Jason, who played football for the Bisons. Friday night football is about the only entertainment in Seminole.

Charlie chuckles at comparisons of his sawmill to John Walton's on the television series but he didn't watch enough of the show to know how he stacks up to the Waltons.

"When I was young," says the forty-two-year-old sawyer, "we didn't have a lot of TV. They were black and white. Sometimes they worked, sometimes they didn't. The Oak Ridge Boys on Sunday morning is about the only TV we sat down for."

# Carter County: Lone Grove

PAT Ratliff tears quarters in half. With his bare hands. I saw him tear three. Two of the quarters came from my pocket, so I know he wasn't pulling a fast one. "You wouldn't believe how much money I make doing this," he says. "I had a guy tell me one time, 'I'd give a thousand dollars to have those hands to pack around. They're money in the bank.' "

The night before I met him, in fact, he took 1,700 dollars from three fellows at an Ardmore restaurant. "Big rollers. They were kind of lit up," says Pat, who testifies that he neither smokes nor drinks.

His feat is all the more amazing because Pat is seventy-eight years old.

To shake hands with Pat is to shake hands with a workshop vise. He is tough.

When he was fourteen, he took a piece of stove wood to a hobo who was beating an elderly couple.

Pat is so tough that people who ought to fear him "are as afraid of me as a possum is of an ax handle." He is so tough that his kinfolk nicknamed him "Bob Wahr," the western pronunciation of the fencing wire that tamed the West.

He is so tough that Robert Duvall followed him around to learn how to be tough before playing his role in the movie *Lonesome Dove*. "He wrote down a lot of notes," Pat says. (I confirmed this through Mr. Duvall, who wants to make a movie about Pat's life.)

Pat met Mr. Duvall through his half-brother, Lawrence Elkins, who played for the Houston Oilers football team. Mr. Elkins met Mr. Duvall at a party in California and told him about Pat. Then Mr. Elkins brought Mr. Duvall to Pat's house in the country.

Pat grew up hunting anything that would fit on the supper table. "There wasn't nothing I couldn't call up out of the woods," he says, and right there on the spot, he demonstrates a turkey and a squirrel call.

"I could do a train whistle that would make you pack your bags. Now I hunt squirrel with a twenty-two pistol. Sorghum syrup, hot biscuits with gravy and squirrel, that's my favorite meal."

He grew up riding and roping, so he was an ideal role model for Duvall. "I loved to rodeo. When I was a kid, you couldn't pull me off a horse."

Pat had a small part at the beginning of Mr. Duvall's movie *The Apostle*. He's the man who picks up a puppy while telling the police where to find the bodies at the scene of a car accident. Then you can hear him telling about the time he rescued an elderly couple from a floating Volkswagen, which is a true story.

Not only is Pat strong, but before doctors replaced his right knee and cut on his prostate recently, he was fast. "When I was a kid," he says, "the only one who could outrun me was my mother."

He doesn't need glasses to read, and his night vision is like an owl's. "My granddad is the only other person I know who could see like that."

His physical strength, he says, is a gift from God. He's never worked at it. He was "muscled up" by the time he was five. Good genes. "My grandfather had a baseball team nobody ever beat. He caught, and his eight sons played in the field. They were such tall, well-muscled men, like a gazelle, like you'd like a race horse to look." ·

His morning milking, a chore that was assigned to him at age five, probably contributed to the strength in his hands. "I milked twenty, twenty-five every day. My hands would be a-tremblin', I would be so tired."

Pat first tried to bend a quarter when he was seventeen, after watching an uncle do it one day on a trip into town.

Pat, his Uncle Walter, several other uncles and some cousins were standing in front of an old mercantile wanting "a red Nehi belly-whopping sodie-water," but they only had one quarter among them. So his Uncle Walter said, "I'll just tear this quarter in half, and we'll buy something for everybody. He was about six-foot-six, a stout old cowboy. I thought he was kidding. It was a silver one. Those were hard."

It took Pat two years, but one day he found a quarter on his mother's dresser and bent it. "You got to get in rhythm," he says. "You got to get it hot. If I can ever get it bent, I got to bend it back real quick."

Pat wears a white Resistol hat, a dark-green western shirt and straight-leg jeans that come down over his Justin boots. When he walks, he favors his right leg with its replacement knee.

He puts his hand to his hat nearly every time he sees a woman and greets each with "Ma'am."

One of Pat's favorite places is Sylvester Johnson's shoeshine stand at the Wal-Mart in Ardmore. As far as Sylvester knows, his is the only Wal-Mart shoeshine stand in the country. Sylvester loves to show off Pat's talent.

But I actually saw Pat bend quarters at the Burger King in Ardmore, where Pat likes to meet his buddies. After we had chatted a bit, I pulled a quarter out of my pocket.

Pat moaned and showed me his thumbs and index fingers. They were still sore from the night before, when he had won his money. "The older I get," he says, "the harder it gets."

But he tore one quarter and then another, each in

less than thirty seconds. While we chatted, Steve Spain, who works in law enforcement in Carter County, came over to the table with a quarter.

"My wife tells me you can tear a quarter," he says and hands it to Pat, who tore his third.

"That's all," Pat says, showing us the dents in his digits. "I'm a sissy, I guess."

## Okfuskee County: IXL

THE spelling of this town's name looks like a typographical error. Buck Spratt, who has lived in these parts for all of his eighty-three years, isn't sure how the town was named, but he says it is pronounced exactly like it is spelled: I-X-L.

Even the authoritative "Oklahoma Place Names" took a pass on explaining that one, even though IXL, on State Highway 48, has appeared on Oklahoma maps for nearly ten years.

Buck was a bit blue on the Monday I met him. The backs of his hands were blue, and his cheeks were lightly tinted. Heavy blue streaks ran into his ear canals and his nostrils. He had spent most of the day sanding blue paint off a Caprice Classic so he could repaint it, a job he has been doing since he was eighteen. (Well, not this particular blue car. He has painted hundreds of cars.)

"You can't miss it," he says of his body shop, on which one of his grandkids painted his name. "It's got Buck writ all over it."

He built this shop in 1948, the same year he built his house and two years after his World War II service in the Army. "I used to build hot-rod engines in here," he says. "I put four kids through college from right here in this building. I sold all my equipment to keep those boys from worrying me about building engines."

One day in the late '40s, a Greyhound bus came calling for him in IXL. The Brooklyn Dodgers had sent the bus because the manager wanted Buck to play baseball.

The coaches knew about him because he had been a member of IXL's Negro Double A team, and while in the Army, he had played against Jackie Robinson. But he declined their offer.

He found his way into the auto body business at sixteen, working as a wash boy for the Chevy dealership in Okemah. Within two years, he was repairing and painting cars.

Buck looks fifteen years younger than his age. He punctuates his stories with streams of tobacco juice. "I've been chewing 'bakker since I was nine, and I still got all my teeth but two," he says, and points to the top of either side of his mouth to show the gaps. He lost those, he says, in accidents with tools of his trade.

He was always fast with his work, often surprising his customers. Once, when a customer was skeptical that Buck's crew could fix his car in a day, Buck replied: "We don't homestead 'em, we don't eat 'em. We fix 'em."

He still has the first paint gun with which he ever "shot" a car, a classic DeVilbiss he still uses.

As for the name of his town, an authoritative explanation appeared years ago in a column written by Robert E. Lee, *The Oklahoman*'s legendary columnist.

Bob Lee gave credit for this bit of edification to W.M. Knight. The name originated as the name of a rural school called "I Excel," founded by the late Herman F. King. The Okfuskee County Historical Society has a picture of the school with students standing under the "I Excel School" sign. Somewhere along the way, the name was shortened to IXL.

In May '99, the same tornado that struck Oklahoma City sent winds through IXL, knocking down half of Buck's garage and a quarter-mile of fence. "My cows were everywhere," he says. "I just sold 'em. I'm too old to run at them any more."

Then he put the sander to the paint of the Caprice Classic and the blue dust flew.

## Payne County: Yale

THIS house was Jim Thorpe's home of sorrows. By the time he bought this two-bedroom frame house, he had already been stripped of his Olympic gold because of his semipro sports activities.

That blow — to fall from his glory as the world's greatest athlete in the 1912 Stockholm Olympics — equaled any blow Jim Thorpe ever suffered in any arena.

But if the first lick cut him off at the knees, the second blow, delivered below the belt while he lived in this house, all but ruined him. He continued to live, work and play, but some who knew him said he never really recovered from the event here in Yale.

That's one of the facts of Mr. Thorpe's life that Alice Cussner imparts as she leads you on a tour of the only house Mr. Thorpe ever owned. He bought it with money from his Indian allotment.

Alice has been working here, off and on, over the last eleven years. She knew a bit about Jim Thorpe before she began working at the house. Now, she can tell you which book about Mr. Thorpe is the best, and she can enumerate the errors in the Burt Lancaster movie about his life.

The area around Yale in Payne County seems to hold as much history per square inch as any place in Oklahoma. Carl Hensley, Yale's city manager, grew up here and knows a lot of it. In the early days of radio, for instance, Yale had one of only five radio stations in Oklahoma: Its call letters were WHAT.

As a boy, Mr. Hensley found arrowheads on the Twin Mounds, which is the site of the first Civil War battle in the territory that became Oklahoma. That battle was fought November 19, 1861.

Carl also hunted for a trunk of gold, supposedly buried here by Creek Indian Chief Opothleyahola, who fought against the Confederates in that first battle.

One account holds that the gold was an annuity meant for distribution to the Creeks, but the war had scattered the tribe and the chief couldn't divvy it up. To protect his tribe's money, the chief put it into a trunk, wrapped the trunk in chains and forced four black slaves to dig a hole and bury the trunk. The chief's companion then shot the four men. A terrified eight-year-old Creek named D.L. Berryhill witnessed all of this, which is how the story was passed down.

Mr. Hensley is one of many who has searched for the gold. "One day, I was squirrel hunting with my dad. I fell down, and the ground was hollow," he recalled. "A friend and I went back with a shovel." But no gold: "It was a hollow log beneath the ground."

Ingalls, between Yale and Stillwater, was the site of a famous gun battle between U.S. marshals and members of the Doolin-Dalton gang. Down at Twin Mounds — or the Round Mountains, as they once were known — a member of Doolin's gang shot and killed Deputy U.S. Marshal Nelson "Pawnee" Rice while he stood on his front porch. The locals buried Rice atop the north mound that day.

Fact mixes with legend in the histories of Payne County and Yale. But Thorpe's time here is well documented. Thorpe moved to Yale because his wife's sister already lived here. Thorpe met his wife, Iva Margaret Miller, while he was a student at the Carlisle Institute, an Indian school in Pennsylvania. He and his wife moved here in 1917.

The house, listed on the National Register of Historic Places, sits a block off State Highway 51.

The bed in the front bedroom is covered with a bedspread Mr. Thorpe and his wife bought in Paris. They were on their honeymoon, which they combined with an exhibition tour with the New York Giants. The spread was embroidered by nuns who spent five years stitching it. Iva's teeny and well-preserved wedding dress hangs in a closet.

On the dresser, next to the bed, is a photograph of Iva holding James Jr. as an infant. There is another photograph of James Jr., who was the source of Mr. Thorpe's sorrow at this place.

The wicker furniture in the parlor belonged to the Thorpes. The only man in history to win the decathlon and pentathlon sat on this sofa in front of this fireplace, which became the site of his heartbreak.

The dining room table, covered with a tablecloth that Iva crocheted, is the table where they shared their meals. As far as Alice knows, the bathtub is the one in which Mr. Thorpe bathed.

A glass case holds twenty-seven of his athletic medals, one dated 1907. "Some have been lost," Alice says. "He had as many more. He let his children play with them."

When he lost his Olympic medals, she guesses, maybe the others didn't mean so much to him.

**A**ND when he lost James Jr., maybe life didn't mean so much to him. It was the influenza epidemic of 1918. James Jr. was three, and was one of the first victims in town. He died in this house, in front of this white-tiled fireplace, in the arms of the world's greatest athlete, who at that moment was most likely the world's most heartbroken father.

## Okmulgee County: Bald Hill

**O**N the south end of this little store, we have something for everything that ails your body. On the north end, we have most anything to fix whatever is ailing your lawn mower. Too tired to mow? Gail Ellis can fix you up with herbs. Allergies making you too sick to cut the grass? That's no excuse – Gail has the stuff.

Lawn mower need a new belt? An idler? A cable maybe?

Go north about ten feet from the papaya mint and see A.D. Ellis.

You've found the part for your mower but you aren't smart enough to fix it? Go back to Gail for Gotu Kola. (That's a brain builder for all you carnivores who have been eating fish for brains all these years.)

"We called the store 'Herbs and Mower' when we had it in town," Gail says. (Get it? Mower. More. "Herbs and More." Slow understanding it? Maybe you need some "mower" Gotu Kola.)

A.D. has been in the lawn mower repair and parts business for more than a decade. People from as far away as Bartlesville and Oklahoma City bring their mowers to his Okmulgee County shop, which, before Gail moved in with her herbs, was known as Southwest Lawnmower.

Gail has been in the herbs and vitamin business for a couple of years, but is only now working full time at it.

Neither one of them has a shop in town anymore. Both are in this cinder block building on Bixby Road, about a mile north of Highway 16. (If you travel there on Route 66, you must go through the town of Slick in Creek County, where the possibilities are endless. If, for instance, you are a pastor in this little town, you would be a Slick preacher. One who sells previously owned automobiles would be a Slick used-car salesman. A lawyer would be a Slick solicitor. You could call a fried-chicken joint The Slick Chick.)

They are peddling herbs and lawn mower parts on a 160-acre Indian allotment that the federal government gave to A.D.'s mother when she was about nine. He was born in a house that stood less than fifty yards from his shop. The only thing left of the original home is the rock brooder house where they raised their chickens.

The original deed, dated December 1902, hangs on a wall in their shop. A.D. also has framed and hung the paperwork on an eighty-seven dollar loan his father took in 1937 when A.D. was two.

The deed shows that his father mortgaged the whole farm, including a Deere sulty plow, a planter, three Oliver cultivators, a black, 850-pound horse named Maud, another just like her named Blackel, a 700-pound bay named Hainy, three cows, five sows and twenty-two pigs.

His mother, Nellie Bruner, was a full-blood Creek Indian whose mother came to Oklahoma on the Trail of Tears. His father, A.D., was a white man from Missouri. A.D.'s brother, Willie, survived the Bataan Death March, several years as a Japanese prisoner of war and the crash of the plane that was bringing him home.

Gail is an Oklahoman by blood, but she was born in California, where her parents moved during the Dust Bowl.

The sign on their shop is more an advertisement now than the name of their business. The sign says, simply: "Herbs — Vitamins." Then below that it says: "Lawnmower Parts."

Most of the time, the door remains padlocked. A yellow note stuck to the door advises the UPS man that their house is a quarter mile to the west. Their house and shop sit in the middle of pastures brilliant in October's ragweed and grazed by cattle.

The mention of ragweed, of course, leads Gail to discuss the virtues of her herbs and vitamins. On top of many of her bottles, she has placed a card extolling their magic. She has herbs for animal dander, bad bladders, overeaters, varicose veins, colic, fever, indigestion and insomnia.

So take some Eyebright Plus (Indians never wore glasses, the card says on this one), and crank up your mower with the new cord you bought from A.D. If the sneezes overtake you, you know where to go for relief.

## Garvin County: Wynnewood

**B**LAME Mike Grissom's mama. He does. "When I was in the fifth grade, they started teaching us social studies," he recalls over a glass of sweet tea and his mama's cookies. "Mama simplified it for me. She told me, 'Lee was the good guy. Grant was the bad guy.' And it stuck. I took it from there."

He's a Rebel — the capital "R" is no mistake — with a cause, which is to preserve the heritage of the people who settled the southeast quadrant of Oklahoma.

"Ninety-five percent of Wynnewood was settled by people from the Old South states," he says. "Wetumka, all Southern people there. McAlester used to call itself the capital of Little Dixie."

Little Dixie, most Oklahomans know, is the name of the southeast corner of the state. In topography, climate and attitude, this portion of Oklahoma is more southern than western. The Indians who came here from the South in the 1830s brought cotton and built plantation homes. When the white Southerners moved here later in the century, they brought in the gins and cotton seed mills. The countryside looked even more Southern than the towns, says

Alma Grissom, Mike's eighty-six-year-old mother who grew up picking cotton alongside Indians in Wetumka.

"That's who we are," Mr. Grissom says, "and it's not so far back. We have people in town whose grandparents were in the Civil War. We have confirmed seventy Confederate graves in our little cemetery. I'm interested in the South. It entertains me like a hobby. As the culture around us disintegrates, the Southern heritage is all we've got to hang onto. I told a man in Oklahoma City one time that, 'The South shall rise again.' He said, 'That's our only hope.' I like that."

Mr. Grissom — full name: Michael Andrew Grissom — is so zealous in his cause that he has written four books, the first of which is a 572-page tome titled, *Southern By the Grace of God*, which he originally published himself. (Pelican Publishing in Louisiana later picked it up.) He also has published *The Last Rebel Yell*, *When the South was Southern*, and — my favorite title — *Farewell to the Accent, or There Goes the Drawl, Y'all!*

*The Drawl Y'all!* includes a small dictionary of Southern terms, such as "rainch: a tool used for tightening bolts;" "okry: what we called okra before we got so bloomin' educated;" "fixin': on the verge of doing something;" and "fur: a real handy little preposition. (Fur cryin' out loud. What are we havin' fur supper?)"

Mr. Grissom came to writing the long way. In college, he studied music, and then he moved to Nashville to break into the business. He changed careers almost accidentally. "I wrote because I was tired of the South getting kicked. I decided if some bona fide author didn't step up and do it soon, I was going to do it and embarrass everybody."

Ever the Southern gentleman, he disdains profanity and refuses to use any words in conversation or in his books that he wouldn't want his mother or his pastor to hear. "I never use four-letter words. I never use anything off-color."

His subject matter and approach have worked. Eleven years and nine printings later, *Southern By the Grace of God* still sells. Mr. Grissom long ago returned to his home town, and now he lives in his childhood home with his mother. He has restored an old Presbyterian church and turned it into the Museum of Southern History. (The church began as a Presbyterian school in 1887, and became an official church after the turn of the century. The church experienced a surge in growth in the 1950s when Doc Poole left the Methodist church because the leaders there didn't like him using the Scofield Reference Bible in his Sunday school class. The hundred members of his class moved to the church with him.)

The original pews, made by convicts at the state penitentiary, are still in the church, as is the original pulpit. With a little urging from me, Mike took to the 1923 Elington piano and played a range of songs from "Dixie" to "Amazing Grace" to "The Old Rugged Cross" to "The Night They Drove Old Dixie Down." He refused to play "The Battle Hymn of the Republic," written, as it was, by a Yankee.

He sells books (his and others) in the basement gift shop of his museum. He sells Confederate flags and bumper stickers that say things like: "I don't care how you did it up north."

He has commissioned, with his own money, a bronze statue that will be placed outside his museum and will have the names of all the Confederate veterans who lived in and around Wynnewood. The face of the statue, which is being sculpted by Sohail Shehada at the University of Oklahoma, will stand nineteen feet tall.

Discussions of the South, of course, always lead to questions about the War of Northern Aggression and slavery, or if you are a Rebel talking, about states' rights. But Mike won't be drawn into those discussions. "The Southern people are not defined by those issues," he says. "The Southern people are defined by the grace, the goodness, the quality of life and examples they left for us."

To that, Mike's mama and General Lee say amen.

# Alfalfa County: Cherokee

HIS name is Dennis Frisk. Now, guess his occupation. Here's a hint: His name is perfect for his job. I met Dennis when he came to my rescue on a dark stretch of Highway 38, between the village of Jet and the spillway at Great Salt Plains State Park.

I first knew I was in trouble down at Coon's Hollow, where I had stopped to watch two couples from Guthrie cast for catfish but mostly what they did was give away their rabbit livers to carp and turtles. "I have turtle-lip prints all over my bait," Charlie said. Or was it Jack? (Rabbit livers are tougher and stay on the hook better than chicken livers.)

The spillway was beautiful. Dozens of white pelicans paddled about, diving for dinner. In the dusk, only the wind in the cottonwoods and the splash of a pelican arriving, departing or diving broke the silence.

After ten minutes of watching, I turned the key on my '53 Chevy pickup with the coveted five-window cab, and instead of a roaring engine, I heard a dragging alternator. A couple more cranks, and she was flooded. Charlie and Jack put down their rods to help me push her off. Nothing. Let her dry out, Charlie said, and we'll try her again. Or was it Jack?

On our next try, she cranked, but Jack (or was it Charlie?) noticed the battery wasn't charging. So I thanked them for the push, jumped in the truck, drove up the hill and watched with heart sinking as the headlights and dash lights dimmed slowly to nothing, and she died. I had traveled just far enough to be close to nothing when my dead truck coasted to a stop on the shoulder in a curve, across from a windmill in the pitch dark.

The night and the place were a perfect place to be stranded. You could almost see by the light of the star-strewn sky; the breeze was gentle and constant. My first telephone call (love those cell phones) was to Oklahoma City for help, and my second was to the Alfalfa County Sheriff's Office. I wanted a deputy to find me so that I could be certain of my location so that I could give good directions to the driver of the tow truck.

Angels sometimes arrive wearing a badge and packing a pistol. Once in a while, an angel even sports a mustache over his lip. Mine did.

Now you know that Dennis Frisk is a lawman, a deputy with the Alfalfa County Sheriff's Office, to be precise. Dennis arrived from the north and parked behind the truck. "You want to jump her off so you can get down to Jet?" he asked. (Jet is a town.)

"Sure," I said.

"Where's your battery?"

"It's, ah, mmm, it's under the hood," I said, though I had never needed the battery so I had no idea where it was. But I had to fake it. It's rather unmanly for a man to be driving an old truck like mine and not know a thing about it, especially something as fundamental as the location of the battery. I lost my manhood within the first three minutes of meeting Dennis.

The battery, you see, ain't under the hood. Had it been up to me to find the battery, I would have concluded that the truck somehow ran without one.

Dennis knew better. He knew the battery was under the floorboard on the passenger's side. (Who ever heard of that? And just so you'll know, the gas tank is behind the seat.) He took up the carpet, showed me the battery and then shined his flashlight under the hood. His diagnosis took ten seconds. "There's your problem," he said, pointing to the alternator. "Wire's broke off."

Long story short, he fixed the wire with tools and a wire from his trunk and jump-started the truck with his cruiser. I telephoned the wrecker driver and turned him back. Then I followed Dennis into Cherokee, where he already had called ahead to the Cherokee Inn and awakened Carolyn, the night manager, who was at the front desk when I arrived.

No surprise here, but that's not the first time Dennis has fixed a car on the side of the road. "That's what I love about this job. You meet a lot of people, do a lot of things, help a lot of people," Dennis told me the next morning. "I try to set an example. At the sheriff's office, we're not out here to be your enemy."

Dennis knew as a child that he wanted to be an officer of the law. He watched all the cop shows. "Dragnet." "Mission: Impossible." "Mannix." "Get Smart." "The Man From U.N.C.L.E." "Cannon." "The Highway Patrol." Thanks to cable, he still watches his all-time favorite: "Adam 12."

He has been in law enforcement off and on for more than a decade. He started in the reserve at Cherokee, joined the police department at Buffalo, then joined the sheriff's department in Galveston County, Texas, for the experience. He moved back to Cherokee, stayed on the police force here for four years, then left law enforcement for four years to work as a mechanic. Four years ago, Sheriff Charles Tucker hired Dennis as a deputy.

The best part of his job is the children in Cherokee County. The morning after he rescued me, he presented certificates and T-shirts to eleven Cherokee Elementary students who had ridden in a bike-a-thon that Dennis organized to raise money for St. Jude's Research Hospital in Memphis, Tennessee. (Brandon Hiller raised 375 dollars and Levi McHenry raised 100 dollars; Keithan Smith rode twenty-six miles around the track next door to their school; all told, the three and Lindsi Calhoun, Anthony Walborn, Kelli Puffinbarger, Brandon Nixon, Kristy Benson, Katrina Bell, Jessica Bell and Shyla Whitely raised 943 dollars.)

The hardest part of his job is to see one of those children hurt. "The worst thing I ever have to do," he said, "is to get involved in the fatality of a small child." Just a few months ago, he helped investigate the death of an eighteen-month-old child who ran into the path of a car.

The sheriff's office covers the entire county with four people. The last homicide was back in '81 or so, and the fight was between two people who knew each other. "We have shootings and cuttings," Sheriff Tucker said. "A lot of times, it's over a woman."

As for his name, Dennis Frisk said that from the moment he went to the police academy, his instructors noted that his name perfectly fit his profession. He has, he allows, lived up to his name a time or two in his career.

# Garfield County: Bison

**B**LANCHE Kathryn Trojan died in this house, early in the morning, sometime between her daughter's trips downstairs. "I'd come down and check on her several times a night," says Ellen Ann Trojan Davis. "She just went to sleep. It was one of her many wishes to live out her life here."

This is the house where Ellen Ann and her two brothers grew up, the yard and the street where they learned to ride horses and bicycles. They were actually born in a house a block north of the Bison Co-op, into the hands of three different country doctors, but this was home. (Ellen Ann actually beat the doctors; she was born into her father's hands.)

Ellen Ann's daddy, Joseph F. Trojan, helped to build this house, with walls that are three bricks thick, the way they built them in Europe. They salvaged the bricks from Bison's old public schoolhouse, where Blanche had taught.

Bison never was much in the way of a big city, although it did have its share of businesses. "We were a little metropolis back when I was growing up," Ellen Ann says.

Bison has dwindled to near nothing, if you are counting population and businesses. That, of course, is not what Ellen Ann counts.

She loves this place, where St. Joseph Catholic Church is the center of the community. Her family helped found the town, which is a Czech settlement. Her grandfather, Joseph Trojan, staked his claim during the land run of 1893. In 1918, Ellen Ann's father became the fourth president of Bison State Bank, a job he held until the Depression closed it in 1933. It is a point of family honor that Joseph's customers recovered every penny of their deposits.

Ellen Ann and her husband, Jim, lived in Texas for thirty years, but when Blanche began to need care at home, they moved back. Her mother died at ninety-six.

Ellen Ann values this town for more than what it appears to be to outsiders. The valley, for instance.

They don't have a name for it, but the valley that falls away from the west end of town stretches out like a blank canvas waiting for God to paint in another sunset. "Oh, it is beautiful," says Ellen Ann, whose yard backs up to the valley.

Ellen Ann's father was among Garfield County's early aviators, and many a Sunday many an aviator would land in his Aunt Mary's pasture to talk and to take up passengers.

Ellen Ann remembers the day that Amelia Earhart flew into Enid to put on an air show. "I remember her crawling out and waving to the people, just like the barnstormers did."

And she tells of other fliers, like her brother, retired Colonel Joseph E. Trojan, who was shot down during World War II and held prisoner by the Germans for two years.

She tells of Bertie Woodring, whose parents built and operated the Hotel Woodring in Bison. Bertie was a barnstormer and a member of the Three Musketeers stunt-flying group. He was killed while testing a military plane at Wright-Patterson Air Force Base in Ohio. Enid's airport is named for Bertie.

Much of Bison's history has been saved thanks to people like Ellen Ann's mother, who recorded her memories and made them part of Garfield County's two-volume history book. "If anyone wanted any history," Ellen Ann says, "they called Blanche."

One thing the history of Bison doesn't include is even one tale of a tornado. "Grandmother Trojan always said the Indians told her we'd never have a tornado through here because of the lay of the land," Ellen Ann says. They never have. On a day like the day I met Ellen Ann, you sense that maybe Bison never has seen trouble, but you know that's not true.

At this moment in time, however, at dusk on an October evening, Bison is a place of peace. There is the lay of the land. Walls built three bricks deep. Lives built upon lives. And souls like Blanche's leaving for home from home, sailing up and over Ellen Ann's beautiful western valley on the wind of eternity.

# Johnston County: In two parts

REAGAN — Johnny Shackleford knows how Noah felt. Noah, the one famous for his big boat, worked on the ark for years under the scornful eye of his neighbors, who thought him a bit eccentric.

Like Noah before him, Shackleford is at work on a project that, at first consideration, makes not a bit of sense.

He lives on a dirt road in Johnston County, far from any place that makes movies. Far from any place, period. The closest town of any size is Tishomingo, which isn't exactly a movie-making mecca.

But for the last ten years, Shackleford has been nailing together a movie set that looks like an old western town. He hopes someone will come here to make a movie.

"The neighbors probably think, 'There goes Johnny,'" Shackleford says and laughs.

His idea, however, may not be as farfetched as it sounds. His inspiration comes from Alamo Village, a movie set in Brackettville, Texas, where movies such as *The Alamo* and *The Return of Josie Wales* were filmed.

And Shackleford, a musician who has toured internationally with several country music bands, knows a few people in the entertainment business. He has played bit parts in a few movies himself.

Shackleford is an Oklahoman who lived most of his life in Reagan. When he was a teen-ager, his family moved to Midwest City, where he graduated from high school.

At twenty-seven, he landed a job playing bass guitar with the house band at Shotgun Sam's Pizza, his first entertainment engagement.

Later, on a trip with a cousin to see Alamo Village, they noticed Happy Shahan, who built and owned the tourist town. Shackleford asked Shahan for a job, and Shahan hired him.

Shortly after that, Shackleford landed a part in *Josie Wales*. He's had parts in other movies, Willie Nelson's *Barbarosa* and *Seguin*, to name a couple. He's also wrangled horses for show business.

But ten years ago, with his parents growing older, he moved back home with them and opened an upholstery business.

And that was the beginning of Sipokni, a Cherokee

word for "old." He didn't want to build an aluminum building, so he built his upholstery shop to look like an old western building. For the purpose of making movies, his shop houses the barbershop and the general store. On down the line, he has built a lawyer's office, the sheriff's office, a Wells Fargo stop, a blacksmith shop, a hotel, a jail and a doctor's office. At least one wall of each building can be pulled out to film interior scenes.

He has been in contact with the Oklahoma Film Commission and others. "I've had about four or five bites," he says. He already has a commitment from one company to film *Five at Dawn*, a western, in October. But he's not spending the money. "Until they set up and start shooting," he says, "they're not going to make it."

His bigger dream, he says, is to turn Sipokni West into a money-making tourist draw, complete with a country band and five shoot-outs a day. He already has about 400 people a year stop by to look over his village and the little museum inside his upholstery shop.

His museum includes the outfit he wore in *Josie Wales* and photographs of him with lots of stars, including Willie Nelson.

Several couples have asked to be married at Sipokni, but he hasn't built the chapel. Nor has he finished the public rest rooms, which is the only obstacle between him and guns a'blazing. "That's the big joke around here," Shackleford says of the incomplete rest rooms.

His buildings are furnished with items of local significance. In the doctor's office, for instance, he has a birthing chair from the Hardy Sanitorium, which was in Ardmore. An old wheelchair once belonged to Della Belle Hardy Young, the mother of his third-grade teacher.

And, in a little house, he has hung a mirror that Isaac Underwood gave to his new bride, Carrie. They were married August 11, 1921. "He traded a mule for that mirror," Shackleford says.

All he needs to succeed, Shackleford is confident, is one big movie. He recalls this advice from Happy Shahan: "Happy said, 'Build it for movies, and the tourists will come.'"

Shackleford hopes for a flood of them.

ဢၪၾ ဢၪၾ ဢၪၾ

MILBURN — They were talking about violence in schools, or rather how to stop it, three polite young men who look like anything but trouble. So one minute we're discussing violence, and the next minute Dustin Meadows bounds from his chair. "You ever felt titanium in an eye?" he asks.

"Give me your finger," he says and leans toward me. I give him my index finger, and he directs it to the skin beneath his right eye, where the bone feels like it is rimmed with BBs. "They call it a blow-out fracture," he says.

It happened the year before, on the last day of September. He was walking down the hall of Milburn High School, carrying his books, his head down. He dropped a pen, bent to retrieve it, and next thing he knew, he was laid out on the floor.

Students scattered. Some cried. A teacher approached him. "What did you hit your head on?" she asked.

"I'm pretty sure it was a fist," he replied.

He wore an eye patch for a month after doctors installed the titanium plate. But even a year later, his vision doubles on him when he's tired, and sometimes his eye sinks into the socket.

Given his firsthand experience with school violence, Dustin has a special interest in his school's "I Pledge" assembly, where students pledge not to fight at school and to leave their weapons at home.

Dustin and his schoolmates, however, are doing more than signing pledge cards. Violence isn't much of a problem anyway — two, three fights a year. But as part of a mentoring program, they hope to eliminate the issues that lead to fights.

His older sister, Amanda Blue, is a VISTA volunteer who coordinates the program. She recruits older students and members of the community to tutor kids in every subject, with an emphasis on reading. The program's goal is to ensure that each student can read and write literately by the end of the third grade.

In a school with 266 students from kindergarten through the twelfth grade, the thirty or so volunteers put in a lot of hours of tutoring. Bob Page, a minister, spends twenty hours a week at the school.

Rick Lyle, who runs The Hungry Ear restaurant in Milburn's old post office, comes on Tuesday mornings to teach skills like budgeting and cooking. (Those who know say Lyle has set up his bedroom in the post office's old vault.) Nalma Osborn, who retired from Milburn Elementary, returns to tutor.

Dustin and his friends, George Hamilton and Dustin Moore, understand the younger students' need for a mentor. "The teacher is the bad guy," George says, "so they need somebody who is not the bad guy.".

But the "I Pledge" assembly is the big event. Violence isn't a problem here, and Dustin, Dustin, George and Amanda want to keep it that way. As Dustin Meadows will tell you, as he looks at you from his titanium eye socket, even one fight is one too many.

## Tulsa County: Jenks

LET'S go ahead and dispense with the jokes about Robert Stemmons, who thinks he may be the only full-time professional whistler in the United States. Robert has heard them all. For instance: Do something wrong around Robert, and he'll blow the whistle on you.

Ethel Stemmons, the woman who gave birth to him, is Whistler's Mother.

When he tours the country, he is on a whistle-stop tour.

He is the Prince of Pucker, the Luciano of Lip, the Pavarotti of Pucker, sometimes known as Hot Lips, and buddy, he is slick as a whistle.

Television news anchors who have introduced their viewers to feature stories about him can't resist this one: "Tonight, we have a real tweet for you."

A headline over his picture in the Billings, Montana, newspaper said: "Lip Service." *The Dallas Morning News* put "Lip Schtick" over a photo of him.

Whistling is not necessarily news. Plenty of people whistle, no mistaking that, and some even make money at it.

Whistlers even have their own International Association of Whistlers and an annual convention in North Carolina, but as far as Robert knows, he is the only whistler whose sole occupation is whistling.

Robert, who began whistling when he was five, picked up the talent from his grandmother, who was quite the whistler.

When he was thirteen, a famous whistler named Fred Lowery performed at Robert's school, Woodrow Wilson Junior High in Tulsa. Robert remembers the moment when the Blind Whistler, as Lowery was known, showed him a whole new world.

"He brought the house down," Robert says. "That's when I began to see whistling as a performance art."

Robert formed a friendship with another young whistler, and throughout the rest of their school days, they whistled together. They would perform things like the school's fight song. "In harmony," Robert adds.

For many years, he never pursued whistling as a career, but he always wondered whether he could go pro.

One day, while Robert was working as a custodian at a school in Michigan, the music teacher heard him whistle while he worked. She asked whether he would like to perform in the school's spring show. They worked up a "little blues number" on the piano.

In 1996, he and his wife, Linda, moved back to Oklahoma, where he read in a newspaper about a talent show. He signed up, figuring he'd lose and then he could relinquish his dreams of performing.

He won.

That was a fluke, he thought, because no one else whistled, and the judges had no one with whom to compare him. Then in April 1997, he and Linda went to compete at the whistlers' convention, Robert thinking all the while: "I'll get beat and put this dream to rest."

Instead, he won second place in Allied Arts, where you combine talents like whistling while you juggle or play a saw. His combo was whistling songs and calling birds.

This year, he won first place in Allied Arts, second place in the popular music category and fourth in classical, giving him third place overall.

In January, he and Linda decided to give his career their full attention. He's the talent, she's the manager.

They have made a promotional video. He has recorded two compact discs: "Whistlodeon" and "A Whistler's Christmas."

When I went to visit him at his mother's house, Robert performed a short concert, demonstrating his trills and warbles and two-note harmonies.

He whistled "What Child Is This." He sounded like a flute. Then he whistled the theme from "The Andy Griffith Show." He sounded like two whistlers, a trick of the tongue. He whistled "Dixie" and the "Hungarian Rhapsody."

ROBERT met Linda Holder when he was twenty-seven and she was twenty-three. By the time they married nine months later, she knew she was in for a melodic marriage. "He whistled all the time," she says. "He would whistle when he didn't know he was whistling. On these long road trips, it gets kind of old."

He hopes to make lots of long road trips, or better yet, air trips on someone else's money.

"I'd like to promote the art and literally breathe

some life back into it. I'd like to promote the idea that
nearly every kid owns and can afford a musical instrument.
Whistlers are associated with happiness. I think if there
were more whistling, there would be more happiness."

# Murray County: Davis

THE frog sat in the crossing and didn't budge at
the approach of the police car. Instead of
running under the road as it is supposed to, the water of
Honey Creek ran over it. We drove within three feet of the
croaker, and neither the shine of the spotlight nor the
wake of the car's rubber tires spooked him.

Moments later, Officer Frank Chambers spotted four
deer in the trees. "Shine your light over there," he said,
and when I did, eight eyes shined back. Their eyes looked
like clear green marbles and appeared to be lit from
within.

Then, as we drove up to the Turner Falls waterfall,
Officer Chambers spotted two more of our friends.
"Skunks," he said. "We don't want to stir them up."

We saw all this on a midnight tour of Turner Falls,
which is a fine way to see the park if you are lucky
enough to ride shotgun with Frank Chambers.

AS so often happens as I roam the roads, I lucked
up on this little journey. I happened to be in
the neighborhood, so I drove to the front gate of the
park. The man at the window told me the park was closed
and that I'd have to return another time.

But as I drove past the booth to leave, I saw Frank
Chambers standing outside his patrol car. Only an hour
before, I had met Officer Chambers at a gas station inside
the city limits of Davis. He told me some interesting
tales about Murray County, like the place down the road
where one of the Dalton gang had been killed. But he
avowed he had no personal stories worthy of interest, and
therefore I quit pestering him.

So when I saw him at the park, we were old friends.
He introduced me to Carl Summers, the man in the entrance
booth, who is a story himself.

In the barefoot days of his childhood, Carl Summers
learned to swim in the Blue Hole downstream from the
famous waterfall. "My aunt, she couldn't swim a lick,"
Summers says. "She threw me in and told me to swim 'cause
she couldn't come and get me."

Back then, when he was five, six, seven years old, when this was a ranch and not a tourist destination, Carl's aunt and uncle lived on the ranch, where his uncle, A.C. Collins, was a foreman. Thus he had free roam of this place, which includes one of the world's best swimming holes, downstream from the seventy-seven-foot, spring-fed waterfall.

Many's the time — goaded at first by his older brother — he has jumped from the rock over which Turner Falls cascades into the pool.

He has lived here his entire life, raised his four children here. And as a full-fledged grown-up with grandchildren, Carl still spends time here.

Turner Falls belongs to the city of Davis, and Carl's job here is to man the entrance booth.

Instead of jumping into the water himself, he tells others where to jump. And to camp. And to hike.

After we had visited awhile, Frank offered to show me around, and Carl gave his blessing. Frank is a part-time employee of the Davis Police Department, and he patrols the park at night.

I saw nooks and crannies and learned stories about campers, like the lonely old man who was driving alone cross-country after the death of his wife.

Frank stopped at the castle and lent me his official police flashlight so I could explore it. You climb fifty stairs to the castle, which was a family home when Turner Falls was privately owned. Inside, cement stairs wind and twist. Without a police officer waiting below, you might be scared. But I had Frank to look out for me, and I had Frank's flashlight.

At the top, you can hear Honey Creek below, and you can imagine sleeping up here in the castle back in the days when Carl Summers was running barefoot, back before you had to pay for the pleasure.

# Kiowa County: Rainy Mountain

THIS mountain is haunted, the Kiowas told me. They don't know why nor by what, but at night, they fear this rocky knob. With the setting of the sun, they say, come the voices of children and the sound of doors slamming. They've never heard the voices or the banging themselves, but that is because they believe the stories. When your ancestors pass down the stories, that is evidence enough. You never will hear the sounds for yourself because you believe and you avoid the mountain at night.

And so I wait at Rainy Mountain, facing west as the sky pinkens, and ragweed bends to the wind, and the shadow of the mountain stretches east. I wait, not because I believe I'll hear anything, but simply to await night at the place the Kiowas both love and fear.

From my spot next to Rainy Mountain, I can see the brick home of the white family, where an hour before, Kiowa elders had circled on comfortable chairs and a leather sofa in the family's den. To the west of me, in black relief against the fading day, stands what remains of Rainy Mountain School's fourteen dorms and classrooms: to the left, a couple of walls of red brick; straight ahead, a building of rock, with one room almost intact.

They all have deep roots in this sparse and dusty plain, the Kiowas and this white family. They had gathered to tell me about Rainy Mountain. This gathering, they hope, will be the first meeting in a campaign to erect a monument.

I wonder, as I recall their stories about the school, if the spirits they fear are the restless souls of the dead, or are the spirit of a people.

Rainy Mountain School is the place where the white man forced their parents to go for education, which meant, really, re-education. In addition to reading and writing, they were sent here to be shorn of their buckskin clothes and what some considered their savage ways. They were sent here, in white man's English, to be civilized.

Whatever it became, the idea for a school wasn't a concoction of the white man alone. Kiowa leaders like Lone Wolf, Big Tree and Gotebo requested of the Bureau of Indian Affairs that the government provide an education for their children.

When the government obliged and built a school, it obliged with the force of government. The government withheld the Indian payments to the families who didn't enroll their children. "My mother always said they were disciplinarians," says Marjorie Tahbone. "They had to march, have inspections, wouldn't let them sing."

Peggy Tsoodle's mother and family traveled to Rainy Mountain from the north, and after that two-day journey, her mother learned immediately what lay ahead. "They pulled that buckskin dress off her and whacked off her hair," she says of her mother's experience. "They had big sticks and would hit them in the head."

One of Marjorie Tahbone's older brothers attended the school. "One thing my brother told me, they were hungry all the time. 'We had chickens, we had milk cows, but we never saw eggs, we never saw milk.'"

If the school was a burden, it was also a blessing. The children learned English, and received the education their forbears wanted for them. "There's a good side to it," Peggy Tsoodle says. "They learned a lot. They taught them how to sew, cook, farm. Taught them personal hygiene."

Luke Toyebo Sr., whose family converted to Christianity under the influence of missionaries, recalls that one of the superintendents was a well-educated musician. "She taught those kids music," he says. "My dad could read music and play instruments. They had baseball and track. They had a band."

Atwater Onco, seated beside his son Eddie, says that of all the people who attended Rainy Mountain School between its opening in 1893 until it closed in 1920, he knows of only five who are alive.

And as members of Atwater's generation die, much that is known about Rainy Mountain School will be lost. That is why the elders hope to raise the money for a monument. "There are people right here in Mountain View that don't know anything about Rainy Mountain or Rainy Mountain School," says Brenda Hawkins, who opened her family's home to the Indians. She and her husband Terry, an Oklahoma City lawyer, are unofficial tour guides for the area. They have named their spread "Rainy Mountain Ranch."

We sat in their den for nearly two hours, and by the end, the elders had relaxed. They mixed stories and laughter with their official business. That is when I learned some of their superstitions. Atwater Onco said to the others, in the Kiowa language, that the Hawkins' stuffed owl was spooking him. "He's looking straight at me."

The Kiowas believe an owl that visits your house brings news of death. "No kidding," he says in English. "When I go home, I'm going to cedar my head." Meaning, he explains, that he will build a fire of coals, top it with cedar chips, then use an eagle feather to wave the cedar smoke onto the top of his head to cancel the curse.

George Tahbone Sr., a man in his mid-seventies who wears his black-and-gray hair in a long, braided ponytail, tells of his close call with danger on Rainy Mountain.

He and Marjorie were traveling the road past Rainy Mountain when a tire went flat. "I couldn't get my spare down, and the sun was going down. She was telling me to hurry. She was already hearing things. I said, 'Let's get out of here and don't look back.'"

Marjorie says, "We don't go that way at night anymore."

N. Scott Momaday, a Kiowa who won a Pulitzer Prize in 1969 for his novel *House Made of Dawn*, knows well the Kiowa legends. In his slim volume, *The Way to Rainy Mountain*, he writes elegantly of this place and his people: "A single knoll rises out of the plain of Oklahoma, north and west of the Wichita Range. For my people, the Kiowas, it is an old landmark, and they gave it the name Rainy Mountain. The hardest weather in the world is there. Winter brings blizzards, hot tornadic winds arise in the spring, and in summer, the prairie is an anvil's edge.... At a distance in July or August the steaming foliage seems almost to writhe in fire. ... All things in the plain are isolated; there is no confusion of objects in the eye, but one hill or one tree or one man. To look upon that landscape in the early morning, with the sun at your back, is to lose the sense of proportion. Your imagination comes to life, and this, you think, is where Creation was begun."

The road that leads past the ranch and to Rainy Mountain is graveled. The drive that turns south and leads to the remains of the school is gravel that turns to hard-packed dirt. The road is two tire tracks split by a median of ragweed that slaps at the undercarriage of my truck.

And so I wait here, at Momaday's point of creation, for dark. As daylight yields to the turn of the earth, the voices I hear on this haunted mountain are only those I conjure myself as I imagine life on this very spot a hundred years ago. The voices I hear, though imagined, are informed by what the descendants have told me. I imagine the whippings and the breaking of spirits on this spot. And I imagine unexpected kindness, and children learning words and music, and playing baseball as they made their forced journey from one world to the next. The thing that haunts here is the understanding of one person's capacity to harm another and the fear that we might ever let it happen again.

## Pawnee County: Pawnee

ON the last day of his short life, nine-year-old Billy Lillie and a friend pretended to be hanging horse thieves. Billy's parents had gone into town.

The ranch foreman was down the road in Yale, visiting family. The boys were home alone with the family's cook, who worked in the kitchen while they played.

Normally, the yard would have been full of children re-enacting scenes from Westerns. Sometimes they re-enacted scenes from movies they had seen at a theater downtown. Sometimes, the re-enactments were from movies made in their neck of Oklahoma, which allowed them to watch stars like Tom Mix at work.

Billy was in a better position than most to see the stars at work. His father, William Gordon Lillie, was known as "Pawnee Bill," who, in a partnership with Buffalo Bill, took a Wild West show around the world.

On the last day of Billy's life, the normal crowd didn't come to play. Only two boys came, and one of them, Earl, left, because he and Billy didn't like each other. So Billy and the remaining friend were left to play alone. They decided to act out the hanging scene from a recent Tom Mix movie.

As the family cook worked in the kitchen, Billy's friend came into the kitchen. *Billy won't play with me*, he complains.

*Oh, he'll be okay*, the cook says. *Go on out and play*.

WILLIAM Gordon and May Lillie were a presence in Pawnee. Neither was native to Oklahoma, but both embraced it as home. Pawnee Bill, a sickly child, reportedly drank the blood of freshly slaughtered cattle to beef up his constitution. May Manning, the daughter of a Philadelphia physician, bridled at her life as a debutante. In Oklahoma, she became a trick rider and all-around cowgirl, a star in her husband's Wild West shows.

Stella Radley Lyon, who lives in Pawnee, remembers that Pawnee Bill loved to drive big cars. "He would drive down the street and flip buffalo nickels to the kids. He flipped a nickel to my little brother. His horn was like a cow mooing. We would holler, 'Honk your horn, Pawnee Bill.'"

The Lillies had one son who died shortly after birth. Because of a surgery, May could never give birth again. So she turned to her husband's Wild West shows and became a star.

Years later, they had the chance to adopt a son from an orphan train in Kansas City. They named him Billy.

Mabel Staley, who was Mabel Potter in the days when she was Billy Lillie's friend, remembers his death. Billy sat behind her in school. The week before he died, she and

Billy were punished for talking in class. "We were talking about what we were going to do the next Saturday," Mabel says.

Mabel's family, the Potters, lived next to the Lillies' ranch and knew the family well. Mabel's father, Marion, was a butcher and a musician who played the mandolin and the harmonica. It was Marion Potter who taught some of the movie-makers how to tie a hangman's noose.

Mabel was so close to the Lillies that after her mother died when Mabel was twelve, she traveled with Pawnee Bill's shows. By the end of her three-year tour, she was jumping through a ring of fire on the back of a horse. "May Lillie was as close to a mother as I had," Mabel says. "She knew I wanted to have a family, and she told me I could get hurt doing those tricks in the show. She told me to be careful."

May Lillie had learned the hard way what could happen to children.

THE Lillie bungalow was a marvel when it was finished in 1910. The Lillies spent two years and 100,000 dollars building the fourteen-room, two-story home that had running water and electricity supplied by a generator in the basement. To the left of the house, if you were facing it, a thirty-foot antenna caught radio waves.

Pawnee Bill called the door that opened onto his front porch a "coffin door," figuring it was wide enough to carry a coffin through, should the need arise.

Many a celebrity walked through that fancy door, people like Buffalo Bill and Will Rogers. Pawnee Bill practiced a little ritual with the door: He brought his guests in through the back door and had them leave through the front in the belief that the tradition ensured that he and May would have even more guests.

On the last day of Billy's life, as he and his friend re-enacted the hanging of horse thieves, his friend became impatient with Billy. The friend already had been inside once to complain to the cook, who sent him back outside.

Billy, however, still wasn't playing, so the friend returned to the kitchen.

*He still won't play with me*, he says to the cook.

*What's he doing?* she asks.

*He's just hanging there.*

PAWNEE Bill learned the sad way that his front door, indeed, was wide enough for a coffin, the one that held his son, Billy Lillie, who accidentally hanged himself on the radio tower while playing cowboy with his friend.

Billy's funeral service was held in his house. His classmates from the third and fourth grade sat together in the bay window. "It was my first experience with death," Mabel Potter Staley says. "I had nightmares about it. I couldn't understand why he couldn't just come back."

The state of Oklahoma now owns the Lillie ranch. They operate a museum that includes photographs, costumes and the stage coach Pawnee Bill used in his Wild West shows. Edwina Rolland, who has conducted tours of the Lillies' home for twenty-one years, knows the history of the silver and the sofa and the buffalo hide on the floor. She points out the amenities of the water closet, an idea Pawnee Bill found in Europe, and the intricate inlays in the wooden floor. She will take you into the room reserved for Buffalo Bill and the one the Lillies set aside for Will Rogers.

To the right of the front door (the coffin door), if you are facing out from the house, you can see the radio tower where Billy died.

MABEL Staley was in grade school when death first hit close. Two years after Billy died, her mother died after surgery in Stillwater. This time, life changed completely. Her father sold his mandolin. The music went out of him.

He thought Mabel could do everything her mother could do. Some days, the pressure overwhelmed her. So she would pour a jar of water, fix a sandwich, saddle a horse and ride up on a ridge that overlooked the Lillie ranch and all of Pawnee.

She would tie up the horse, lean against a tree and look out over the world. The hill provided peace and sanity for a young woman forced too soon to grow up.

All these years later, Mabel remembers it all clearly. "You know that Scripture, 'I will lift mine eyes unto the hills from whence cometh my help,'?" she asks. "I always tell people you just need a hill."

# Kay County: Ponca City

**S**I, says Byron Looney, he did fly all the way from Wichita, Kansas, to eat Mexican food at this little airport restaurant. And Byron, as I learned, isn't the only pilot to fly a few miles for a fajita. On the Saturday I was there, several pilots and passengers entered Ponca City airspace for an enchilada. Owner Enrique Avila says that on one Saturday, forty-two planes were parked outside for his restaurant.

In the world of flying, pilots know where to find the best fly-in restaurants. When pilots are out for a joy ride, with a restaurant as their destination, they call these joy-ride meals the "hundred-dollar hamburger." By the time you fly to your destination, eat and return, your hamburger has cost you some money.

In Byron's case, however, it was the "hundred-dollar frijoles." Byron, an employee of Cessna in Wichita, learned about Enrique's from his flying instructor. "I was doing my first dual cross-country," he says, "and we came here for lunch."

Enrique's is popular with more than just pilots. In Ponca City, I asked a family on the street where I should go for Mexican. Without pause, they gave me directions to the airport.

Enrique, who came to the United States from Cuba in 1973, opened the restaurant in the city's airport terminal in 1983. "I didn't know anything about business. I was a professional painter. ... I didn't know anything about cooking Mexican food. I'm from Cuba."

His wife, Irma, was born in Nuevo Rosita, Mexico. She became the cook. Enrique waited tables, cleared tables, cashiered and washed dishes. The first year was not so good, but the second year, business took off.

From his small start with two employees (his wife and himself) and twenty tables, he now has eighteen employees and 100 tables. His wife has retired from the business. She stayed home to raise their four children.

The food is authentic Mexican. On the menu, dishes are rated with peppers: a one-pepper rating is mildest; a three-pepper dish will cause spontaneous gastrointestinal combustion.

Besides its location, Enrique's is an unusual Mexican restaurant in another regard. Enrique's is closed on Sunday, he doesn't allow smoking, and he doesn't sell alcohol. "I'm a Christian," he says. "We used to close on Wednesday nights too, for Bible study."

They make everything fresh. This isn't a restaurant review, but I must say, the guacamole was perfect, the nachos were worth the drive, and the three-pepper burritos lit me up. For the burrito sauce, they stir in 100 grilled jalapeno peppers per pot. "That wasn't hot at all," Enrique said of the batch I sampled. "When it's really hot, people sweat."

I'm torn between writing about this place and keeping it a secret, so I've hit upon a compromise. I'll make it easy, but not too easy. You know which city, and you know where in the city. But you'll have to find the airport yourself.

That, however, won't be too hard. Watch the sky for fire-breathing pilots and follow their jalapeno vapor trails.

# Coal County: Coalgate

I stand barefoot in a country cemetery, under a nearly full moon at half-past ten on a fifty-degree night. I hold my loosely clinched fists chest high. In each fist I hold a wire that extends in front of me, like two parallel antennae running parallel to the ground.

Then I close my eyes and walk.

Odd though it may sound, my behavior is perfectly rational. I am behaving scientifically. I am looking for graves. Specifically, I am testing Doris Breger's and Verdell Clark's method of finding graves.

What they do is find graves with what amounts to divining rods. This is not magic. For whatever scientific reason, they can find graves and pipes with these pieces of wire. They don't claim to have any supernatural gift. Anyone who can hold the wires ought to be able do this.

I wanted to see for myself.

FIVE years ago, while Joe Avanzini was mayor of Coalgate, he asked his father, Bill, to identify the graves at the Coalgate Cemetery. Bill Avanzini's task had two purposes: For the sake of history, townsfolk would like to know who is buried where; for the future, they need to know where they can bury new arrivals.

Bill estimates the 110-year-old cemetery has 10,000 plots, and many of them are unmarked. They have found about 3,700 marked graves and figure another 2,000 don't have headstones.

Bill is an architect who worked in Oklahoma City for

six years, but in 1966, he moved his family back to Coalgate, the town of his birth. He and his wife, Joy, wanted to raise their three children in a small town. He took over the hardware store his grandfather opened. "My grandfather came to Coalgate and Lehigh in 1887," Bill says. "I married the girl next door. Well, two doors down."

After five years on the cemetery project, Bill had wearied of the work. Then, at a Coalgate School reunion, he ran into Verdell Clark, who was born and raised here but had been out in the world for thirty years teaching philosophy to college students. He was about to retire from Green Bay, Wisconsin, to Arizona.

Bill told him about the cemetery project, and Verdell developed a new retirement plan on the spot. "I knew immediately I was going to come back," Verdell says. "Ain't nothing here, but it's home."

THE idea for using divining rods to find graves came from Doris Breger, who is working on the cemetery project with Bill and Verdell. Doris, who grew up in Coalgate and raised her family here, married thirteen days shy of her fourteenth birthday. "I couldn't have done better if I'da waited until I was thirty," says Doris, who is sixty and still married to Odell Breger. "He is a fine man."

Doris learned about "witching" for graves a year ago at a genealogy seminar in Shawnee. "The first time I tried it, it worked," she says. "I wanted to throw down the sticks and run."

Bill and Verdell were skeptical until Doris demonstrated for them. After he saw it work, the soft-spoken Bill remarked: "Doris, I think you are on to something."

They have found hundreds of graves this way, and they have confirmed the graves with a probe. But that isn't good enough for the official map of the cemetery. To confirm the graves, they will have to use sophisticated electronic equipment, which will cost anywhere from 3,000 dollars — if they contract for the work — to 12,000 dollars if they buy the equipment and do the work themselves, which is their preference.

Verdell's divining rods are made from wire about the same gauge as a clothes hanger. He bends one end of each into an L-shape. That's the handle you hold loosely in your fist.

You hold your fists about chest high and hold the wires out in front of you so that they are parallel. Then you walk slowly. When you cross a grave or a buried pipe, the wires cross. Or so Verdell said.

They can't explain why the rods work, but they don't believe it's a supernatural phenomenon. "I think there's a scientific explanation for why it works," Doris says. "You can use these things to trace out a water drain. You can find a mine shaft. You have to decide if this is a body you are finding or it's where the dirt has been disturbed."

Says Verdell: "I think it's a magnetic phenomenon."

MOONLIGHT transforms this cemetery into a landscape of pale white and black silhouettes of cedar, sycamore and leaning tombstones as Verdell demonstrates his new skill.

First, he takes the rods and walks along the cemetery road. The rods remain parallel. Then he walks into the grass and over a grave. The wires cross. Still, I'm skeptical.

So he gives the wires to me. I walk over a grave. The wires cross. I do it again. They cross. For the next five minutes, I walk past graves with mixed results.

Then Bill takes the rods, and his success is limited, too.

By this time, I have removed my shoes, which is Doris' preferred method. Bill and Verdell take me a couple of rows up, where I don't know the layout. I close my eyes so that I won't know where I am, thus minimizing the chance that I'm subconsciously manipulating the rods. They set me on course.

After a few steps, I feel the rods move in my hands. The right one swings all the way round and hits my left arm. Verdell confirms I've just passed a grave. I walk for another minute as the rods continue to cross and uncross.

For whatever reason, the wires cross as they pass over foreign objects in the earth. So our night-time foray ends quietly, with the world awash in moonlight, and the three of us leaving the cemetery with eye-witness testimony but no explanation, and me having to explain why I happen to have grass between my toes at midnight.

# Stephens County: Duncan

ROSELLA McQuain understands why the city's founders didn't want people to spit on the sidewalks. Rosella doesn't want you spitting on the sidewalks of Duncan, either. She knows that you can't have great expectorations and great sidewalks, too.

Duncan's anti-spitting law, which prescribes a twenty-dollar fine for spitters, went on the books in the early days of this Stephens County town. And on the books is where Rosella wants it to stay.

Rosella, who owns Victory Silks and Tack in downtown Duncan, has good reason to be so spit-persnickety. As past president of Main Street Duncan Inc., she is overseeing the installation of Duncan's new downtown sidewalks. Like many business people in downtown Duncan, she is helping pay for them. Spit and shined she wants, but that's all.

The project began four years ago when the city council decided to replace downtown's deteriorating sidewalks and saw this as a chance to build something bold, something other than a generic white sidewalk.

Main Street Duncan hired Tulsa architect Michael Hall to provide inspiration. So Hall dreamed up a plan that now is set in stone. Or a bunch of stones, to be precise.

For starters, Hall suggested that the city create sidewalks that resemble the region's native sandstone, easy enough to do (if a bit more expensive) with a bit of red coloring in the cement.

Then, he suggested, create a trail — to symbolize the Chisholm Trail — through the downtown area by engraving Duncan's history in blocks of granite and then laying the blocks at intervals in the sidewalk.

So that's what they have done. Many of the blocks offer a precise moment from history: "In 1906, a baseball argument resulted in the death of umpire Ed Lewis. Two brothers were indicted." Another notes first lady Cathy Keating's tour of the state in 1997.

To help pay for the project, the sidewalk committee sold stones to families and businesses, who could engrave anything they wanted. Forty-four regulars at The Grill, for instance, collected money for one and had their names cut in the rock.

Actor and director Ron Howard, who was born in Duncan but left for Hollywood when he was five, will have a star in front of the old Palace Theater. His star will be next to former U.N. Ambassador Jeanne Kirkpatrick's. She's also a native of Duncan.

Rosella, who grew up here, knows much of the town's history and learned more in doing the research for the stones. She knows, for instance, that Ron Howard's aunt once owned the Wade Hotel and spread her large collection of ceramic dogs throughout.

Julia Speegle's hotel was right beside Wall Street, which really was an alley where oil men made hand-shake deals. "It was," Rosella says, "like a spit-and-whittle corner." Hoyt Axton's mother, who wrote "Heartbreak Hotel," was thinking of the Wade when she wrote that song, Rosella says.

The city dedicated the sidewalk on December 4, just in time for Christmas, but the sidewalk was luring shoppers and tourists downtown way before that, says Tim Florence, Rosella's son-in-law and executive director of Main Street Duncan. And in the reversal of a trend, stores are moving from the mall back to downtown.

Tim, a native Kentuckian who moved to town about four years ago, has become Mr. Main Street. He shamelessly plugs his adopted city where he found his wife. He brags that Duncan is the antique capital of Oklahoma.

I don't know about that, but at Bobbie High's Antique Market Place and Tea Room, I did find an old woodpecker toothpick holder like my grandmother's. The metal woodpecker sits on a metal tree limb, which is hollow. You put toothpicks in the log, push the woodpecker's sharp beak into the log, and he springs out with a toothpick.

And at Forever Friends, Carol Roland and Teresa Barnes made a soda-fountain Cocola for me.

Tim has learned the points of interest in Duncan, like the backward "N" in the name of the First National Bank, which was built in 1900. The bricklayer was from France, and he wasn't yet fluent in English. "They convinced him to do it right on the other side," Tim says.

Only two miles from town, he says, you still can find ruts from the Chisholm Trail. And, Tim says, Duncan's J.C. Penney is the only real Penney store in the United States that is still downtown and not in a mall.

As for spitting on the sidewalk, Rosella had that city ordinance carved in stone and it will be well displayed on the new sidewalk. "I thought it was still important enough," she says, "that we put it in two times."

A word, then, to the wise: If you decide to break that law in Duncan, take care that you are not within spitting distance of Rosella when you do.

# Pushmataha County: Clayton

CONVERSATION lags at the family table. No sound except the clink of forks on Nita Lewark's fancy dinner plates. But the silence is a good silence, the silence of people comfortable with one another. The silence of friends who don't need to fill every moment with chatter. The silence of contentment and peace.

Outside of Bill and Nita's cedar home atop a ridge in Pushmataha County, the sun of November has evaporated the morning chill. Bill Lewark, retired Air Force colonel and pilot, has erected a flag pole in front of their home. The U.S. flag and the Oklahoma flag ripple occasionally in the breeze.

Out of the quiet, Ellis James speaks in his gentle tone. "Only two people are missing from the table," he says. "Daddy and Mary."

What Ellis means is that after all these years, their family is almost intact. Only their father, Hogue, has died. Mary is not there because she is traveling with her husband, Donald.

This is a remarkable gathering of family for many reasons. All the brothers and sisters remain friends: Ellis, sixty-nine; Mary, sixty-seven; Charlie, sixty-six; Nita, sixty-four.

And the in-laws are as much in the family as the rest: Bill, Nita's husband; Jo, Ellis' wife; Donald, Mary's husband; and Gloria, Charlie's wife.

They are gathered at the table of Nita and Bill, in a house that is remarkable for many reasons. When Nita and Bill built this house on land that Nita's parents bought more than a half-century ago, they didn't start from zero.

They started with the home in which Nellie and Hogue raised their four children. They took it down to bare boards, then rebuilt it. So Nellie sleeps in the same house where she has lived for decades.

Then Nita and Bill added their two-story lodge with fireplace and wooden floors.

So as the siblings and their mother dine, they dine only feet from the original room where they ate as a family.

They always seat their mother at the head of the table. Nellie is slight of frame and snowy on top. She never fills her plate until everyone else has filled one. She just won't.

She doesn't talk much, but misses nothing. But she is happy to share stories of her life if you ask.

She grew up in Carlisle, Arkansas, and when she was twelve years old, she came to Jesus at a two-week Billy Sunday tent revival. "I'd been attending night after night. All day the day I was saved, I knew I was going to go up that night," she says. "I prayed about it that day. That's when I was saved, I think. Not at the meeting. When Billy Sunday called for people to go up that night, I must have been the first. I cried. I guess I cried tears of joy. It's a feeling I think you have when one is completely converted."

Fifty-four years later, the peace endures. The peace of her Savior. The peace of this mountain ridge. The peace of family. "It really is a good feeling," she says. "It's really a peaceful feeling. It's a very good feeling. I'm very fortunate to have as many children around me all the time. I get to see all of them often."

She has all her children but the youngest, who died after only eighteen months of life. Her children produced children, sixteen of them. Her grandchildren have produced thirty great-grandchildren who in turn have had nine great-great-grandchildren. "I didn't think life would be like this. I didn't think I'd ever be ninety-five. I didn't think life would be this nice at ninety-five.

"My faith has always been very strong," she says. "It has certainly caused me to reach this age, I'm sure. I always depended upon the Lord in my troubles. He has certainly been good to me in answering prayers and giving me advice. My children have brought me much happiness because they are so very good to me. I was happy when I was saved. I was happy that my boys came home from the war safely. I am happy that all my children are Christians."

The years have changed them, but so much remains the same. They can still walk down the steep creek bank to their swimming hole. Outside, at Nellie's end of the house, the bucket still hangs on the well and the water is clear and cold.

No life is free of trouble, nor was theirs. Nellie lost her youngest child. Hogue has been dead for twenty years. But through it all, she has stayed afloat on a current of peace, the sort of peace that exceeds our understanding.

So they gather at this table, Nellie's children, and everything has changed but nothing has changed, because all that is important has survived. You know that when Nellie sits at the head of the table. There is the smile on her lips, and the glow from her eyes that comes from a full heart.

# Bryan County: Durant

For a guy from the young generation, Alfredo Bernali sure talks a lot about hard work. "Some people disagree with work," he says, "but it's good. I don't believe in fun. I always work. Thanks to my mom and dad, I know how to work. I like everybody to work. I don't like laziness."

Alfredo is thirty-two but he could pass for twenty-five, and by his telling, he's been working for twenty-four years. His mother owns Gaby's, a restaurant north of Puerto Vallarta on Mexico's Pacific Coast.

"In Mexico," he says, "if your family has a business, you have to work in the business."

He waited tables, he cleaned fish, he cooked on a grill and on a stove top. "In Mexico," he says, "you have to do everything when you are a little boy."

Alfredo grew up the third oldest of fourteen children. He valued the work ethic of his parents, but as a teen-ager, he decided that the restaurant business was not the work for him.

Alfredo wanted to be an actor. His career began while he lived in Rincon de Guayabitos. His first job was as a model in Puerto Vallarta when he was fifteen. Soon, he was skipping school to model for advertisements.

His parents, however, disapproved, so he made what was the Mexican equivalent of a move to Hollywood. With money he had earned at his parents' restaurant, Alfredo ran away to Mexico City where he attended acting school and worked for the modeling agency Bellas Artes Baguel. He worked in exotic locales like Cancun and Acapulco.

By 1990, though, he quit the modeling business and returned to the business he knows best. He had been to the United States once in a while. He has lived, among other places, in California and Texas. While he owns a home near the beach in Rincon de Guaybitos, the United States is the place he loves.

Through a series of twists, turns and words of mouth, Alfredo settled in Durant. When he didn't find any restaurants that reminded him of home, he started one. One of his sisters, Gabriella — named for their mother — moved to town to help run the restaurant. Thus did Maria Bonita open its doors in downtown Durant, down the road a mile or two from a place that advertises "Tex-Mex" on its sign, which is no temptation to Alfredo.

Maria Bonita — both in taste and in decor — is

tropical, like the town where he was born. "Authentic," is how he describes the food in his restaurant. "Tex-Mex," he says, "is not Mexican to me."

# Comanche County: Lawton

F IRST, Matthew Simpson falls into the path of a train and is killed. A year later, a tornado-like wind knocks down his family's home. One year. Two tragedies.

"Tornadoes are like life," says Matt's father, Phillip, a professor of political science at Cameron University. "They are very capricious. You never know when you are going to get hit."

By the time their house blew down on Memorial Day 1999, Phillip and Linda Simpson knew houses aren't that important. Yet, coming as it did so close to Matt's death, the loss of their home was like a second blow on a fresh bruise. "I'm trained as a social scientist to try to put order on things," Phillip says. "But a lot of this is just pure chaos."

In his death, however, Matt preserved a bit of order for the rest of his family. "In a sense," Phillip says, "he reached out and saved our lives."

M ATTHEW Phillip Simpson was their red-stocking baby, born two days before Christmas 1975. Matt died twenty-two years later, the day before Easter 1998.

Matt had been a student at the University of Oklahoma. He was killed when he fell in front of a train in Norman. The crew members didn't realize they had struck him until they arrived in Oklahoma City. Matt's watch was still on the train's running board. "That was the hardest thing I've ever had to do," Phillip says, "lower my son into that ground."

But the Simpsons had another son, and a friend had warned Phillip against mourning Matt's death to the neglect of Joseph. Phillip took the advice, and that's likely why he's here to tell the rest of the story.

O N May 30, Phillip and Linda Simpson traveled to Oklahoma City, and while they were in town, they stopped to see the destruction of the May 3 tornado. The next night, the Simpsons were having a quiet end to their Memorial Day. Linda's mother and Phillip's sister were at their home.

Phillip was in the den, settling in with a Clint Eastwood movie. His mother-in-law was in the living room. Joe, Matt's younger brother, was in his room. Phillip's sister was in the room that once was Matt's, watching the local news report. Linda was in the hallway.

Mary Beth appeared in the den to announce that Channel 7's Andy Wallace had warned of a strong storm cell approaching. Phillip immediately rounded up his mother-in-law and his son, neither of whom was eager to retreat to the safe room they had built next to their house.

If the storm had threatened a year before, the Simpsons would not have had the safe room for shelter. They had it because of Matthew's death.

In taking the advice of the friend that he should be careful not to neglect his surviving son, the Simpsons had built a music room for Joseph, an aspiring musician.

And with money left from Matthew's insurance policy, they built a safe room next to Joseph's music room.

That concrete vault is where they gathered on the night of May 31. "It got real quiet, then our ears began to pop like there was a dramatic change in pressure. Then it sounded like hail was pounding the room. That was two-by-fours hitting the wall. I finally opened the shelter door. The tornado got our house twenty feet away, but it didn't get the safe room or the music room.

"Joseph's room was especially hard hit. I came real close to losing my second son. ... Life is full of hills and valleys. We've had two hard valleys."

THEY spent the summer digging out, and now the Simpsons are in a different house on a different patch of land. They left the premises, but not the lessons. "Losing Matthew and losing our home has changed us a lot," Phillip says. "My emotions are nearer the surface. It has made me a better teacher. ... I can tell my students that even though tragedy happens to you, you've still got to get up and try to make a contribution."

Politics and government, as Phillip understands them, are man's effort to impose order in a chaotic world. His life has been a striving for order. Then the deputy knocked on his door with the first bad news. Then Andy Wallace said to take cover.

"A lot of human existence is real chaos," he says. "We hang by a string. It's been a real hard couple of years. I'm ready for some good news."

# Jefferson County: Ringling

THESE are the tales of the banker and the baker's
daughter, neither of which has a thing to do with
the other except that both occurred in the town that
almost was winter home to a famous circus. The person whom
the stories have in common is Elena Jones Cain, who grew
up in Ringling but now lives in the village of Edmond.
Elena is the one who shared the stories with me.

Jimmy Ingram was the baker, and Elena was a friend
of his precocious daughter, Latrell. (Much later,
Latrell's son David Ford married Elena's cousin Linda
White. Linda's mother's maiden name, by the by, was Snow,
her husband's last name, of course, was White. The
Ringling Eagle published a story about the wedding of
Snow-White.)

David Ford, whose mother is Latrell and whose
grandfather is Jimmy the baker, provided a photograph of
his grandfather in his shop. The photograph has nothing
to do with the story of Jimmy's daughter, except to show
the face of the man whose child showed such derringdo.

Take a magnifying glass to the picture, and you will
see that the Griffin Grocery calendar hanging on the wall
in Jimmy Ingram's bakery says January 1936.

Move the glass to the left, and you see the sign on
his glass display counter: "Today's suggestion. DOUGHNUTS.
Golden Brown. Light. Sugary." To the left of the sign,
there is a telephone, the type that you pick up and talk
into while holding the receiver to your ear.

Jimmy, the baker, leans against the counter with his
left arm, his right hand propped on his hip, and either a
pencil or a cigarette gripped between his fingers. (Since
he later became a Baptist preacher and insurance salesman,
we'll give him the benefit of the doubt, but don't look
too closely.) His cash register shows his most recent
sale: thirty cents.

He's dressed in white from his hat to the bottom of
his apron, except for the dark tie knotted neatly at the
neck. His apron advertises White Dove Flour.

Jimmy is husband of Jewel Pruner Ingram, who
presented him with the mischievous little Latrell, who
grew up to be somewhat well-known in Oklahoma City, as did
Jimmy the baker.

Jimmy Ingram eventually moved to Oklahoma City to
become chief baker at Crescent Market. Jimmy baked in
large quantities, as evidenced by the recipe book his
grandson David Ford still has.

In now-yellowed lined paper, Jimmy wrote his recipes for lemon pecan cake (yield sixteen cakes at one pound, two grams each), Burnt Sugar Cake, Toll House cookies (three pounds of brown sugar; four pounds, two ounces granulated sugar; twelve packages of chocolate chips; yield eighty-five dozen); and Post Toastie cookies, which called for three boxes of Post Toastie cereal and one ounce of ammonia (that's what he wrote) to make thirty dozen cookies.

Jimmy Ingram grew up in New Mexico and did a bit of everything — including a stint as a boxer — on his way to Ringling. (Ringling, on the eastern edge of Jefferson County, almost became the winter home to the famous circus, thus its name. But the circus people, Elena says, decided Oklahoma was too cold and didn't stop until Florida.)

Latrell, Elena's friend who was the daughter of Jimmy the baker, grew up to be, among other things, Karen Kerr, the personal shopper for customers of Kerr's Department Store. (She often shopped for servicemen, who would write and ask her to shop for their wives or girlfriends.) As Karen Kerr, Latrell (who later became David Ford's mother) wrote an advice column the store published with its ads.

In her first column, published September 27, 1950, in the Oklahoma City Times, Latrell offered hints for all sorts of life-threatening problems. "When we serve appetizers before a meal, it always causes a problem. That old trick of a grapefruit with the toothpicks is something that always irritates our family, and so the night we brought Porky-the-Pig home, we caused a sensation! Porky is a gay little ceramic pig with holes all over his back, and colored toothpicks sticking up like a porcupine. He'll solve your problems as he did ours, for olives, cocktail sausages and other tidbits. He's only $1, too."

Next to her column, Kerr's advertised a nineteen-inch Eye-Witness black tube and Golden Throat Tone RCA television for 445 dollars. "Clearest, steadiest picture in a matchless furniture setting!"

In the days before she was selling for Kerr's, it was the fashion to climb the Ringling water tower, which stands to this day. At nine, Latrell was younger than most who made the climb, but when one of her friends dared her, she was quick to accept the challenge. The trip up was fine. The trip down scared her. One of her friends ran to Latrell's parents. "You'll never guess where Latrell is! She's on the water tower. She's too afraid to climb down."

The chief of police climbed the tower to rescue her. Elena only heard about that story, but she was there the night the fellows robbed the bank president at his home, which was kitty-corner from her father's gas station on Highway 70. "My dad always called him W3," she says. The banker, W.W. Woodworth, was her father's fishing buddy. "I don't know why they robbed him at home," she says. "He didn't take the money home with him. They scared everybody to death."

Beyond those stories, Ringling was a fairly sedate town, she says. She worked at her father's stations. "I pumped gas and checked oil like everybody else," she says. "My brother fixed flats. That was his spending money."

People wanting gas knocked on her father's door day and night. "He would always give them gas," she says. At least most of the time: "If they had been drinking, and they come up wanting gas, he wouldn't sell it to them."

## Haskell County: Whitefield

MONT Webster says things in ways you can understand. For instance, as he and I looked out over Belle Starr Canyon, he described how Belle and her gang often fled the law in Porum, racing horseback over the mountain and hiding in the hollow below us. (From Mont's mouth, hollow comes out "holler.")

The outlaws hid in the thick woods where pursuit would have been foolhardy. "Nobody was going to go in there after them," Mont says. "That would be like sticking your head in a barrel with a bear."

Mont knows this country. His fingerprints are all over it. He gave a running narrative of the landscape as we toured Haskell County. He not only knows the roads, he knows where the old roads were. He can point you to Belle Starr's hard-to-find grave and to the collapsed Younger Bend schoolhouse in the Younger Brothers' neighborhood. (As to the cause of Belle Starr's death, Mont favors the story that has her son shooting her after she whupped him for stealing her horse.)

As a jack of all trades, Mont built many of the houses around here, or bricked them, or built the cabinets for the kitchen, or laid the tile, and he remembers every one from Stigler to Enterprise.

When Mont wasn't working, he was running his wolf dogs. Before the Corps of Engineers built the dam at Eufala Lake here, Belle Starr Canyon was one of his favorite wolf-hunting places. "I've built many a fire where that rest room is," he says.

As a tour guide, he throws in editorial comment: He points out that President Lyndon Johnson came here in the mid-'60s to dedicate the dam, but the disdain in his voice is clear. LBJ decidedly was not one of his favorite presidents.

Mont and Velma live in a house that he built from the foundation up. He cut the timber at his own mill and collected the stone with which he rocked his walls. "I drove every nail in this house."

For nearly fifty of their seventy-three years, they have lived here. The house stands as a testimony and as an example of the good things about their lives: the endurance of family, the value of faith in God, a willingness to work, the common sense to work with what you have and the thrift that allows you to have enough with which to work.

When they bought the land for their house, they depleted their savings. So they lived in a cracker box of a house while Mont milled the lumber until he had enough to frame the house. Once it was framed and walled, they moved in, but another two years passed before he had enough stone to rock the outside walls. "If you didn't have the money," he says, "you let it alone until you did."

Seventy-three years they have been married. They laugh when they recall the people who said their marriage wouldn't last. Mont spotted Velma at an Apostolic revival meeting in Atoka and plopped next to her in the pew, under the glare of Velma's grandmother.

Velma was only fifteen, but she told Mont she was sixteen. She turned sixteen two months after they married. "I robbed the cradle," Mont says, "and I didn't even know it."

Mont's father went with him to buy the marriage license, but they didn't tell Velma's grandmother their plan. Then they drove to Atoka in Mont's father's 1923 Model T and found a preacher who didn't invite them inside for the ceremony. He married them while they sat in the car. "We never got out," Mont says. "I gave the preacher a five-dollar bill. It was half of the money I had, but I had a wife and five dollars left."

THE affection is obvious between Mont and Velma, a sweet familiarity in the way she rubs his arm when they talk or as she sets his fried eggs and bacon in front of him at breakfast. They have lived two-thirds of their lives together in this rock house, which they built fifty years ago. They built it amid the trees, beside a dirt road that has become a paved, busy highway. From the highway, their house looks like any of the other dozens of rock houses you see all over Oklahoma.

Like all houses, however, the house of Webster has a story all its own. To this day, Mont remembers the origin of many of the rocks. He knows which ones came from Arkansas, which came from the quarry down the road, which came from friends.

Two stones, however, set this house apart from all other rock houses. When Mont was rocking the walls, he took a hammer and a chisel to two large stones and shaped them into hearts. He laid one heart in the wall at the front door and one at the back. Two hearts, one at each end of the home. Two hearts, one rock-solid home.

Mont's sweetheart turned eighty-nine years old the day I visited, and we went to the Hilltop Cafe for her birthday lunch. We left the house by the back door, going past the back-door heart.

From where we sat at the Hilltop, we could hear the chicken-fried-steak oil a'bubbling in a skillet. When our lunch came, Mont asked the blessing over the meal in an unembarrassed voice that covered the dining room. He sounds like Grandpa Walton when he prays.

Then Mont went to bragging to friends at the next table, including Coy Few (who, as Mont says, "is few and far between") about how long he and Velma have been married. "They said it wouldn't last, but I never, ever thought I'd made a mistake," he says. "I never regretted it. Somebody asked her the same question once. She said, 'I'll take the fifth.'"

She laughs at his joke, almost shyly, a joke that surely she has heard a hundred times, and peers over the top of her cup of coffee, which she holds to her mouth with both hands. Her devotion is clear. Earlier in the day, when they posed for a photograph by their back-door heart, she had cupped his chin in her hand and stroked the top of his head. Now over he coffee, Velma looks at Mont with those same eyes of love. Then Mont says something else in a way you can understand. "If we had to go another seventy-three years," he tells the Few and the far between at the other table, "I'd tell you we'd make it."

# Love County: Rubottom

THE story of Rubottom Cemetery's start took the long way 'round to arrive here in print. The route it took is almost as interesting as the story itself, because it illustrates the hand-me-down, long-way 'round that most local histories take before they eventually arrive in some form of print.

An amazing number of Oklahoma stories have made it to the print stage; almost every county has an official — often hard-bound — copy of the county's history, as do many of the towns.

Such is the case with Rubottom in Love County.

I came upon Rubottom while looking for a place to land in Love County. In planning my trip to Rubottom, I badly miscalculated the travel time from Clayton, in Pushmataha County (I didn't figure in the burrito stop in Doo-rant, as the natives say it), and by the time I arrived, it was eleven p.m.

So I spent an hour wandering the dark cemetery with my flashlight. The night was perfect for a walk in the cemetery. The flags flapped noisily. In the distance, coyotes yelped, yipped, barked and howled.

Cemeteries tell their own story, especially the small community cemeteries, but often you need a local historian to fill in the gaps.

A sign at the front of the cemetery gave a telephone number, which I called (but not at midnight). The woman who returned my call referred me to Afton "Curly" Williams, president of the Rubottom Cemetery Association.

Pay dirt. Mr. Williams sent me a slim red volume titled "Rubottom: Its History and People," which was compiled and written by Gladys Mobley Bradshaw.

But here's where you really have to pay attention: In telling about the beginning of the Rubottom Cemetery, Gladys Mobley Bradshaw was quoting newspaper reporter Sharon Burris, who was quoting Phyllis Dewbre-Costello, who heard the story at one of the annual cemetery workings at Rubottom. Hardly the horse's mouth.

Here, then, is the story as it appears in Rubottom's official book of history:

"'A horse thief was caught, summarily hanged on a tree, dropped and buried on the spot with no marker to commemorate him,' Costello said. 'Such was the frontier justice in 1900 and such was the beginning of the Rubottom Cemetery.'

"Costello said the second burial in the cemetery,

that of W.P. Rubottom, was also the result of violence, although slightly more legitimate.

"'The story goes that Mr. Rubottom had put up fences around his crops and some outlaws told him they were coming through with their cattle,' Costello said.

"'He responded that he would have a gun if they tried to cross his fences. They did, and gunfire ensued. Mr. Rubottom was killed about as quickly as the horse thief, but was buried with more ceremony, including a handsome marker that stands today.'"

The beauty of these history volumes is the clarity with which they are written. Often, individual families will write the history of their own family and how it ties into the history of the town.

These are some of the stories from the Rubottom volume:

Once, Bob Mobley, Walter Cates and several other teen-agers convinced a "pompous young peddler" to stay overnight for a snipe hunt, which everyone knows is a joke on the "hunter." As the pranksters were leaving their victim, he said to them: "Boys, it's spooky here. Would someone lend me a gun?" They gave him a gun. Then as they walked away again, he said: "I'm cold, would someone lend me a jacket?" Someone gave him a jacket.

An hour later, when the group returned to finish the joke, they called out to him and heard no response. They rushed to the place where they had left him. The salesman, the gun and the jacket all were gone, never to be seen again.

This one is about William Allen Warthen, husband of Ora Lee Fletcher Warthen: "Grandpa Will was a tall, large-boned strong man who would amaze his family and visitors by dragging a huge tree on his back from the woods. Many times he would be bent almost to the ground from the weight. He enjoyed cutting wood and always kept a ready supply for the family's use. One of the funny things that I remember about him was that after a family gathering at Harvey Warthen's house, he was asked if he would like to ride in the car to the Ramsey's place. His answer was, 'No, I'm in a hurry; I'll just walk.'"

Mr. Williams, who sent me the book, says the biggest problem with the cemetery is its size. "We're running out of space," he says. "It's such an old cemetery there's not much of a way to be buried near your relatives."

# Adair County: Stilwell

THE turkeys scatter, pushing, flapping, shoving toward the far end of the barn. The driver of the '53 Chevy pickup motors into the barn, goes right past the automatic feeder line, stops and turns off the engine.

The gobbling grows louder. The turkeys won't come within twenty feet of the bright orange-red contraption with a shiny silver nose and silvery grin.

"What is it, Sister?" Turkey Lurkey, the hen, asks Turkey (Soon To Be) Jerky, another hen.

Turkey Jerky pauses before she answers, stopping to peck (rather stupidly) at a chain, wagging the red thing-a-ma-hickey that hangs from the middle of her beak and flops into her feed sometime.

"That," Turkey Jerky — TJ to her friends — finally answers, "is The Truck that our mama's always warned us about."

If turkeys gasp, a gasp goes through the flock of 8,000. If turkeys could stop gobbling for half a second, the barn would have be silent.

For all their lives, all thirteen weeks of it, these turkeys have talked of nothing but this day. Few of them, however, know what a truck is. But they know to be afraid.

The more observant of the turkeys had a suspicion that The Truck was something like the contraption that had brought them to this place east of Stilwell on Highway 100.

TJ remembered the day in Muskogee when that noisy contraption arrived. The contraption stopped near the house where she had hatched only the day before.

A large, featherless creature scooped up TJ and 14,999 of her sisters (a few brothers slipped in, too) and loaded them on the contraption.

For the longest, then, TJ and the others jostled, until the contraption stopped, and they were herded like cattle (oh, the indignity of it), into a much bigger home than the one they had left. ("Can you imagine," TJ said at the time, "anything worse than to be born a cow? I'd rather be dead than red (meat). The day I moo is the day I die."

Most indelibly seared in her bird brain, though, were the words of Tom Turkey, the old man of the brooder house.

"Beware of The Truck," he had gobbled as she passed him. "Tell the turkeys. Someday ... The Truck will come."

RAY Merriott went into the turkey-growing business in 1979, and by his reckoning he has sent hundreds of thousands of turkeys, millions even, to an untimely (by turkey standards, anyway) end.

When he began raising turkeys twenty years ago, he raised "table turkeys," meaning he raised them to go straight to the dinner table. They arrived 22,000 at a time, and in about three months, they were ready for the butcher in Springfield, Missouri.

Now, instead of turkey turkeys, he raises birds destined to become turkey breasts, turkey bologna, turkey ham. He grows them larger than the birds intended to be placed whole on the Thanksgiving table.

Thanksgiving turkeys usually are no bigger than fifteen pounds to twenty pounds before processing. Now that he tends his turkeys until they are thirty pounds to thirty-five pounds, he only receives about 15,000 in each batch.

The chicks start in one house, and after five weeks, he divides the flock in half, putting each into one of the two barns. "It's amazing," he says of their growth. "They bring 15,000 birds in here on one bobtail truck. It takes eleven semi tractor-trailers to take them out of here after seventeen weeks."

He picks up a turkey — we think it is TJ — so I can make a photograph of them together. When he throws her back with the flock, a dozen startled turkeys flap their wings and take to the air, blowing our hair and creating a swirl of dust, dung and feathers.

'SISTERS," TJ shouts. TJ holds court on the west end of the barn. To the east, turkeys stretch as far as she can see. They are pushing, flapping their wings, crawling on the backs of one another, falling onto the ground. (The man who drove the '53 Chevy pickup into the barn would write on his notepad that the scene looks exactly like a shopping mall on the Friday after Thanksgiving.)

TJ observes the man with the notepad. He wades among her sister hens, who part before him. Suddenly the man from The Truck turns and waves the yellow notepad. "Shoo," he says, in his best turkey-herding voice.

To his left, The Featherless Creature Who Feeds Them removes his jacket and shoos the birds. Both men drive the birds toward the truck, but the word has spread: Be afraid of The Truck. (The man from the truck will write in his notepad: "A group picture with turkeys is tough.")

After thirty minutes, the two have shooed enough

turkeys to the truck for a photo. Mr. Merriott bends to pick up Turkey Lurky.

"There, there," Farmer Ray says. "This li'l ol' '53 Chevy pickup isn't going to hurt you. This fellow only wants your picture for the newspaper."

Turkey Lurky glances over at TJ. "See?" Turkey Lurky says. "Your story about the truck is baloney (pork, not turkey). This creature feeds us. He's our friend."

"Gobble, gobble, gobbledy gobble," TJ says. (Translation: "It's a trick.")

Farmer Ray turns to the wildly gobbling TJ. "What's that you say, ol' girl?" he asks.

Turkey Jerky, who still thinks this is a trick, is quick on her clawed feet. "Moo," she says without a moment of hesitation. "Moo."

## Atoka County: Atoka

NOBODY on the streets of Atoka knew what, exactly, was happening inside the Reba Room at the Best Western. (Reba McEntire, that's who. She's from Stringtown, over to the east. She sings for a living.)

The meeting had been billed as one of the semi-regular reunions of the Atoka High School, Class of '44. But on this day in September, something far more significant transpired.

Most of the participants, to be sure, were members of that class, but what they saw that day will shake the world far beyond the halls of Atoka High School.

The man responsible for the intrigue is a fellow who didn't move to Atoka until his last year of high school. But in that one year, Boyd Glover played basketball well enough that coach Hank Iba gave him a full scholarship to Oklahoma A&M, which, as everybody knows, now is Oklahoma State University.

Boyd hitchhiked to Stillwater with two dollars and ten cents in his pocket, but when he realized how far he was to be from his sweetheart, he gave up his scholarship and went to East Central State in Ada, where coach Mickey McBride gave him a replacement scholarship.

Now, all these years later, Boyd Glover returned to Atoka with an invention that will rattle the rafters of tradition.

WITHIN weeks of his arrival in Atoka in 1940, young Boyd Glover spotted the girl he would marry. After fifty-nine years, fifty-seven of them in wedded bliss, Boyd still delights in telling the story.

It was the first week of school. Boyd sat in the hall, studying, when he noticed a blue-eyed brunette in bobby socks and loafers. "During that fifteen to twenty seconds, I said to myself, 'That's the girl I'm going to marry.'"

A young man of action, Boyd wasted no time. On Saturday, he walked the two miles from home to downtown Atoka, where all of the county went to see and to be seen.

Sure enough, after a spell, along came the freshman student of his dreams. Boyd invited her to a movie, and she accepted.

They married in 1942, after he had left college to join the Army-Air Force, which he did after the Japanese bombed Pearl Harbor.

The woman he married, Bonnie Phillips, is a native of Atoka and a member of that Class of '44. Her father ran the Cyclone, a filling station east of town. When she was three, Bonnie remembers, two men stopped at the station about ten o'clock one night, knocked on the station's door and asked for gas.

"My dad gave my mother the shotgun. One of the men pretended he couldn't get the gas cap back on. My dad bent to help him, and one of them shot him. The bullet went through his cheek and out his neck."

Bonnie doesn't remember many of the details herself, but she does remember all the blood.

Her father survived and went on to open another filling station. The armed robbers spent time at the state pen in McAlester.

Bonnie married Boyd, they moved away for a while, and after Boyd left the service, the Glovers returned to Atoka in November 1943. In 1954, they opened a Western Auto.

ON that day in September 1999, Dean Loveless, Jesse Downs and Janice Bussy joined Boyd Glover at a table in the Reba Room. Quietly, and without ceremony, Boyd took the lid off a newfangled version of a centuries-old game.

Boyd Glover believes he has built a better game of dominoes, and the Class of '44 was there for its Atoka debut.

This isn't Boyd's first invention. How do you know when Boyd Glover is thinking up a new contraption? His heart is beating.

He invented and patented a concession stand on

wheels that concessionaires pulled behind their vehicles. (The Restaurant That Comes to People.) It was shaped like a barrel, had three sinks, all the plumbing, electricity, and in 1966, a microwave oven. (He built the prototype in his garage; to take it out of the garage, he had to let the air out of the tires and cut a notch out of the frame of his garage door.)

His other patented invention was an air purifier that cleared smoke out of the air. Honeywell manufactured his original design, but now many companies build air cleaners that operate on a similar principle of attaching a charge to a smoky particle.

He has folders full of his other inventions — like the hamburger grill that puts on the mayo, mustard, et cetera, and then spits out the fully wrapped burger.

He has invented windshield wipers that use air instead of blades and an electric razor with blades built into a glove. (You shave by stroking your face.) He hasn't patented those.

But he has obtained the copyright and trademark for "Wishbone Dominoes," named for Barry Switzer's famous offense. Document disclosure was filed with the U.S. Patent Office in August 1999. The rights are up for auction on the Internet, starting at 100,000 dollars.

The game is pretty much like traditional dominoes. Instead of rectangles, however, the dominoes' corners are trimmed off, creating an elongated octagon with a place for two numbers at each end of the domino.

The result is that scoring is much higher. Boyd has calculated that a player can score at least 2,030 points with Wishbone.

On that day in September, when he unveiled his new game, he and the members of the Class of '44 played four hands. The three beat the inventor at his own game. "I had the lowest score," he says.

As of this writing, Boyd has not had a bid on his Wishbone Dominoes, but he's thinking of someone who ought to make an offer: "Barry Switzer should buy this."

## Marshall County: Madill

MEGAN is older than her years and at the same time younger, skittish of strangers, shying away and hiding her face with her upheld hand, palm out, as if shielding her eyes from the sun.

She looks frail, but frailty hardly could have

survived all that she has survived. Her eyes have absorbed things no child should see.

We'll call her Megan, so that we may preserve her privacy. Her story is one of sadness beyond endurance, yet she endures. Her face of innocence — her pretty, classic nose and the cut of her cheeks — makes the story of her former life seem all the more jarring.

Some of the children who live here at this home for children would rather live at their real home. Not Megan. She is happy here. "In all my time in child care, ten being the worst, her situation was a nine," says Art Brown, administrator of the Baptist Home for Girls. "The type of abuse she went through, the severity of neglect. She never had the chance to be a child."

Megan has been here for a year. Kindness by kindness, Megan has risen from the emotional poverty of her life. Her ascendancy has a well defined starting point. On the time line of Megan's life, you could mark the day of the bicycle as the start of her journey up.

**W**HEN Art Brown tells the story of Megan and the bicycle, his eyes disappear behind tears that never run down his cheeks. Her story isn't the only one that brings him to tears; many of the children in his charge at the Baptist Home have stories of sadness and triumph.

Megan's story, though, hits an especially tender spot.

Art came to the home in 1991 as assistant administrator, and now he is in charge. The short version is that when he was twenty-four and his wife, Dawn, was twenty-three, God called them to care for hurting children, and not only their physical needs. Their calling is to bring children to Jesus even as they comfort them.

The Browns became house parents at the Boys' Ranch in Edmond, a job which led eventually to Madill. The Browns have two children of their own: Austin, thirteen, and Kay Lynn, nine.

The thirty young women and two young men who live here aren't orphans in the technical sense. They are social orphans, children whose families can't — or won't — care for them.

Life for these children is hard all year long, but Christmas often can be the toughest, especially for those who can't see family for the holidays.

As the season approaches, many embrace the hope that this is the year Mama and Daddy will come. Some parents promise to come and then don't show.

But Christmas also is a happy season as churches and neighbors go out of their way to give the children presents and parties.

For more than a decade, First Baptist Church of Marietta has provided bicycles for all the children who don't have one. Last year, Megan's name was on the list.

THE Rev. Tommy Higgle does the fun part. Others in his church in Marietta raise the money and buy the bicycles. He delivers them.

Last year, he arrived the Saturday before Christmas. "You should have seen her face," Art says of Megan. "It's probably the nicest gift anyone ever had given her."

While the other children tried out their new bicycles, shy, frail Megan, who still was new to the home, motioned Brown over to her and made a quiet request. "Mr. Brown, when they leave, will you teach me how to ride?"

Art Brown cries when he tells this part, because he is not telling a story about a six-year-old's first bicycle. Megan is eighteen. "She didn't have anything. Can you imagine being eighteen and never knowing how to ride a bike? She didn't have one, and nobody to teach her."

When Pastor Higgle left, Megan's house father, Nick Charlton, took her and the bicycle to the cottage, and he coached her, while many of the staff and house parents watched from behind windows. "When she started," Art says, "everybody was crying."

A week later, Megan came around to show Art how well she was riding, an accomplishment that was the first of many accomplishments in her life. She made a trip to Washington, D.C., her first ride on a plane. She attended a "Girl to Womanhood" conference in Louisiana. She aspires to be a hair stylist.

"She's got a dream," Art Brown says. "When she came, she didn't have a dream."

## Pittsburg County: McAlester

MARGARET Jones is Santa's officially designated U.S. postal clerk, here in the heart of Little Italy. As such, she handles all of Santa's mail that arrives at the post office in McAlester.

Margaret, mother of three and a ten-year veteran of the U.S. Postal Service, is well-qualified for the job, which she has held for three years.

The first qualification is an unqualified belief in

Santa Claus. Her second qualification is that she has delivered mail on a route so she understands Santa's pressures and special needs.

As Santa's agent, Margaret is authorized to answer letters on his behalf and to share the letters with others, which is a way of spreading the fun of Christmas.

The McAlester post office was pretty busy the day I arrived, mostly with people buying stamps. But Margaret took time out of her busy day to share some of the letters with me.

She has received only two since Thanksgiving, but it's early yet. A young lady named Kathryn wrote to Santa on a computer and printed it out with red ink. Kathryn, as you'll see, isn't staking everything on Santa:

"For Christmas, I want a Barbie Shop With Me cash register, Mambo #5 CD. Maybe some other things you can think of for me. I also want those white fingernails with GLUE, not those stickers. If you can't get none of this stuff, that's OKAY. I'll probably get it for my birthday."

The other 1999 letter is from Robert L., who has so much faith in Santa that he didn't stamp his envelope, which isn't unusual with Santa's fans. In addition to asking for toys and chocolate candy, Robert was very specific in his request for double A, triple A, C and D batteries.

Margaret's favorite letter came in 1998 from a lass named Lacey: "If you would please try to get the following list. But first, I'd like to say I'll never forget to give you cookies and milk. And I've tryed to be the nicest girl I can. Here's the list: 1) Dear Diary Clueless, pg. 598, Penny's catalog 2) Wheel of Fortune cartrige, pg. 632 3) Just tiny surprises 4) Quiz wiz. Thanks."

Margaret was amused that Lacey took the time to include the page numbers from the catalog. Says Margaret: "That's a true woman."

As long as Margaret can read the author's return address, she sends a reply from Santa. "If they write to Santa," she says, "they should get a letter back."

I was in Pittsburg County because people all over Oklahoma have been bragging about the Italian restaurants in McAlester and in Krebs. So I pointed my '53 Chevy pickup southeast, and within a couple of hours I was smelling spaghetti sauce. After I finished at the post office, I headed for supper.

If you come from Oklahoma City, the first Italian place you'll encounter is Giamoco's in McAlester. Then a hop, skip and a meatball down the road, and you are in

Krebs, the land of lasagna and linguini.

Krebs is so synonymous with Italian food that many diners come to town looking for a restaurant named Krebs. The town of Krebs has more Italian food than Santa has jingle bells.

The three most famous restaurants are Pete's Place (the first in town), Isle of Capri and Roseanna's. Since the first two don't open until four p.m., I settled in at Roseanna's, where Elizabeth Prichard shared a bit of the history of the place.

Pete Prichard, her grandfather, came to the United States as a young boy. His father came to Oklahoma to mine coal.

Her great-grandfather changed their name from Piegare to Prichard at the request of the coal mine bosses, who couldn't spell Piegare. Pete started his restaurant so he could leave the coal mine.

The other three well-known restaurants, including Giamaco's in McAlester, all are descended from Pete's; each of the families that owns a restaurant is related to him.

While the menus are pretty much the same, Elizabeth says, the recipes are slightly different, as the families have adapted them to their own tastes.

One thing you can order at Roseanna's that you can't at the others is gnocchi — pronounced "nee-oh-kee," an Italian dumpling made with eggs, milk, flour and potatoes. That was a treat their grandmother cooked at Thanksgiving and Christmas.

In Margaret's family — extended and otherwise — the men, all the way back to Pete, cook the meals. Three of Elizabeth's six brothers cook, while one waits tables with her. Elizabeth has five sisters.

Elizabeth's father, Frank, named the restaurant Roseanna's after her mother, Rose Ann. He thought that sounded better than Frank's Place.

It opened as a carry-out place, but popular demand encouraged Frank to buy some paper plates and tables and to open for sit-down.

The families don't compete for customers, Elizabeth says. "There's business for all of us. We go to their places to eat, they come to ours," she says. "You drive by on Friday and Saturday night and everybody's packed."

When the family isn't eating Italian food, they go for Mexican. "My dad used to say we all should have been born Mexican," she says. "It used to aggravate him."

# Greer County: Granite

WHETHER he's at work or at home, Bill Willis cannot escape the stony gaze of Will Rogers. That's because Bill has built a granite mosaic of Will in his back yard.

The mosaic is the first phase of an unfinished tourist attraction that Bill started in the mid-'70s after a friend proposed that he build an Oklahoma version of Mount Rushmore.

Bill was a natural for the project. He and his family have been in the granite business since about 1950, when Bill's father, J.R., bought the quarry and equipment from Pellow Brothers, which opened the quarry in 1902.

Bill liked the idea, but the granite mountains that anchor the north end of Granite were all wrong for a sculpture.

Bill proposed, instead, that he build 108-foot-tall mosaics of Will Rogers, Sequoyah and Jim Thorpe. He charted the course with the head and shoulders of Rogers. (To give you a sense of the size, I stand six-foot-three, and Will's tie from the knot to his chest is taller than me.)

Bill dedicated the top third of Oklahoma's most famous humorist in November 1979, and that's where the project stopped. "I've sort of given up on it, I'm so old," Bill says. The mug shot of Will cost Bill and his father 50,000 smackers to build.

Bill, whose children and children-in-law work in the business with him, works in 25,000-pound blocks of granite. Their biggest diamond saw grinds up 6,000 dollars worth of diamonds every two months. "That's a hundred dollars a day for diamonds," he says.

As the blade slices the granite into manageable sizes, sixty gallons of water run over the saw every minute to cool it.

The town of Granite sits at the intersection of Oklahoma's Highway 9 and Highway 6. The population varies between 1,500 and 2,000 people, says Rafe Murray, depending on whether the counters include the inmates at the state medium security prison here, which is one of Granite's claims to fame. "When you meet people and tell 'em you're from Granite, they ask, 'Are you in or out?' That's the joke," says Rafe, whose ancestors came here in 1907.

Opal Norman, Rafe's seventy-eight-year-old grandmother, has lived here all her life. Her sons Johnny,

Joe and Roger are in business in Granite. Rafe lived here all but the early years of his life. Now Rafe, his wife, Tonya, and their four-year-old son Kal live in a new house whose north window looks out on Devil's Slide, a round, slick face of Granite Mountain.

Granite, the town, generally is a quiet place. The Granite Cafe serves cheeseburgers and fries for less than three bucks, and has one non-smoking booth tucked on the south side of the dining room.

The only crime of note was the 1987 murder of a schoolteacher who lived in a house on Main Street. Esther Steele was stabbed to death in her sleep; two students went to jail for the killing.

IF Bill Willis ever finishes his 308-foot-tall mosaics, and Granite becomes a tourist stop, it won't be the first time. In the early 1900s, the town was famous for its sulfur springs, which became a place of relaxation and healing for visitors who came to drink and swim in the medicinal waters.

Promoters built a skating rink and a hotel beside the mountain. Mother Jones, the famous Socialist, once spoke to a group of 3,000 here, according to an old issue of Prairie Lore.

Lupe Arredondo, seventy-eight, oversees what's left of the resort. He took Rafe and me down a trail to what once was the swimming hole. It now is a dry and dusty bowl ringed by cedar.

Bill hopes that his children will someday finish the granite mosaic of the three Oklahoma heroes. It's been twenty years since he finished Will's head; he figures it will cost 3 million dollars to 4 million dollars to complete the project. "I need," he says, "a 5-million-dollar angel."

## Jackson County: Martha

I was looking for Friendship, but instead I found Velma in Martha, not to mention pipe organs and a Volkswagen graveyard. Friendship is only a dot on Oklahoma's official state map, which I could see, but I couldn't figure how to go there, because the map doesn't show a road. Judging by the map, you would have to hike in or charter a chopper.

So I called the Jackson County Sheriff's Office, where a Deputy Kidd told me how to find Friendship. (About two miles north of Altus, if ever you are in need of Friendship; on Highway 183, look for the Friendship Baptist Church sign.)

It was on the way to Friendship that I passed the place where Volkswagen Beetles, Volkswagen vans and Volkswagen Karmann Ghias go when they bug out. Except for a fellow with a flat tire — who was taking shelter at the Baptist church — nobody was stirring in the cold and rainy weather of Friendship.

So I drove west, north and — when I saw the sign that said Martha — west again. I stopped in downtown Martha, which consists of the post office, town hall and Cotner's Pipe Organs. (The Martha Speedway sits east of downtown.)

Most every town you find in Oklahoma will have a post office and a town hall (and many will have a race track or rodeo arena), but Martha is the only town in the state with a company that builds pipe organs, at least according to Tom Cotner's sign.

Tom, who grew up in Altus, always loved music, according to Pat Cravens, Tom's office manager and gatekeeper. She grew up across the street from Tom. "When we were growing up across the street from each other," she says, "he would practice the piano, and we would sit on the front porch and listen to him."

Tom chanced into the organ building business. One day after college, he was in Wichita Falls, Texas, and encountered a couple who installed organs. "I went in to say hi," he says, "and they put me to work."

He apprenticed with them, and he's been working on organs since.

Before he opened his own business in Martha in 1982, Tom was in business with Paul Haggard, a craftsman who cared for many of the pipe organs in Oklahoma City.

When Mr. Haggard retired, Tom came to Martha, where his parents were living. In his shop, Tom builds organs from scratch, restores organs and converts organs to electronic organs, which aren't really organs at all, he says. "An organ is like any natural instrument," he says. "It's a natural sound. The sound has a life of its own that isn't there when you try to imitate it with anything else. It's a substitute."

Tom's most recent contribution to the world of organ music is the acquisition of the pipe organ from St. Paul's Episcopal Cathedral, which is across the street from the Murrah Building, which now is the site of the national memorial to the victims of the April 19, 1995 bombing. During repairs after the bombing, church members decided to purchase a new organ. St. Paul's Episcopal in Altus bought the old one. "We took it apart and brought it back to Altus," he said. "We saved a very fine state treasure."

Pat showed me around the factory. "This is an antee-q," she says, playing with the word "antique." Pat, who hired on with Tom in January, does a bit of everything in the shop. Ron Gignac is the shop's jack-of-all-trades and Jane Lingrel and Dave Roberson work mostly in electronics.

One day a truck driver with a delivery called for directions to Martha. "Go until you get to a sign that says, 'Martha — that-a-way,'" Pat told him. She is high on the town, even though she lives "upstate" in Mangum. "You don't have to worry about locking your car. ... The biggest problem with traffic in Martha is getting people to stop at the stop signs."

Across the street, at Martha's Post Office, Velma Smiley has watched with sadness the departure of families she has known during her twenty-nine years at the post office, twenty-six of them as postmaster. Even she and her husband have moved in closer to Altus. They live next door to a daughter in the neighborhood where Velma grew up. "The older I get, the more I realize family is all we've got."

In moving close to Altus, she has given up her extended family. "The town is my family," she says. "When people live alone, and they don't show up to check their mail, sometimes I send my husband to see about them."

Velma tells of a recent incident that illustrates what has happened to Martha. She received a telephone call early one Saturday from a woman in Texas whose father lives in Martha. She was concerned because her father wouldn't answer his telephone. She had checked the Martha telephone directory for someone to summon before she finally called Velma down the road.

As she told Velma: "None of these names in the telephone book means anything to me."

# Beckham County: Elk City

**N**EVER mind that the time is ten minutes before ten p.m., that the temperature is thirty-four degrees, and that the grass is frosted. These children will not be stilled.

They stand under twenty-seven strings of green light bulbs that stretch forty feet from the ground to the top of a pole, which is bejeweled with a lit star.

The strands of light form a Christmas tree, and the gaggle of children is inside it. They tilt their heads. They whirl and twirl and giggle and squeal until they stagger and wobble and fall down under a sky of spinning green stars. Then a girl jumps up and sits on the chest of a young lad who has been slain by dizziness and total, unself-conscious joy.

I have my note pad, scribbling my descriptions by the glow of Christmas lights, trying to capture the moment on lined, yellow paper. Then comes the part of my job that I so often dread — I who am more intro than extroverted, more insecure than confident — the moment when I must intrude into the lives of strangers and ask them for their names and how to spell them and can I put them in the newspaper.

THE tree under which the children twirl stands on the back side of Elk City's park, which has been given over to miles of lights strung over acres of park.

Many of the displays are traditional, with mangers, Marys, Josephs, magi and shepherds. Some are whimsical, like the seven-foot angels playing baseball on the diamond. (But there is a serious side to this one: It is in memory of a child who won't ever again play here.)

Santa is ubiquitous, riding a train here, a stage there. Some displays have nothing at all to do with Christmas, except that they are built with Christmas lights, like the coyote howling by the cactus and the cowboys cooking over a campfire.

I have found that riding the roads of Oklahoma is like panning in a stream for gold. I pan and sift out gray and black and ordinary, then a fleck catches my eye and suddenly I find a multicolored gem like the Christmas display at Elk City.

ELK City's Christmas display wasn't the only jewel I found in Beckham County. On my first pass through, during daylight, I stopped at the intersection in downtown Carter and saw to the east the remains of a rock gas station.

Best I could tell, the station never had been updated before it was abandoned. The gas pump was the early type: You pump the gas into the glass measuring tank, then drain the gas into the car.

The station — across the street from what once was the Tilton Hotel and down the street from the café — is built of small, smooth round rocks. Ditto the pillars that hold up the cover over the drive-through.

Just over the county line, in the Greer County village of Willow, I stopped to study what is left of the Willow Beauty Center. Whoever abandoned the little shop left it laughing. A three-foot-tall stuffed doll sits in the shop's picture window, her yarn hair tangled in what look like a machine for electrocuting people.

The machine is, in fact, a primitive permanent wave machine. Twenty-two curling clips, that look like hair barrettes, hang down from a steel halo; their wires are covered with the old-fashioned cloth insulation.

To the left of the permanent machine is a hood hair dryer on wheels. With the sun just right, the shadow from the words painted in the window spell "beauty" on the hood of the dryer.

This is Route 66 stuff.

So the children twirl until they fall down, and then another group of squealing children arrives. Instead of going dizzy, they weave in and out of the light strands.

I stand back in the dark and watch and think of my own two daughters back home who probably aren't in bed yet, either. I have my note pad and my pen, and I know I should walk into the tree and interrupt their play and ask them for their names.

There will be that uncomfortable moment when the children and the grown-ups see me emerge from the darkness and wonder if they should be frightened. I'm nervous, wondering if they'll tell me to beat it or if they'll be happy to oblige.

Finally, I decide not to do it. It would have spoiled this green-light, star-bright moment for them and for me, and these Christmas childhood moments are few enough and too far between as it is.

## Woods County: Alva

When last we checked in with Durward Brown, he was a seventy-three-year-old retired teacher who collected and restored old cars. Twelve years later, little has changed. Now he is an eighty-five-year-old retired teacher who collects and restores old cars.

Last time we checked, he figured he had bought license tags for twenty-seven cars with a total value of about a quarter of a million dollars. "And," he said, "I'm building another one."

I met Durward and his wife, Jadeena, on a cold night in January 2000 as they prepared for Alva's football hero parade. The next morning, a Friday, I followed Durward as he drove a 1966 Mustang convertible to a gas station. The temperature was twenty-three degrees, and he was driving with the top down.

Durward stores his cars and trucks all over the place, from his garage at home to his "museum" on U.S. 64 to a barn on his farm. In his garage, he keeps a 1966 Rambler and a 1957 T-bird. On his driveway, he keeps a 1959 Studebaker pickup.

The truck is one of five Studebaker trucks in his collection. Another is a one-and-a-half-ton, dual-wheel 1953 work truck, which Brown bought new and still uses. The museum collection includes a Model T pickup that Jadeena's grandfather bought. Three generations of Clen Leeper's family worked that truck into the dirt. "It wound up in the iron yard," Durward says. "That's where I got it." (Clen, a farmer, bought the first combine in the state of Oklahoma. Durward keeps the carburetor in his shop.)

The museum also is home to a Ford Phaeton, which Durward found buried in a gully. Durward dug it up, fixed it up and took his granddaughter, Stephanie Richey Coon, to the junior-senior prom in it.

The Browns own enough antique cars to make their own parade, but that isn't necessary, since there's always a parade somewhere. Like the day after I met them when they drove the Mustang and the Rambler in the parade, which was held to honor the football team at Northwestern Oklahoma State University. The Rangers won the national NAIA football 2000 championship, the first national title the school has won in any sport in its more than 100-year history.

The T-Bird officially belongs to Jadeena. Durward gave her the keys to it on their fiftieth wedding anniversary.

That was eleven years ago.

"I still haven't driven it," Jadeena says. "I'm afraid I'll wreck it."

I went to see the Browns after reading a story that Jim Etter wrote about them in 1988. Jim Etter used to write for *The Daily Oklahoman*. He was always digging up interesting people like the Browns.

I wanted to hear about their cars, but they have so many other stories that I was in their living room forty-five minutes before we talked about automobiles.

Durward grew up near Slapout, and came to Alva to attend college in 1934. He was one of the last students inside "The Castle on the Hill," a grand old building on the Northwestern campus that was destroyed by a fire on March 1, 1935. The origin of the fire has been a mystery, but Durward has a theory.

The night before the fire, Durward was studying in the library, which was in The Castle. At ten p.m., the final bell rang. He went to the rest room in the basement, where he saw several boys playing shinny — batting a can down the hall with sticks.

When Durward left the rest room, the boys were sitting atop a stack of bags of floor sweep, the oil-soaked wood shavings used to clean wooden floors. They were smoking a cigarette.

Durward walked to the house he shared with his sister and a cousin. At four a.m., his sister awakened him with the news that something on campus was burning.

The investigation never revealed the source of the fire, and Durward won't say the boys started it with their cigarette. But he always has wondered. "I can just tell the story," he says. "I don't have to draw any conclusions."

Two years later, Northwestern dedicated the Jesse Dunn building, which replaced The Castle. The building is named for the lawyer who became Oklahoma's first supreme court justice.

By this time, Jadeena had started school at Northwestern. She studied home economics and planned to teach.

Somehow, the college convinced Eleanor Roosevelt to be on hand for the dedication service. She arrived by train and stayed at the Bell Hotel, which still stands in Alva.

As part of the celebration, the home economics students threw a party for more than 250 very important people. Some of the students served the diners. Jadeena was part of the team that prepared supper. "We had green beans," she remembers. "I don't remember the meat. It's been more than sixty years."

THEN there is Slapout. "I was there," Durward says, "the day it was born." He and Joe Johnson were on their way home from school one afternoon when they encountered Tom Lemmon and a team of horses pulling a small building south toward the new highway the state was building. (It's now State Highway 3.)

"What'cha doing?" Durward asked.

"I'm going to start a town," Tom replied.

His plan was to open a store and to trade with the mule skinners and others who were building the road. "I'm going to call it Nye," Tom told Durward.

"N-Y-E?" Durward asked, spelling it.

"Right."

"Why?"

"I plan on selling nye near everything," Tom replied.

Well, Tom did very well. So well, in fact, that he traveled to Woodward every day to restock. While he was gone, he left his sister in charge, and she's the one who gave the corner the name that stuck.

Anytime someone asked for something that was sold out, she would say, "We're slap out of it."

A fellow who gave everybody nicknames soon took to calling the corner Slapout.

After a year, Joe Johnson, who had leased the land to Tom for his store, decided that Tom was so successful he wanted his corner back. So he didn't renew Tom's lease.

Tom moved his store across the street, and Joe put up his own building. Joe and Durward's daddy painted a sign for the Joe's store that said "Slap Out."

About that time, a representative of Eason Oil convinced Joe to sell gasoline at his store. When Eason manufactured its own highway maps, they put Slapout on the map so that everyone would stop there for gas.

Across the street, Tom opened his store, called it Nye, and sold "nye" near everything but gasoline.

DURWARD Brown knows cars, and after years of study, he has his own philosophies about the horseless carriage. "Statistics show," he says, "that the people who spent their money trying to build a better car aren't here any more. But the people who spent their money advertising are."

At his shop, Durward has hung a photograph of his Uncle Charlie Hagan with the guts of a Model T spread out on a table. Charlie is reassembling the engine as his final exam at Sweeney's automotive school in Kansas City.

That was in 1912, two years before Durward was born. Maybe Durward's passion for internal combustion engines was inevitable: "I grew up under his feet, looking at the kind of stuff."

## Woodward County: Woodward

WITH teachers named Dixie and Ethel, you know Mary Robertson was destined for culinary greatness. Dixie Snow and Ethel Turner took Mary into the kitchen when she was only sixteen. Mary was a new bride who had learned her way around the kitchen at the elbow of her father during a year when her mother was bedridden.

Her professional career began when she hired on as a waitress at the Wayfarer Inn and then asked to be moved to the kitchen. "They taught me the best way," she says. "They just turned me loose. They cooked everything from scratch. They don't teach like that any more."

Over the last twenty-nine years, Mary has cooked at restaurants all over town. Now she's down town at the Polly Anna Cafe, Woodward's oldest restaurant.

Mary starts work between five and five-thirty a.m. She bakes more desserts by ten a.m. every day than most people make for Thanksgiving and Christmas combined. Her meringues are Mount Everests of egg whites. One of Mary's cinnamon rolls has the heft of a loaf of bread.

The Polly Anna has been in the same family since 1953, when Al and Jane Williams bought full ownership. (They started at the Polly Anna with Charles Pappe, the man who went on to found the Sonic restaurant chain. The first two Sonics were in Woodward and in Shawnee, according to Al Williams.)

Al and Jane started in the food business in Virginia, where they put in two Tastee Freeze restaurants. "But it was too far from home for me," Jane says, and so they returned to Oklahoma and went in partners with Mr. Pappe.

Five years ago, they sold the Polly Anna to their son Lyndon, and chances are looking good that it will stay in the family for at least another generation. Many is the morning that Lyndon's young son has helped Mary in the kitchen. "I keep telling him, 'One of these days, I'll be working for you.'"

Mary's art extends beyond the kitchen. It extends, in fact, from her ankle to her shoulder. Mary paints, and her son, Shawn, moonlights as a tattoo artist. So she painted roses and vines, which he transferred to his mother's skin. "I was forty-one when I got my first one," says Mary, who is forty-five. "We started with a rose on the front of my ankle. Over the years, we've kept adding. I figured if I was going to have them, I ought to use my own art work."

She paints at night, after ten-year-old Katie is in bed. But for now, she expends most of her artistic energy at the Polly Anna, where her coconut cream pie is the biggest seller, followed closely by the lemon meringue. "I cannot follow a recipe," she says. "The only ones I can follow are the ones in my head. If I measure something out, it doesn't turn out right."

JOE Cheap's feet look ordinary enough, but that's deceiving. The feet hinged at the bottom of Joe Cheap's shins have covered a few miles in his life, a bunch of them on the football field. When, for instance, he was a running back for the Buffalo Bisons up in Buffalo, these feet carried him to score fifty-six points when Buffalo beat arch rival Beaver 68 to nothing. He scored eight touchdowns and eight extra points.

Joe went on to play college ball at Tulsa, where in 1958 he ran back a punt eighty-six yards to beat Cincinnati and set a school record that stood until the '90s. "They punted to us three times," he says. "The first two times, they were off sides. On the third time, I guess they were so tired, they couldn't catch me."

Joe has owned a sporting goods store here in Woodward since 1970. January 21, 2000, was his thirtieth anniversary, which is why his son Jeff invited me up to meet his parents. Joe and Lanus Cheap, Jeff wrote in a letter to me, are two of the "truly great people in the world today."

But don't ask Joe or Lanus. If you want to learn something from Joe Cheap, you have to ask, and don't expect a long answer. For some, talk is cheap. For Joe and Lanus Cheap, words come at a premium. They are quiet people whose lives speak for them.

Joe does the selling. Lanus buys for the store. Joe lets shoes out on credit, or just for a trial run in someone's house. ("That drives my mom crazy," Jeff writes.)

In thirty years, Joe says, no one ever has cheated him.

His last name, he admits, has inspired jokes, especially after he left his home town. Sometimes his business shows up in the telephone directory as "Cheap Joe's."

Joe knows his place in the world. In high school, for instance, when he and Lanus began to court: "She was a cheerleader, I was just a player," Joe says, noting the current parallel in their ownership of the store: "She runs it. I just do the work."

# Harper County: Buffalo

**B**ASKETBALL practice is over. The work day fades into supper time as the young women leave their gymnasium. A thumbnail moon grins down on them as they disperse through this town in northwest Oklahoma.

For two hours, I watched these young women run nonstop. For two hours, they reminded me that I can't do that anymore. My mind skittered back to my days of high school basketball.

"I could do this," I thought, and then I reminded my self that I can't. I sadly admitted that probably I could work back up to it, but at this moment, any attempt to run with these women would result in embarrassment and really sore knees.

Darin Jones, in his fourth year as coach, understands that youth is short. Ten, fifteen years from now, they won't have the freedom, the stamina, the opportunity to do these things.

He pushes them through practice. When they look back on this time, he wants them to know they performed their best, to know that they couldn't have run faster, jumped higher, played harder. They lift weights. And on beautiful days like this one, he runs them outside on the track, to run with the wind, as it were.

"Let's go Olympic," he shouts, and they run three-by-three down the court, trying to score 100 points in five minutes.

"Follow the leader," the coach shouts. "Vegas," he barks, before they catch their breath.

They huff, sweat darkening the hair above their foreheads. "Free throws," the coach shouts, "and if you miss, do the dot drill."

Shoot. Hop. Run. Whatever they are doing, the players never are still.

"Let's go," he shouts, gathering them for a five-minute scrimmage. "Make it, keep it."

The starters against the reserves. They are coming off a 34-27 loss to Laverne, their biggest rival. They are looking toward Vici and then to their annual invitational tournament, a thirty-eight-year tradition in which some of these players' parents played.

This will be the last go-round for Crystal Robison and Alicia Buss, the team's two seniors. They know, Jones says, time is short.

The rest work as hard: juniors Lauren Hudson and Cassie Prophet; sophomore Rachel Hudson; and freshmen Karen Roberts, Kristi Zollinger, Courtney Adams, Katherine Jeffries and Amanda Klingenberg, who are also on the middle school team.

Jones concedes he's rough on his players, but it's because he loves them and wants to contribute to their success, which doesn't necessarily mean winning but performing beyond their potential. "I really appreciate how hard they work for me," he says. "They listen to me yell at them and tell them all the things they are doing wrong. These girls are exceptional. I have a five-year-old daughter, and I hope she grows up to be as good as these girls."

He isn't talking about their basketball skills.

On the day I watch, they reward his coaching by doing all that he asks. No opponent, he says, runs them in a game as hard as he runs them in practice. Yet no one complains or groans. No one curses, not once.

He said his players are first rate because their parents are involved in their lives, and because Buffalo is a great place to grow up without big-city intrusions and distractions.

For two hours, I watch this court-full of potential, the future running on ten feet clad in squeaking basketball shoes. The future for them, the past for me.

I want to tell them that if they'll work at it, maybe they can delay the moment that they'll look back and wonder where life went, the moment when their knees began to complain.

But after seeing their determination even as their tongues dragged, I know they don't need me to tell them anything. Someone already is teaching them some of the most important lessons.

Instead, they inspire me to think that even when the years of youth have passed, they really haven't passed completely unless I let them. I have my own daughters to teach, and so I best find a good pair of floor-squeaking basketball shoes. Shoes that will be kind to these worn-out knees.

# Delaware County: Jay

OF all the days to forget my camera... I could have posed by the Jay Water Plant. The Jay city limits sign. The Jay American newspaper office with the

American flag painted in the front window. The Jay water tower with Jay Bulldogs painted on its side. The Jay post office. The green "City of Jay" trash bin.

I came to Jay because, well, how often do you have the opportunity to tour a town that bears your name? It is empowering, let me tell you.

Another thing we have in common, this town and I, is that nobody can say exactly why either of us was named Jay. My parents said they liked the name but aren't sure how they came up with it. It's not short for Jacob or Jason or Jake or Jerry. Just plain Jay, which I like, because I haven't run into too many other Jays, and not a single other Jay Grelen, because I am the only one in the entire world, which gives me something else in common with the one and only Jay, Oklahoma.

I learned about the founding and naming of Jay in the big green book (yours for thirty-five dollars) that tells the history of Delaware County. Jackie Marteney, curator of Delaware County's historical museum, let me browse in a copy for free.

According to the book, the seed for Jay was planted July 27, 1908, when a group of men met at Muskrat Springs to organize the Delaware County Improvement Association. They hired surveyors to determine the geographic center of Delaware County, which, as it turned out, fell in the allotment that belonged to Thompson Oochalata, a full-blood Cherokee.

Since government restrictions kept the association from doing anything with his land, Claude L. "Jay" Washbourne Jr. donated ten acres of land that lay east of Oochalata's property.

On December 8, 1908, voters chose Jay as the county seat, moving it from Grove, which caused no end of hard feelings and accusations that the Jays stole the election. Before the brouhaha was settled, the Supreme Court and the governor had become involved, a couple of militias had formed, and the original courthouse in Jay "mysteriously" burned.

That is how Jay came to be. As for its name, there are two stories. The first is that Dick Walker, one of the surveyors, named the town for his only son, Jay.

The second is that it was named for Jay Washbourne, who had donated the land. Washbourne supposedly picked up his name from a flour-sack shirt his mother had made for him. A large "J" printed on the cloth wouldn't wash out, and thus he was named for his shirt.

The green book also includes the directions for washing clothes, as explained on a sign at Brewster's

Laundry:
1. Build a fire to het kettle of rainwater.
2. Set tubs so smoke won't blow in eyes if wind is pert.
3. Shove one hole cake lie soap in biling water. (*Must have been painted by the same person who painted Loyd's sign. Keep reading.*)
4. Sort things in three piles. One pile collard, one pile white and one pile britches and rags.
5. "Starch": Stir flour in cold water to smooth then thin down with biling water.
6. Rub dirty spots on board. Scrub hard then bile, rub collard but don't bile, just wrench and starch.
7. Take white things out of kettle with broomstick then wrench and starch.
8. Spread tee towels on grass, hang rags on fence.
9. Pore wrench water on flower bed. Scrub porch with hot soapey water and turn tubs upside down.
10. Go put on a clean dress, smooth hair with side combs. Brew a cup of tea, set, rest a spell and count your blessings.

JAY is forty miles north of Tahlequah in pretty, hilly country. The stretch of Highway 10 between the towns is lined with impressive stone bluffs, cute resorts and plenty of places from which to rent canoes.

One of the most interesting buildings in Jay is a vacant, weather-beaten old place that once was a house of commerce. Most recently, judging by the faded words painted high on the store front, the building was home to Loyd's Tire Shop, House Full of Bargains, Holesale & Retail. A "W" later was added to Holesale. You can tell it came later because it isn't in the same style.

Before Loyd's moved in, the building was occupied by Jay Used Furniture. Those letters are bleeding through Loyd's letters.

So that I could say that Jay fully experienced Jay, I ate pizza at Papa Shawn's downtown and bowled two games at J Lanes (115 both times, which is high for me).

Don't think that just because Jay is small that it is backwards. Jay is home to one of Oklahoma's only two drive-through convenience and food stores, owned by none other than Bubba.

Bubba discovered drive-through stores in the northeast while driving eighteen-wheelers for J.B. Hunt. For years, he had wanted to start his own business. "I was the kind, when I saw a business for sale, I'd put on a coat and tie and go in and say, 'Is this establishment for sale?' I'd have my note pad. Of course, I didn't have no money," he says.

When Bubba discovered drive-through stores, he knew he had discovered his niche. So he drove and saved and waited. Then one day while in Jay, he saw a piece of property for sale. "I said, 'This is it. This is where Bubba's going to plant his feet.'"

He had designed his store in a motel room in Kansas City while he waited on a load of freight. Now that he had his land, for which he paid cash, he was ready to go. His store has been open for four years, built beside a highway, he says, that carries 10,000 cars a day. "I'm across from Wal-Mart, next door to O'Reilly Auto Parts. You couldn't ask for better," says Bubba, whose given name is Tim Foote and who grew up in Muskogee. "Everybody has a dream, and this is my dream."

The dream has produced its comic moments. Not everyone, for instance, is sure what business he conducts when they drive into his building. "People still stop by," he says, "and ask me to fix their air conditioner."

## Cherokee County: Tahlequah

THEY never know, over here in the office of the registrar of the Cherokee Nation, what they might find when they open the mail. They receive little bags of sage, X-rays and photographs of tattoos from people, all of whom are hoping to certify their Cherokee ancestry. "People send us blood drops on paper to see if we can test them," Registrar Lela J. Ummerteskee says.

Lela and her staff are the keepers of the official Cherokee roll — part of the Dawes Commission Roll — which closed in 1906. To be certified as a member of the Cherokee tribe, you must be able to prove you are a direct descendant of someone on the roll.

Lela, who went to work for the tribe twenty-two years ago as a file clerk, is half Cherokee. Pam Hood, who spends most of her day at the front counter in the registrar's office, is $17/256^{th}$ Cherokee.

They never see a slow day here, with anywhere from fifty to eighty people arriving for help every day. The months from May through September are the busiest. People wanting to trace their ancestry plan vacation trips to Tahlequah. "They are from all over," Lela says.

The roll changes daily, and Lela updates the total every two to three days. On the day of my visit in

January, the Cherokee Nation population was 211,220.

Ninety-five percent of those tracing ancestry are doing so in order to take advantage of the benefits afforded tribe members, Lela says. The other five percent simply want to know. "The majority of people coming in know who they are," Lela says. "They just haven't bothered to get their certification."

Degree of blood doesn't guarantee certification. Your ancestor must have registered with the census by 1906, Lela says. Those who didn't are the "too lates," Pam says.

"We have full-bloods now who can't be certified because their ancestors didn't sign up," Lela says.

They have seen people become emotional when they authenticate their Cherokee ancestry, and they have seen people angry when they can't. "We never tell anyone they're not Indian," Lela says. "We just tell them we can't certify them."

Some Indians didn't register because they feared they were giving the government control of their lives, Lela says. "Others said, 'Why should we register as a race when no one else has to?'

"Whites at that time didn't have to get a number. Why should we have to prove who we are? We are the only race of people who has to prove who we are."

Even now, a century later, suspicion still raises a wary eye. On Thursday, as Pam worked the counter, a mother and daughter arrived in search of help. Before they would talk to Pam, they needed one answer: "Do you work for Cherokee Nation," one of them asked, "or the federal government?"

# Sequoyah County: Gore

THE members of the high school band may not know it, but if Al Gore becomes the next president of the United States and keeps his promise, they'll be marching in his inaugural parade.

It would be mighty appropriate, seeing as how the town of Gore is named for one of the vice president's relatives, although no one is sure exactly which one.

And it would be a nice gesture in return for Gore's support of Gore. Of the 186 votes cast in the 1988 presidential primary, Gore gave 153 of them to Mr. Gore.

Gore originally was named Campbell, but it was one of two Oklahoma towns with that name, says Paul Eichling, the man with all the answers to questions about Gore.

Since it needed a new name anyway, the Campbell in Sequoyah County saw a way to make hay in the process.

The town's first-rate Indian baseball team needed uniforms. So town leaders contacted Sen. Thomas P. Gore, one of Oklahoma's first two U.S. senators, with an offer. If he would find money for their team's baseball uniforms, they would name the town after him.

Or at least, that's the way Eichling has heard it. "How much truth there is to that, I don't know," says Eichling, who has been Gore's town clerk and treasurer for twenty-six years, only slightly longer than Bill Summers has been mayor this time around. "I've looked for documentation, but I've never been able to find it."

Thomas P. Gore, who lost his sight in a childhood accident, is regarded as one of Oklahoma's more colorful politicians. As for his relationship to the current Vice President Gore, some think he is a distant cousin, some think a great uncle. "I haven't been able to determine that," says Eichling, who is fairly certain Thomas Gore's family was from Tennessee.

Far more certain is that Thomas Gore was the grandfather of the novelist Gore Vidal.

Aside from its town with a famous name, Sequoyah County is known as the trout capital of Oklahoma, thanks to the trout stocked in the Illinois River.

Eichling's grandfather was a doctor and grocer in town, and the first white man ever to dine with Cherokee Chief Red Bird Smith. When his grandfather was robbed and shot, members of the tribe traveled en masse to his house to pray for his recovery.

As the town's designated historian, the townsfolk send all seekers to Eichling. Once a fellow came in search of his grandfather's records. "We finally found him on the 1910 census," Eichling says. "He was in the Sequoyah County jail."

As for that promise from Vice President Gore: During a past presidential campaign, the Gore High School band played at a rally at the Muskogee Civic Assembly Center.

When Mr. Gore noticed the band's name, he talked to some of the band members, signed his autograph a few times and assured the band members that if he was elected president, they'd be marching in his parade.

So if they start the cake sales and car washes now, by January 20, 2001, the Gore musicians could have enough money to make the trip to Washington.

To hedge their bets, however, the musicians in Gore might want to work a revenue-sharing deal over in Rogers

County. Come inauguration time, the town of Bushyhead just might be wanting to send some of its musicians to Washington, and they might be needing some traveling money.

# Hughes County: Wetumka

JACK Herring readily admits he probably would have been one of the suckers in the summer of 1950. "I probably would have been the biggest sucker of the bunch," he says. "Anything the American Legion could do to make a little money, we'd jump on."

That was the summer that F. Bam Morrison came to town, telling the good people of Wetumka that he was advance man for a circus that was coming. Jack was commander of the American Legion, a fact that Morrison learned from some of the town folk.

Ol' F. Bam went from business to business, lining up sponsors for the circus. He tried to line up Herring Hardware, but Jack was out installing a television antenna. (Television came to Wetumka in 1950, and Herring Hardware sold Zenith TVs.) When F. Bam stopped by the store for a third time, Jack's father told F. Bam he was becoming a pest and recommended he bother someone else.

Mr. Morrison, who later became known as the Flim-Flam Man, found plenty of gullible Wetumkans eager for entertainment. He traded circus tickets to druggist Bill Love for a prescription; he traded tickets to Ray Meador for a hotel room. (The hotel was three stories tall and had an elevator.) He traded circus tickets for meals at the Wide-A-Wake Cafe. He traded an Indian blanket to a local doctor in exchange for a shot of penicillin.

He convinced local businessmen to lay in a supply of frankfurters, buns and soft drinks. And hay for the elephants.

Then F. Bam Morrison disappeared, leaving a lot of tickets that weren't worth the paper on which they were printed.

But the brave citizens of Wetumka didn't let that spoil their week. Instead, they inaugurated Sucker Day and served free hot dogs and soft drinks and let the kids scramble for money hidden in the hay. "We just swallowed our pride and had a big day," says Jack, who is seventy-nine.

For fifty years now, the town has celebrated Sucker Day on the last Saturday of August. And F. Bam Morrison has been immortalized in a children's book by an Oklahoma author. The book, titled simply "The Flim-Flam Man," was published in 1998 by Farrar Straus Giroux.

Author Darleen Bailey Beard learned about F. Bam Morrison from a co-worker at a tailor shop where Darleen worked part time. The next summer, she went to Sucker Day and interviewed several people, including Jack and Jo Herring, PeeWee "Mr. Wetumka" Nolen, Orville Gammill, Elgie Absher and city manager Don Kardokus, all of whom she thanks in the front of her book.

Her research took her to the library and the historical society. "I read the articles that F. Bam Morrison actually wrote and put into the newspaper advertising his carnival," Darleen says. "He said he had forty rides, forty shows. Even had a guy named Tex Walker."

She tells the story through the eyes of a fictitious character, Bobbie Jo Hailey, a little girl who stutters.

While Darleen isn't from Wetumka, she is genetically an Oklahoman. It's not her fault her parents lived in Pennsylvania when she was born and for the first twelve years of her life.

She was a shy girl, she says, who loved to write. Her father worked at a newspaper and once invited a young reporter to dinner so Darleen could meet a real writer.

Darleen gave a manuscript of one of her stories to the reporter, but was too shy to watch the reporter read it. So Darleen excused herself to bed and went upstairs. Then she sat at the top of the stairs and heard the reporter proclaim her story "really cute."

Her fifth-grade teacher, Jacqui Schickling, also was an inspiration. Every week, the teacher required her students to write a story using the words from the current list of spelling words. Sometimes Darleen wrote two or three stories. She dedicated her first book to the teacher, whom she tracked to a houseboat in Florida to tell her about the book.

As an Oklahoman, Darleen has found plenty of material in Oklahoma. Last year, Darleen's latest book, "Twister," was released in March, just two months before the May 3, 1999, tornado.

Now Darleen is working on a historical children's novel about the Babbs Switch fire, which killed thirty-six people in a one-room school house on Christmas Eve 1924.

Meanwhile, *The Flim-Flam Man* has drawn international attention to Sucker Day in Wetumka. To this day, no one knows whatever became of F. Bam Morrison, who could still be alive.

But there were sightings. At a book signing in Tulsa, a man stopped to visit Darleen. "He said he was from Texas and said the Flim-Flam Man came through his town too. This guy promised the same things. Then he took off."

As if the Flim-Flam Man and Sucker Day weren't enough Americana for one town, television arrived here at just about the same time. Jack Herring was a pioneer in the field, a high-tech visionary who saw the future in picture tubes and tall antennas.

The first TV to come to town was the Philco, which Lawrence Massey sold out of Massey Hardware and Furniture. Jack and his father, Grant, who ran Herring Hardware, were only seconds behind, introducing seventeen-inch Zenith sets. The next brand, RCA, came to town much later, he says.

"I sold seventeen-inch," he says. "The smaller the tube, the better the picture. Magnify the picture, magnify the interference. My competitors were selling twenties and twenty-ones. Everyone told me, 'You've got the best picture.' I never did tell them why."

Jack was quick to adopt the new technology, and he was a pretty good salesman. To attract customers, Jack set a television in one of the windows at Herring Hardware.

People would gather in front of the window, sitting on the sidewalk and car bumpers. "About the best show they had was professional wrestling," he says. "That and baseball were the two main deals. That's what I tuned it to. That would get them in. That helped sell some TVs."

Sometimes, the picture on the TV screen would roll, and of course, Jack had to leave whatever he was doing at home to fix it, sometimes at nine o'clock at night.

Jack reckons his family was the third in Wetumka to have a TV at home. A TV, of course, required an antenna, which stirred up a lot of curiosity in his neighborhood.

Jack built his own antenna, and also erected one at every home where he sold a television. Many of those antennas stand to this day, he says.

And what of Jack Herring, the man who rode the cutting edge of technology fifty years ago? "I still have an antenna," Jack says. "We can't get cable out here."

# Tillman County: Loveland

THE roads that lead here are gravel roads, sure, but they are mighty fine gravel roads. "You have to go five miles to get to pavement," says Bob Simpson, who has lived here all his seventy-two years. "That's one thing that's hurt us. We never were on a highway."

Bill Simpson, son of Bob and Virnitia, doesn't live here anymore, but he *does* remember the isolation of living at the end of a gravel road in southwest Oklahoma. "When the creeks get out, Loveland becomes an island," says Bill, who was visiting his parents the day I stopped by. "We circulated a petition to get pavement. They told us they would build a road in two years. That was ten years ago."

Isolation and fine gravel roads, however, aren't Loveland's claim to fame. Loveland, ZIP code 73553, is one of the towns in the United States that receives an avalanche of mail for Valentine's Day.

People send tons of mail to the Loveland post office because they want their cards to carry its postmark. And since 1926, the Simpson family has canceled all the mail, Valentines and otherwise.

Loveland, in Tillman County, was founded in 1907, and the post office was established in 1908. From 1908 until 1926, the town had five postmasters. From 1926 until 1998, Loveland had only two postmasters, and both of them were related to Bob Simpson.

Postmaster Number Six was Lydia Simpson, Bob's mother. Postmaster Number Seven was Virnitia, his wife. Loveland won't, however, have a Number Eight. The U.S. Postal Service closed Loveland's office November 16, 1998.

BOB was born the year after his mother became postmaster. As a kid, his job was to fetch the early mail delivery at the train depot and then deliver the day's dispatches. On Sundays, a bundle of *The Daily Oklahomans* would arrive for him to sell.

The post office was in his home, the same home where his mother gave birth to him.

The quarter-section his grandfather homesteaded in 1907 is smack in the middle of the region known as The Big Pasture. The rubber stamp Virnitia used for stamping envelopes had a big heart that encircled the words: "Valentine Greetings from the Heart of the Big Pasture, Loveland, Oklahoma."

JIM Cardwell moved to Tillman County as a child, when his parents returned to care for Jim's grandfather, James Allison Cardwell. Like many others who grew up here, Jim left after he finished high school. If you weren't a farmer, Tillman County didn't offer much.

"They had an Army-Air Force base in Frederick," he says. "That closed after World War II. Then they opened a helicopter manufacturing plant. Then they started manufacturing brassieres. (When) the missile site came in ... they closed that down."

Jim's love of the place is rooted in the memory of his grandfather, whom his friends called Bud. Bud was an auctioneer who fiddled at barn raisings.

Bud's farm was west of Manitou, about a third of the way to Tipton. Jim knows the Loveland region as Hackberry Flats, and it was there, in 1905, that his grandfather hunted wolves with Teddy Roosevelt. "My granddad was a staunch Democrat," Jim says. "Teddy was a big Republican. I was kind of surprised he was in on the hunt."

Jim, who is fond of the exclamation "shucks," has to pause for a wave of emotion as he recalls his grandfather, who died shortly after Jim's family returned to the farm. "I heard him play the fiddle. Boy he could do that," Jim says. "He was a grand guy. He brought his family in a wagon to Oklahoma. Raised three kids. Started in a dugout in the side of a hill — half sodded, half dug out."

The team that pulled the wagon from Kansas was a pair of Clydesdales, which Bud's father gave to the family. The family settled briefly in Oklahoma City on a patch of ground by the North Canadian River. Bud sold the plot for a hundred dollars, another wagon and a team of horses, and the family moved to Manitou.

The Clydesdales ate a lot and were cantankerous plow horses, so Bud took them to Frederick and traded them for two mules. "My grandmother almost divorced him for that," Jim says.

Ben and Bessie, two freed slaves, sharecropped on Bud's farm and took care of Jim. "They had a little ol' shack south of our house. I was down at Ben and Bessie's one day. Bessie, she always took care of me, spoiled me rotten. She had the tub turned upside down in the yard. 'Don't you turn that tub up,' she told me. 'I got a possum under there.' I asked, 'What are you going to do with that?' She said, 'I'm going to cook him for dinner.'"

And she did. "I tried a little bit of that possum," he says. "That was the greasiest meat."

Jim and his friends had one other memorable encounter with animals. Occasionally they would play near an Indian graveyard behind his grandfather's farm. One day they heard something scratching and coming out of the ground over a grave.

"We didn't know what it was," he says. "There were six or seven armadillos come out of a coffin. We was hoping it wasn't someone coming out of that ground."

THE historians aren't sure how Loveland was named, but the theory persists that the name may have been suggested by a Mr. Duncan, or Tom McCracken, the first postmaster, who may have lived in Loveland, Colorado at one time.

The other part of the theory holds that when the residents of the town couldn't agree on a name, they wrote all the suggestions on slips of paper, put them in a hat and someone pulled Loveland.

Thousands of letters have passed through Loveland. Thousands of Valentines and wedding invitations arrived in boxes and manila envelopes, already stamped and awaiting only the Loveland postmark. "I've had people drive seventy-five to a hundred miles to deliver two boxes of invitations," Virnitia says.

When Steve Simpson and Jennifer, his wife, were mailing their wedding invitations, they bought the stamps at Loveland, stamped them in Loveland and canceled the stamps at Loveland.

One July 4, a couple arrived unannounced and wanted to be married in front of the Loveland post office. They stirred up a preacher from Grandfield, and Bob's mother Lydia, who had been canning beets, was a witness in her beet-stained apron.

Until about 1974, the Loveland post office operated out of the south room of Lydia Simpson's house. When Bob and Virnitia built their house, they enclosed one side of their two-car garage and that became the post office.

Now Bob and Virnitia are remodeling the post office into a living room.

At its peak, Loveland's population swelled to about a thousand, and the town had several businesses.

The last surviving business, a grocery store and filling station, closed in 1968, the year Steve Simpson was born and the year his mother became postmaster. When the Loveland post office closed in 1998, Steve's son Brandt was about five months old.

At twenty months, Brandt Simpson is the youngest resident of Loveland, whose population has shrunk to fourteen. "When Bill's here," says Virnitia, looking at her oldest son, "there's fifteen."

# Cotton County: Cookietown

**N**O, this is not the home of the cookie factory. That's Marietta, east of here, over in Love County. This place really is called Cookietown.

Proof? There's the "Cookietown" city limit sign, and there's the "Cookietown, Oklahoma" sign on Marvin Cornelius' falling down old store.

Cookietown is on Oklahoma's official state map, and you can't ask for more credible evidence than that. Its spot on the map may have been in danger a few years back, but Terry Neese aims to keep it on there.

Terry, the Republicans' nominee for lieutenant governor in 1990, was born here, and she made certain that everyone on the campaign trail knew it.

In years past, others from the area — assuming no one would know where Cookietown was — would say they were from the surrounding towns of Randlett, Temple, Devol or Walters. But not Terry. When someone asked, she told them she was from Cookietown. "I think all of that kind of rallied a lot of the people in Cotton County," she says, "especially around the Cookietown area. I think I brought a pride for them."

Terry realized about ten years ago that Cookietown's status might be in danger when a man updating the map called her to ask if Cookietown was incorporated. If not, he said, it couldn't stay on the map. "It was natural to roll out of my head, 'Well I'm sure it is incorporated.' Why they have to be incorporated, I don't have a clue."

Incorporated or not, Terry figured they'd better spruce up the highway intersection where Cookietown sits. That meant, primarily, that she called Duckie Myers, who led the project to put up the sign on Cornelius' store.

By preserving Cookietown, Terry is preserving her life. "My grandfather and grandmother lived two miles west of there for fifty years," she says. "My dad was born there and lived there seventy-eight years. Both of my sisters were born in the house two miles west of Cookietown. It's an important point for me. I want to make sure we keep Cookietown on the map."

The origin of Cookietown's name is not clear. The more colorful of the two tales that Terry tells holds that a truck loaded with cookies collided with a car and spilled its load.

The more likely version, she says, is that a hungry

surveyor working in the area went into Cornelius' store, where Marvin Cornelius had only cookies to sell that day. So the surveyor ate cookies and named the town in honor of his lunch.

Like Jim Cardwell next door in Tillman County, Terry remembers the stories of Teddy Roosevelt hunting in Cotton County. Roosevelt camped on Deep Red Run Creek on land that Terry's grandfather owned.

Her father, Clifford, played on the Union Valley school's championship basketball team with Doyle Parrack, who went on to coach at the University of Oklahoma.

The night Terry was born, a storm dropped six inches of rain. The flood prevented her father from driving home. So he swam the quarter-mile to their house. "I don't know why," she says, "he thought he needed to get home so bad."

Maybe, I'm thinking, for the same reason she needs to keep home on the map.

# Noble County: Perry

THERE we sat, in a corner booth at the seventy-five-year-old Kumback Cafe, and who should join us but Zen Glimmer, the quiet and unprepossessing new editorial cartoonist for the local newspaper. (He's not paid; it's his version of a letter to the editor.)

As Providence would have it, Anna Lou Randall had shown me his first two cartoons only moments before Zen and his wife, Jill, arrived.

His first cartoon showed a snowman and a pile of snow melting in a city dump truck. The punch line...

Wait, first you need to remember that Perry is in Noble County.

Now ... the snow is beginning to melt, and the punch line, in bold letters above the cartoon, says: "NOBLE WARMING ..."

Zen's real name is Glen Zimmer, and he grew up in Oklahoma City. But he and Jill, who were living in Edmond, decided Edmond was too big and wanted to raise their two daughters in a smaller place. So now they are renovating a 100-year-old, two-story rock building that originally was a hardware store.

Jill won local fame in 1999 when she opposed plans for attorney Stephen Jones to sell copies of his book while he was speaking at the Carnegie library in Perry. Jones was the attorney for the man who bombed the Murrah building in Oklahoma City.

Speaking of the bomber, who should walk by our booth but Second Lieutenant Charlie Hanger of the Oklahoma Highway Patrol, the man who arrested the bomber ninety minutes after the bombing.

Lieutenant Hanger lives in Perry. A photograph of him in his uniform, posing at the Kumback's lunch counter, hangs in the restaurant. "Town hero," it proclaims.

Then who should come by our booth but Craig Kemnitz, whose parents Charles and Laura Kemnitz have run the Sinclair station on the same corner for forty-five years. They still check your oil, wipe your windshield, pump your gas, and Laura Kemnitz will gauge your tires, since her husband's eyesight isn't what it was.

Craig tells us Darren Dreifort, the million-dollar pitcher for the Los Angeles Dodgers, was in the Kumback just the day before. Darren knows Craig because Craig is the brother of Brent Kemnitz, who is the pitching coach at Wichita State, where Darren played his college baseball.

Craig helps his parents run the Sinclair station, which Charles Kemnitz bought for lack of other opportunities. "I got out of the Navy, and I couldn't find a job, so I bought this station," he says.

"He bought us a job," his wife says.

The station started as DX, became Total and now is Sinclair. Craig sells petroleum products to Ditch Witch, the international machine company that began in a Perry blacksmith shop and is the driving force in this town.

Speaking of Ditch Witch, the company was having a school this week, which meant a lot of out-of-towners were here filling up the restaurants. Our plan was to eat lunch at the Kumback and then to eat pie at Barbara Lancaster's Shady Lady, which is just down the street from the two-story house where Grandma Dalton once lived. Once the Dalton gang came to see grandma, Barbara says, and decided to rob the train station while they were in town. The restaurant, which once was a rooming house, stands next to what once was the infamous Hell's Half Acre.

With Ditch Witchers everywhere, all but one piece of Shady Lady pie was gone. "This," says Anna Lou, "is the place where you order your pie first."

Over at the barbershop, we met up with Jack Dorl, who is the only barber left in his four-chair shop. He is not, mind you, a stylist. "No way," he says. "I'm an old-time barber. Mostly flat-tops."

Zen Glimmer pays Jack to flatten his top.

My day in Noble County began in Red Rock at The Homestead Bed and Breakfast at the GT Ranch. I pulled up to a plate of waffles that Glenda Riddle made in the waffle iron her grandmother used, the kind that you set over a gas fire to heat.

Glenda was my tour guide, my foot in the door with the nice people in Perry. After our day in town, we returned to The Homestead, where she raises longhorn cattle. Most of them are pets, like the ancient Outlaw, which she keeps for the entertainment of visitors. But she fattens up a few of them, so that her guests at The Homestead can expect a big steak for supper.

This place is under a big sky, land unbroken as far as you can see. As we looked at Outlaw and her other longhorns, Glenda spotted the promise of rain hanging low to the west and wished for some. Before her words had dissolved into the east wind, however, the horizon cleared to blue.

To the northeast, a curve of a wide-band rainbow appeared. The rainbow didn't descend into a pot of gold, and it disappeared into the clouds. The rainbow – God's reminder that He won't again destroy the Earth with a flood.

Glenda doesn't want a flood, but three inches, she says, would be nice.

# Washington County: Bartlesville

IT's nothing more than an odd-shaped slab of concrete now, with nothing to denote its importance in history. Ed Ririe, who showed it to me, says that many of the locals don't even know it's up here, but this slab once was a foundation in the United States' national defense system.

Technically, this site a thousand feet above Bartlesville is in Osage County, but everything up here has a Bartlesville address. This hilltop once was home to the 796th Aircraft Control and Warning Squadron. A radar dish, covered by a giant rubber balloon, rotated and searched the skies for airplanes flying into its territory.

The locals who *do* know about this place still call it Radar Hill.

Sites like this one were built around the United States starting in about 1950, a response to the chilly relations with the Soviet Union. These were the eyes of the Cold War.

On Radar Hill, the highest point for miles, some of

the original buildings remain. Connie and Doug Freebern, founders of the Red Dirt Soap Company, built their plant and retail store in what once was the operations building.

That is the building where Air Force officers watched radar screens. When an aircraft showed up on the screen, the officer would radio the plane's location to men at the other end of the room, who then plotted the location on a giant plastic grid of the area.

Ririe, who moved to Bartlesville to work for Phillips Petroleum, was stationed at the 769th ACWS in New Mexico during his time in the military. That base was laid out pretty much like this one, so it looks familiar to him.

He and his wife Alice have their candle-making company, Keepsake Candles, in what was the gymnasium building.

Ririe moved from a mountain-top radar station in New Mexico to a hilltop radar station in Oklahoma. He's a living vestige of the Cold War whose family is letting its candlelight shine from a hill.

**E**D might never have found his way to a hilltop candle-making factory if not for the time a game warden in New Mexico stopped him for speeding.

The game warden had a daughter, and in spite of the circumstances of their first meeting, he met the officer's daughter, Alice, married her and moved her to Bartlesville.

In 1969, Ed's mother, Florence, asked Ed and Alice to help with a fund-raising bazaar for Oak Park United Methodist Church. She wanted them to make a candle from an antique, cut-glass toothpick holder.

So Ed made a mold, and Ed and Alice appropriated their daughters' crayon supply and made candles.

Karen Ririe Distefano, who was telling me this history, paused at this point to say of her parents: "They stole our crayons. All we got to play with were the black, gold and silver, because they wouldn't melt and blend in well. We were crayon deprived. That explains why we are like we are."

Their candles, nonetheless, were a hit, and, as Ed likes to say, the candle making "was a church project that got out of hand."

They moved from the kitchen to the garage and hired their first employees, the Ernst brothers — Cliff and Lee — from down the street. Then they moved into another building, and when they found out the old Radar Hill gymnasium building was available, they moved to the top of the hill.

Now they make about 200 candles a day. They make molds from antique glass, canning jars and lots of other things. The outer shell is made from a wax with a plastic additive, so that it has a higher melting temperature; the heat of a candle flame won't melt it. Then they fill the shell with a scented candle.

"That's why we call it Keepsake," Karen says. "We were using family keepsakes and once the candle has burned, you get to keep the shell."

The candle shells look so much like glass, they eventually began shrink-wrapping them to protect their product on the shelves. "People would look at them and say, 'That can't be wax,' and they'd scratch them with their fingernails," Karen says.

B ECAUSE he worked on a radar mountain, Ed Ririe knows much about the history of Aircraft Control and Warning Squadrons. Because he's met many of the men who once worked on Bartlesville's Radar Hill, he knows something about the local history.

The ACWS was preceded by the Ground Observer Corps, a nationwide band of civilian volunteers who scanned the skies for airplanes with binoculars. The lookout post in Bartlesville was atop the Hotel Phillips, he says.

As an early warning defense system, the binocular plan had its shortcomings. So the Air Force built the radar stations.

The shelter for the radar dish was called a Radome. It was an inflated bladder made of several layers of Goodyear rubber.

To enter the Radome, airmen had to pass through an airlock so that the balloon wouldn't loose its pressure. It was heated by banks of automobile lights.

That was then. Now, it's an odd-shaped slab of Cold War history, graying quietly atop the hill that bears its name.

## Nowata County: Nowata

U NTIL the dispatcher directed Deputy Billy Scott to return to the sheriff's office, the night had been fairly quiet. Deputies Scott and Tom Ledington had stopped a couple of speeders. Together, they toured a couple of bars looking for underage drinkers. They warned a bar owner about two men in a corner playing cards with poker chips.

The deputies were about to pay a surprise visit to a gathering place called The Picnic when dispatcher Richard Miller asked Scott to return to the office.

About five minutes past midnight, Miller had taken a call from a man who reported his elderly uncle had just died. Miller dispatched Scott to the home.

So just that quickly, Scott changed gears. Now he wasn't a tough cop protecting the county. Now his job was to gently help a family in its first moments of grief.

B ILLY Scott chooses to work the six p.m. to five a.m. shift so that he can spend more time with his children. He has taped to his radar unit a small picture of himself with Bryson James and Brianna Maria.

Before he entered law enforcement, Scott served in the Army, where he was a combat infantry soldier. "There is not," he says, "a lot of call for that in civilian life."

He has been in police work five years, and dreams of someday working for the Oklahoma Highway Patrol. In the meantime, he has learned the roads of Nowata County.

On weekends, his patrol includes checks of the out-of-the-way places where teen-agers congregate for outdoor parties: Devil's Backbone, Custer's Cove, to which you travel along Junk Yard Road. The roads to these places often are rutted, sometimes muddy and barely negotiable. "They think we don't drive down here, but we do," he says, as he points out the water on one side of the Devil's Backbone and the steep drop-off on the other side. "We cover anything that's got dirt on it. We're out here in areas some people don't know exist. We cover everything from disagreements to unintentional deaths."

He is there to stop crime, prevent tragedy. That's why he goes to the back-road hangouts, not because he likes to harass young people — at twenty-seven, he's not much older than them — but because he wants to intervene before they do something tragically dumb. So we drove the back roads until death called.

T HE house west of Nowata, invisible from the dirt road, sits back in the woods at the end of a curving dirt drive. A man in a white pickup truck, headlights marking the drive, awaits Billy's arrival. "You want to follow me?" he asks, and then drives to the house.

The man leads the deputy inside, through the kitchen and into the bedroom where the eighty-four-year-old man had died. A niece stands beside the man, comforting her aunt, who cries quietly.

Billy silently surveys the scene, makes his presence known, and then backs respectfully from the room.

For the moment, instead of patrolling the roads of dirt and asphalt, Billy Scott is helping a family steer the path from life to death. From ninety miles-per-hour to the rhythm of life. From the streets of Nowata to the back roads of Nowata County.

**B**ILLY Scott's goal is to keep his county safe, to go wherever he is needed. The photograph of his children reminds him of the importance of his job. "I like being able to get out and drive the country side," he says. "I like knowing people. I'm not confined to the city. I like the freedom."

His freedom, though, lasts only as long as he pays attention. "That's what keeps me alive," he says. "If I get casual about a traffic stop, it could be my last traffic stop."

## Craig County: Vinita

**V**ICKY Smith remembers that first purchase like it was — well, like it was forty-one years ago. She was ten years old when she bought her first collectible — a set of books for which she paid three dollars. "I bought them because of the covers," she says. "I think they were about travel."

As a child, she collected comic books and toy guns, especially those issued with the name of television stars like Roy Rogers, Gene Autry and Davy Crockett. "Everyone who was on TV had one," she says.

Now, Vicky, of Vinita, owns an entire antique mall filled with antiques and collectibles that belong to fifty vendors who rent space from her.

Collectible is a rather flexible word in Vicky's business. They could be, for instance, those Peanuts glasses you picked up at McDonald's fifteen years ago. In your neighborhood, they are garage-sale items you sell for a quarter. At Vicky's antique mall, those same glasses are "collectibles" that fetch four bucks and fifty cents. "You go by the old, 'One man's junk is another man's treasure,'" she says.

Vinita happens to be home to the world's largest McDonald's, which you would know if you ever have traveled past Vinita on the Will Rogers Turnpike. The one in Moscow claims to be the biggest, but John Morin, owner of the Vinita McDonald's, says that at 29,135 square feet, his is bigger by 6,000 square feet than the one in Russia. This McDonald's spans the turnpike. Even if it wasn't the biggest, it surely has the world's biggest golden arch.

But you won't find the collectible Peanuts' glasses there. For those, you'll have to go into town to see Vicky, who has been dealing antiques for twenty years. She's been interested for far longer than that, however, and her inclination is hereditary and environmental. "We were all pack rats," she says of her family.

She didn't intend to make a living at pack-ratting. She had rented a building in which to store her treasure. "People would stop and try to buy things when I was moving in," she says. "So I decided to start a shop to support my habit."

Her first sale was a Victorian walnut child's bed. "I sold it for the princely sum of probably 150 dollars. Now it's probably worth a thousand."

She travels near and far for antiques, which doesn't always make her family happy. "I shopped my way to Florida one year," she says. "We were headed for Disney World. It took us two weeks to get there."

Her most unusual collectible was a basket that was made in the early 1900s in Texas. "It was an armadillo basket. The head and the tail made the handle."

## Osage County: Near Pawhuska

JOHN and Nicole Hurd both grew up so far out on the range that they don't know what to make of all this asphalt running by their country home. "It's unreal," John says. "We ain't used to having a paved road. We're used to traveling ten to fifteen miles of gravel."

They live about seven miles up the road from Pawhuska, the closest either of them ever has lived to a town. Even so, they live closer to gravel roads than they do to Pawhuska's city limits. But to ranchers, only seven miles between them and town is suburban crawl.

John, who was riding horses by the time he was four, is the assistant foreman on the Tallgrass Prairie Reserve. He's in charge of the herd of 918 bison on the place.

Nicole's father was a rancher, and she and her sisters began riding young also. Now the young couple's three children already are more comfortable in a saddle than they are strapped into an automobile.

Corey, ten, is training his three-year-old horse Poco, a quarter-Shetland mix. Bailey, five, rides a horse named Scooter. And while I was there, three-year-old Macy sat astride her daddy's big quarter horse and declined the chance to climb down when her father offered.

If you needed a cast for a movie about a cowboy family, the Hurds are complete and perfect and won't even have to act. The Hurds are the authentic item. John spends 500 dollars for handmade cowboy boots because he needs them to fit for long days in the saddle, not because he wants them to look good on a boot-scooting floor.

The urban cowboy craze hurt the real cowboys, because it forced up the price of boots and hats. A real cowboy, John says, usually can spot the pretenders. A cowboy who works in his hat, for instance, has his own way of shaping it. "Some of the guys look like they just took their hat out of the box and put it on their head. Once you've been a cowboy like we have, where it's your livelihood, you can pretty much see if they fill the boot," John says, "or if they don't."

John and Nicole know a fancy hat when they see one. The higher the X-factor, the better the hat. The X-factor has to do with the quality of the felt. "You're looking at a hundred-dollar bill to buy a 5-X hat," John says. "I've never owned a 100-X hat. I just hear about them."

The Hurds are modest and gentle, quiet spoken, quick to laugh and loving with their children. Nicole sat in a child-size wagon, cuddling Macy and watching the two men in her family put two horses through their paces. Bailey climbed fences and begged her daddy for a ride.

John has a saddle, among other awards, to attest to his skills. At a ranching rodeo at the Lazy E in Guthrie, he was named Top Hand. (He didn't volunteer that information; his wife did.)

For men who make their living as cowpokes, John says, these rodeos are to them what a Sunday afternoon softball game is to other men.

On the Tallgrass Preserve, John and his co-workers round up the bison with four-wheelers and pickups. Once a year, they pen them and scan the computer chips on the bison's ears.

In his off time, John breaks horses for other riders, a skill he is passing on to Corey. Their dream is to rope as a team once Corey has Poco ready.

Even young Bailey, who is about to turn six, is a worker. She has left home with her father at five in the morning and spent the day on horseback as they worked cattle. "It's like a family," John says. "If you have a child out there, everybody looks out for her."

The Hurds aren't nervous for their children to ride. Six months ago, a horse threw Corey and his parents told him to climb right back on the horse.

Restoring the rider' confidence isn't the only reason for climbing back on the horse that just threw you. It teaches the horse a lesson, too. "If you don't get right back on him," John says, "next time he's liable to throw you again."

## Latimer County: Wilburton

AT the moment, Terry Stanford is only twenty-eight quilts behind, which is a sight better than the way she started 1999. "Last year," she says, "I had fifty to start on after Christmas."

Ask her why she does it, and she wonders how anyone wouldn't know the answer to that. The answer is as plain and to the point as the needle on Terry's quilting machine: She quilts because she loves to quilt, and she loves to quilt because she loves quilts.

"I guess a quilt is the feeling of home," she says. "I would prefer to have a quilt that's been handmade over any blanket."

Terry lives and quilts in the country — her driveway cuts off from a gravel road — thus the name of her enterprise: Country Time Quilts.

In the region where robbers once roamed, she walks the short distance from her house to her shop, where dozens of bolts of colorful fabric stand along the walls, and rolls of white batting (that's the lining inside a quilt that makes it heavy) lean against a wall.

Her love of quilts is a natural outgrowth of the hours she spent watching her grandmother sew and quilt. Terry would snuggle down into her grandmother's feather bed, hunkering under layers of quilts.

In her grandmother's day, fabric was hard to come by, so like many resourceful seamstresses of the day, her grandmother salvaged the multicolored fabric from chicken feed sacks. Her grandmother allowed Terry to pick fabric. "She'd make me dresses and quilts," she says.

Terry began to sew when she was in the seventh grade, and she hasn't stopped. She made three-piece suits for her sons, and prom dresses for her daughters.

She went into quilt-making full time four years ago after she bought a quilting machine in Missouri. Some customers stitch together their own tops, and hire Terry to put the quilt together with the lining and backing. Some take scraps to her and hire her to do the whole thing. "I get to see so many pretty quilts," she says. "They all do such good work."

She has in her shop a quilt made completely of old feed sacks like the ones her grandmother used. She has another made of old handkerchiefs that someone found in a closet after the death of a relative. She has finished quilt tops that were started more than fifty years ago and stored before completion. A friend of the family hired her to make a quilt from T-shirts.

The quilting machine, which requires the muscle of two men to lift, makes the task much easier than the days when quilters stretched a quilt across a frame. The machine runs easily along a track so that she can sew the full length of a quilt. Tracks that run crosswise allow her to sew the other direction so that she can make curves and circles. It is a skill that must be honed. "I used up lots of old sheets practicing," she says.

The machine allows her to stack the top, lining and backing "to where," as she puts it, "the quilt's not all whomper-jawed."

She wants it known that she couldn't be doing all this quilting without the help of her husband, Luke, and their blended family of nine children: Alan, David, Judy, Linda, Michael, Robert and the triplets, Ashley, Jeremey and Lesley.

When making quilts, she must be careful what she lets these helpful members of her family see. She points to a quilt draped over her machine. "Luke cabbaged on to that blue one," she says. "He won't let me sell it."

# Custer County: Clinton

FUNNY the change in the role of Route 66. The fabled highway began as the Main Street of America, the first road to connect one end of the United States to the other (never mind the minor detail that it only went as far east as Chicago).

The Mother Road, as John Steinbeck called it in *The Grapes of Wrath*, was the road to prosperity, the highway to happiness, the path to the future.

Now, as Route 66 yields to interstates and the elements, the Mother Road is the path to the past. It is the highway back to the good old days when the automobile was changing our lives, and for the better we naively thought at the time. The days when soldiers hitchhiked, we didn't dead-bolt our doors and "carjack" was something you used when you had a flat on Route 66.

A leg of historic Route 66 runs right through this Custer County town, right up past the museum built in its honor. For a mere three bucks, you can learn quite a bit about the old road and see nostalgia-inducing artifacts dating all the way back to the origin of the road, including a couple of Dust-Bowl era trucks that look as if Tom Joad had just parked them (except they aren't dusty).

The town of Clinton, which is doing its bit to hang on to Route 66, has modernized enough, but you can find people and buildings that hearken back to the glory days.

Even though the Clinton Domino parlor wasn't there fifty years ago, it's in a bank building that was built in 1903, so it looks the part. I wandered in there one day recently, expecting to find people like my Southern Baptist grandparents playing dominoes.

This is not, suffice it to say, my grandparents' brand of dominoes. It's a bar with dominoes, where the players knock on the tables and keep score on the table tops with chalk.

Across the street, fifty-eight-year-old Jack Majors repairs guns at Shamburg's Sporting Goods, where he has worked since he was a high school freshman. He started as a floor sweeper.

The Shamburg family has owned the business for seventy-five years, although it started as a gasoline station down the street. "They started selling fishing tackle," Linda Farmer says of her grandfather, D.C. Shamburg, "and when they started selling more tackle than gas, he went into the sporting goods business."

They moved into what was Hawk's Hotel, named for owner Sam Hawk. Eventually, they bought the entire building. Jack took me on a tour of all three floors and the basement, from the well-named stink-bait room in the very bottom to the rods and reels upstairs, with guns, tackle boxes and obsolete athletic shoes scattered about.

On the third floor, Jack has a room where he stores guns for parts. The floor is carpeted with springs, barrels and gun bolts. A gun ought to last a lifetime, Jack says, if you keep it clean. "Dirt in Oklahoma wears out more guns and machines than anything else."

Life for this domino parlor and sporting goods store, however, is about over. The state is widening Highway 183, and to do so, they'll have to take out both buildings. "They say that Jack's work bench is about where the stop light is going to be," Linda says.

A few blocks down, Dr. Jim Rhymer's office is safe from the widening, so this man from the good ol' days (but not that old) won't have to move. Doc, as most everyone calls him, is known as the Tootsie Roll doctor. Since 1961, Doc has kept a supply of Tootsie Rolls for his patients, whatever their age.

His wife Colleen (pronounced ko-leen) should have credit for the tradition. Doc began with bubble gum, but one day when he ran out, she gave him Tootsie Rolls, and they were a hit.

He still makes house calls, and sometimes, when someone is hurt at night, he'll have them come by his house for a look. His son Jim, a pharmacist who owns the Exchange Pharmacy at the stockyards in Oklahoma City, says his seventy-one-year-old father shows no signs of quitting.

Doc and Colleen are reserve deputy sheriffs in Dewey County; they scuba dive and snow ski. He is a pilot, and he's team doctor for several of the athletic teams in the area.

"His practice is still full," Jim says. "He's full time plus now. He really works too hard, but we can't get him to slow down. He never turns anybody away. One of the things that he didn't intend to teach me, but he did, is that sleep is secondary. Do what you've got to do, you can sleep later."

ONCE we drove it into the future, now we drive Route 66 into the past. We have our domino parlors, our Jack Majors, our Doc Ryhmers, which link us, like the old road, to what once was. If we're smart, we'll keep the road in good repair.

# Ellis County: Arnett

CLIFF Hanan moved to Ellis County in covered wagons, and he actually remembers the move. He was a kid, of course, when they arrived in 1926, but he remembers, he assured me, that the covered wagons were like the ones in the movies.

"We moved here in three covered wagons," he said. Two sets of grandpas and an uncle from Waynoka helped them move. His mother drove ahead in the family's Model T, and she would estimate where they would have to stop for the night. Then she would send the kids to scrounge for firewood so she could prepare supper.

Cliff's father, who was a school teacher and dairy farmer, loaded his Holsteins and chickens into a boxcar to make the trip to Gage. He traveled in the boxcar with them so he could milk his cows.

Because of the train's circuitous route, frequent stops and a breakdown, the trip from the Hanons' home in Hillsdale, near Enid, to Gage took three days. His family on the covered wagons arrived at the same time he did.

You hear those kinds of stories if you hang around Ron Miller's office at his car lot. I was there by invitation, and Ron, Cliff and Rex Holloway knew I was there to hear stories. But Jane Gross and her customers down at the Circle G cafe say the trio doesn't need a newspaper hack with a pen and a tablet to prompt their stories.

Ron's little office ranks right up there with coffee shops and barbershops as a place to loaf. Cliff sat in a regular chair, shifting his walking stick from one hand to the other. Rex sat in an antique barber chair, which was closest to Ron's wood-burning stove, where cedar logs popped and three steaming tea kettles humidified the air.

Ron and Cliff prompted Rex to tell about his days as a first sergeant in the U.S. horse cavalry. During World War II, Rex led troops and a mule train over the Burma Road to deliver ammunition to soldiers on the front.

The three of them recounted the history of Ellis County, and how Arnett came to be the county seat. Before statehood, the area was divided differently and included Day County. A little village called Ioland was the county seat. One night, however, the courthouse burned (a politically inspired arson, many suspect) and lo and behold, the next morning, the county records that didn't burn turned up down the road in the town of Grand, which its citizens immediately declared the new county seat.

That didn't last too long, for upon statehood, the area was redivided, and Oklahoma created Ellis County from portions of Woodward and Roger Mills counties. Day County was dissolved. Then, because of Grand's proximity to the North Canadian River, which was prone to flooding, Arnett became the county seat and Grand became a ghost city almost overnight.

Now Rex Holloway owns the land that once was Grand, including the spring that made it such a good spot for a town. He pipes the water to his cattle.

Sometime in the next couple of years, Cliff says, you'll be able to read all about it in a book his brother-in-law, John Rider, is writing. He is a retired university professor with a doctorate in accounting.

Down at the Circle G, which the Gross family has owned since 1979, they aren't discussing where the county seat should be. They're talking triplet calves and girls' basketball, both being of high importance, but the basketball is the more urgent matter at the moment.

Once again, the highly talented Arnett girls' basketball team is contending for the Class B state championship. The folks lingering over hamburgers, fries, coffee and cigarettes know all about the strep throat that has knocked out one player, but she's on antibiotics, they say, and ought to be good to go by game time.

S O now you have Circle G and Ron Miller's car lot. If you can't find a story in Arnett, you ain't trying.

## Dewey County: Vici

D ON'T fret that Dixie Salisbury has sold the Vici Restaurant. The Liars' Table isn't going anywhere. The table, which sits smack in the middle of the restaurant's front dining room, was here when Dixie began work here twenty-three years ago, and when she bought the restaurant eleven years later, she didn't disturb it.

Now, new proprietor Michele Randall says the table stays.

The Liars' Table is the meeting place in Vici (pronounced Vigh-sigh). At the Liars' Table, the tall tales fly most of the day every day. It is one long table with legs that fold up; eight chairs surround it at all times, with room for one more at each end.

The Formica tabletop is worn from hours of elbows and thousands of cups of coffee. "I never did teach them to keep their elbows off the table," Dixie says.

The Liars' Table fills up before the restaurant opens. The coffee drinkers begin arriving about four-thirty a.m.

As they have aged, members of the Liars' Club have slowed a bit, and they don't usually arrive until five a.m. Richard Dryden is usually the first.

"They come knocking on the back door, and we let them in," Dixie says. "They take care of themselves and pour us coffee. We keep the table filled up until about nine of a morning. Sometimes they let the Methodist preacher sit there with them. There's more conversation than coffee."

Dixie was forty-two with grown children when she went to work waiting tables at the Vici Restaurant. Thirteen years ago, when her boss decided to close it, Dixie bought it so the employees wouldn't lose their jobs.

Now, at sixty-five, she's ready for other things, like time with her sixteen grandchildren and one great-grandchild. "I decided it was time to let somebody else have it," Dixie says. "Michele's worked for me ever since she was old enough to work."

The restaurant has lost another veteran, Juanita Moss, who has been the morning cook for thirty years. At seventy-nine, she, too, was ready for a break, Dixie says.

A lot of hunters and a few state celebrities have eaten Juanita's biscuits. "I think ol' Barry Switzer has been in here a couple of times," Dixie says.

The weightlifting team from the Vici High School ate in here three times a week. "They called themselves the Biscuit and Gravy Club," Dixie says. In the years that she has had the restaurant, she has added a back dining room, which is the regular meeting place for the Lion's Club.

In a nod to the times, a section of the back dining room is for nonsmokers, but even in the middle dining room, few smoke. The smokers usually alight in the front. "They really let the smoke fly out here," she says. "I'm half allergic to that smoke any more."

While the time is right for her retirement, she has other plans for John, her husband of forty-five years and father of their seven children. He runs a barbershop behind the restaurant. "He won't retire," she says. "I can't let him do that."

The Friday night I was there, her last Friday night as owner, Dixie took time to sit at her counter to tell me about the Liars' Table. Two days after that, on Sunday, she baked her last biscuits.

Then, on Monday afternoon, I checked in with her by telephone to ask about her first day of retirement. She slept in Monday morning. Late. "Until about four."

# Washita County: Forty One

YOU won't find any city limits signs for this place, named for the highway that once passed through it. But it is still on the official Oklahoma state map, which shows that Forty One is about halfway between Cordell and Sayre. So when my odometer rolled over the seventh mile west of Cordell, I looked for signs of the town. The only way I knew for sure that I was in Forty One was when I stopped and asked a fellow who was mending a fence beside the highway.

He showed me where the town had been, and showed me which house to visit to learn the history of Forty One. At the house, I could hear a television, but the occupants were appropriately suspicious of a big-footed stranger who came calling at sunset. They didn't answer my knock, but their friendly collie and cat greeted me and then snuggled together in the stiff end-of-the-day wind.

Forty One, where the cat and the collie lie down together.

My second destination in Washita County (which is pronounced wash-E-tah, unless you are from there, and then you would say it WaRsh-e-tah) was Bessie, but before I tell you about Bessie's Whole Hog Pancake Supper, I'll tell you about the late Seventeen Burdine, whose name is sort of like Forty One's. (This is a true story. I actually talked to Seventeen.)

Seventeen Burdine was born in rural Alabama, the seventeenth child in his family. When his parents told the doctor they had run out of names, the helpful doctor suggested they name him 17. The parents took the suggestion to heart, and that's just what they named him. (Two more children followed, but their parents found a couple of more real names.)

For the first years of his life, Seventeen wrote his name as 17, but when he joined the Army, somebody made him spell it out. Thus did he become Seventeen.

The name sparked much conversation, as you might imagine, and caused a fair amount of trouble. While he was away in the Army, for instance, and called home collect, this is how the conversations with the telephone operators went:

"I'd like to make a collect call," Seventeen would say.

"What's your name?"

"Seventeen Burdine."

"Not your address. Your name."

And so on.

On my way to Bessie, I stopped in Dill City and Burns Flat, and circled the pretty domed courthouse in Cordell. And then I crossed the railroad tracks, passed the Farmland Co-op, and I was in Bessie, where you can feel whole-hog excitement.

Thirty-four-hog, 8,500-pound excitement, to be

exact, because that's the number and weight of the animals
that are giving their lives for the 41$^{st}$ Annual Whole Hog
Pancake Supper to raise money for the Bessie Volunteer
Fire Department.

Every year, Bessie volunteers cook the hogs,
every last morsel. Nothing of these animals goes
to waste, from the pug snout to the tail. They only thing
they don't cook is the oink. "Nothing is thrown away but
the bones," says Deadra Buffing, who has volunteered year
after year. "They boil the heads, the teeth are still
intact. That's what they use to make the head cheese."
(The head, not the teeth.)

On Whole Hog Saturday, volunteers make sausage and
all the other meat products they will sell. The lines are
two blocks long. "People stock up," she says. "Some people
come in and buy fifty pounds of meat."

Newcomers to Bessie who find themselves at the back
of the long line can gaze upon the statue of Ben Kiehn, a
banker who, in January 1928, gave his life defending the
town's bank.

"He and his brother ran the bank in 1928," says Jim
Crane, who was hanging out at Hank Svitak's garage when
Hank recruited him to tell the story. "Ben was sitting at
a desk when the guys pulled their gun at the cashier's
counter. Ben pulled a gun out and was going to resist the
robbery. They had a little gun battle. The two robbers
fled west on country roads. A group of men got together
and chased them down."

Zelma Buffing, who grew up in Bessie, remembers the
day of the robbery. She was about fourteen. The statue of
Kiehn stands on property that abuts her front yard. "I
remember seeing Ben Kiehn when he was shot and lying on
the floor," she says. "I always remember it."

In spite of his injury, Kiehn hit his mark. He
mortally wounded one of the men, whose body was put on
display in Cordell, says Zelma, who is the grandmother of
Bret Buffing, who is Deadra Buffing's husband. Zelma's
husband Andrew, who died several years ago, had a vivid
recall of the events, which he related to *The Daily
Oklahoman*'s legendary writer Jim Etter: "The town was just
loaded that day. And the next morning they all took out
like huntin' a coyote" to search for the surviving robber,
who escaped with most of the 701 dollars and left his
wounded partner to die in a dry creek bed.

You won't have to worry about bank robbers in
Bessie. The bank is gone, lock, stock and safe. You can go
hog wild without fear and eat your fill of pancakes,

which, Deadra proclaims proudly, they make with whole milk
and cream. "They are like eating sugar. You don't even
need syrup. You can eat until you are sick. It's the
county event of the year."

If you are going, Bessie is seven miles east and
about that many miles north of the town of Forty One. For
more precise directions, ask any one you happen to see out
mending his bob-wahr fence.

# Grant County: Wakita

THOSE Hollywood storm chasers in the movie *Twister*
looked pretty wild and brave, but when the real
thing threatened, you couldn't find them anywhere.

Robyn Rapp, who, along with her husband, Richard,
owns the local hardware store, was in Enid one day in
1995, when tornadoes threatened. By the time she returned
to Wakita, however, the sun was shining but the streets
were empty. "There was not a movie person here," she says.
"They were terrified."

The movie crew had evacuated to Ponca City, where
most were living while they filmed the hit movie.

That is only one of the amusing stories the townfolk
tell about the half year Hollywood occupied their town of
450, give or take a few dogs, cats and possums.

Their visitors from the West Coast arrived with lots
of equipment, money and preconceived notions about people
who live in Oklahoma. Robyn Rapp, for instance, was going
to call Richard in his truck when one of the movie hands
expressed amazement: "He has a *phone* in his truck?"

"They thought we were so backwards," Robyn says. In
*Twister*, every car was a junker and every yard had a
clothesline, "as if," Robyn says, "no one had clothes
dryers."

WHILE the movie-makers were collecting stories
of Okie-lahoma to tell their fancy friends back
home, these same "sophisticated" people inadvertently
created legends of their own.

They decided, for instance, the ripening wheat
fields weren't green enough for their movie and asked,
Richard Rapp recalls, if they could paint the wheat green.
While the entire story takes place in northern Oklahoma,
one storm-chasing scene includes clouds shot in Texas; the
footage included Texas highway signs, which the movie
makers failed to edit out. "Hollywood," says Linda Wade,

"didn't know the difference between Oklahoma and Texas."

When the movie finished, however, most everybody agreed the experience was a good one. Four years after the release of *Twister*, Wakita still is capitalizing on its stardom.

Wakita's garden club, officially named the Twister Garden Club, maintains a *Twister* museum in a building that Linda and Tom Wade own. Linda, by virtue of ownership and as president of the Garden Club, is the museum's curator. "Steven Spielberg actually walked on my floor," Linda Wade says of the famed filmmaker, who was part of the executive staff on the film and visited the museum during the weekend he spent in Wakita.

The museum's artifacts include doors and storefront windows saved from the movie, and the Dorothy I. (If you have seen the movie, you know all about Dorothy.)

The museum's most recent acquisition is a *Twister* pinball machine, which Bill Paxton, the male lead in the movie, donated and shipped to Wakita.

Of all the actors who worked in Wakita, Paxton — who was in *Apollo 13* — was by far the most popular. "He was the most outgoing of the Hollywood types," Linda Wade says. "He carried a football and played catch with the kids."

Kayla Rapp, a thirteen-year-old, agrees that Paxton was a good sport. "My grandmother got a picture of him without a shirt, and his arm around her," she says.

If you look hard and fast, Kayla says, you can see her in her role as an extra.

Kayla and the other students in Richard Barr's Spanish class at the Wakita school all have seen the movie several times, and most of them own a copy of it. More significantly, Kayla, Kacie Miller, Bo Moreland, Travis Horning, Kelsey Blye and Jeremy Hull all have seen a real tornado, or at least tornadic weather. They and their 159 classmates have rushed (in a calm and orderly fashion, no doubt) to the school's storm shelter, which doubles as the school's band room.

The movie provided a fair amount of money for the little town and many of its people, who sold or leased lots of stuff. "I actually gave them a laundry basket and mop handle out of my back yard," Linda says.

The day they needed a 1960s bedroom suit, Richard Rapp offered the set-builders bedroom furniture that belonged to his parents, who were out of town and none the wiser. "We rented it to them twice," he says. "They paid more than it was worth new to rent it. Two days later, they were unloading it, and my folks drove up."

After the movie makers buried Wakita in storm debris, they spent two months cleaning up the town. When they left, Wakita had three blocks of new streets, the farmers' co-op had an updated scale, and eyesore buildings had been knocked down and cleaned up.

And, of course, there is the *Twister* museum, which has been featured on "Good Morning America" and now has Bill Paxton's pinball machine. Since the release of the movie, nearly 7,000 tourists have visited Wakita. "Our normal tourist rate before the movie was zero," Linda Wade says. "The movie made our name."

WHILE the folks from Hollywood held some wrong-headed notions about the good people in his town, Richard Rapp will concede that sometimes the townsfolk lived up to Hollywood's preconceived notions. "At the premiere," he says, "we cheered for our water tower."

# Wagoner County: Okay

THEY'VE been playing music together for thirty years, these two sisters-in-law, but here they are in the dark of a Saturday night, practicing again.

"We're starting a revival tomorrow," explains organist Kay Hopkins, who married Connie Faulconer's brother George Hopkins. "We're making a list of our songs."

Connie, the pianist, was the first of the pair to play for the First Baptist Church of Okay. Shortly thereafter, someone donated the organ, and Kay became the organist.

Connie grew up in Okay, and Kay grew up in Tulsa. Kay moved here as a teen-ager when her parents bought Robins Roost Resort from Connie's grandfather, Leo Robbins. (The resort became Robins when a sign painter assumed it was named for the bird with a red-breast and spelled it with one "b.")

"I had never heard of Okay, and I did not want to move out here," Kay says. "Moving from Tulsa was a big adjustment."

After she moved to Okay, Connie became Kay's best friend, which eventually led her to love with George. For a while, George and Kay lived in Tulsa. Small-town George hated it, though, and even Kay admitted she missed Okay. "It's nice living where you know everybody," Kay says.

"It's a small, friendly town."

In other words, Okay, OK., is A-OKAY, says Kay.

This hundred-year-old town has had a tough time maintaining its identity. One of its first settlers was Nathan Pryor of the Lewis and Clark expedition, which was based here when the site was called Three Forks.

The first post office, established in January 1891, was named Coretta, according to George Shirk in *Oklahoma Place Names.*

In 1893, the post office was closed. On November 16, 1900, the post office reopened as Rex. On May 1, 1911, the name of the post office was changed to North Muskogee.

Finally, on October 18, 1919, the post office was named Okay, taking its name from Okay Truck Manufacturing. The name has stuck, at least for the last eighty-one years.

The name presents its problems. There is the confusion when the unenlightened think Okay means "all right." As in: Kay only married an Okay man, not a great one. Or Connie shops at an Okay grocery and dines at an Okay restaurant. The Okay sisters-in-law were preparing for a revival at their Okay church, where the Okay pastor Ron Forrest has invited the Rev. Mark Hester to help revive his Okay congregation.

And there are the times, for instance, when they try to order something over the telephone. Sometimes, when the operator asks for the town's name and the answer is "Okay," the operator thinks they mean the abbreviation for the Sooner State and will ask: "What town in Oklahoma?"

Or they have exchanges like this:

Operator: "What's the name of your town?"

Kay or Connie: "Okay."

Operator, undoubtedly thinking the person on the other end means simply *okay,* replies: "Okay, I'm waiting."

"That," says Kay, "is when you spell it."

# McIntosh County: Hanna

AS screen doors go, this one is heavy duty and pretty impressive, though it could stand a bit of fixing up. Shirley Leeper apologizes for it as I walk into the Bounty Ministry, but a perfect door is not high on Shirley's list, and she quickly is talking about what is happening in this place.

The screen door opens to a large room that, in previous incarnations, has been a grocery store, a restaurant and a movie rental store, among other things. Now the room brims with clothes for the needy of McIntosh County. "God provides it all," Shirley says of the inventory. "God wants us to do something here. God has His hand on this place."

The Bounty Ministry is the work of the House of Prayer, a church that started here four years ago. The members meet in the building next door. They recently acquired this building for their clothing ministry, and they have their eye on the bar on the other side of the church.

"We call ourselves Christians," Shirley says of the church, explaining that the House of Prayer does not affiliate itself with any denomination. "God wasn't a God of names on church doors. Man did that."

Shirley works at the prison at McAlester, where she was a guard — or corrections officer, as they are called — and now is a corrections counselor. Her husband is a native of Hanna, but they met in California, where both their families had moved in search of steady work.

They married in California and started their family there, but eventually moved home to Oklahoma. Now they are working with other families who also say they have been called of God to bring comfort, clothing and the Gospel to the people here. "I never planned to be in Hanna," Shirley says, "but God put me here."

Little is left on Hanna's main street, and the House of Prayer is easy to find, especially on Saturday nights when the church members hold Gospel singings. Sometimes musicians come in from other places to play, and sometimes local musicians provide the songs.

For the moment, the House of Prayer provides clothing for the body, food for the pantry and sustenance for the soul. But once Bounty Ministry is better organized, the members plan to use the restaurant equipment in the kitchen to cook free hot lunches. The senior citizen center across the street provides meals for fifty cents, but Shirley knows people who have trouble scraping together two quarters.

Two of Shirley's daughters-in-law volunteer their time down here, and one of them told Shirley of a woman who was in such straits that she didn't have shoes.

As she recounts that story, Shirley fans her face with her hand in a vain attempt to stave off the tears. She pauses in the middle of the story to regain composure. Women like that, she says, are the reason she and the others are in Hanna.

"We pray over everything we get," she says. "We

believe when they use the laundry soap we give them, that God's anointing is on it. We give our help with no strings attached. We want them to know about Jesus. This is not about filling up anybody's church. This is about souls."

# Major County: Glass Mountains

Y OU can see right off why they call them the Glass Mountains, or the Gloss Mountains, depending on whether you are reading the official state map or the sign on the highway.

The name of the mountains has been in debate for years, going back to the legend of how they were named in the first place. An English surveyor supposedly named them the Glass Mountains, but pronounced it "gloss."

However you say it, the source of the surveyor's inspiration glistens from the reddish soil of the hills and mesas along Highway 15 on a sunny afternoon. The mountains are one of the county's claims to fame.

Jerry Jantzen grew up down the highway from these hills, in the community of Ringwood, population about 200.

Life seemed hard, then, Jerry says, but in retrospect, he wouldn't trade it. He hit his father's wheat fields by the time he was six, and by the time he was eight, he was spending the entire day working them.

Before he could legally drive, he was hauling the harvest ten miles, which the farm kids were allowed to do so long as they drove straight to the elevator and then back to the farm.

Most of the time, they worked and went to school, but life had its moments, times like turtle races at the Ringwood Fair and Watermelon Festival and at Vacation Bible School at the Mennonite church, where Margie Wedel was his favorite Bible school teacher.

"There were no stop lights in Ringwood," says Jerry, who lives in Oklahoma City and owns Route 66 Tire and Auto on Edmond Road. "Main Street consisted of about a two-block area. The school was on one end, the telephone office was on the other. Once a year, they'd block off Main Street for two days."

The annual watermelon festival was the first weekend of September. The old-timers tossed horseshoes, the kids ran foot races, hopped in gunny sack and three-legged races, and cheered for the turtle races. "About a month before the fair, we'd collect maybe ten or eleven turtles. Every kid had a sandbox back then, and that's where we'd keep them. We'd check to see which was the fastest.

"They always had a parade, Saturday morning at ten o'clock. I always got to ride a horse in the parade. When I was little, I got to ride a tricycle or bicycle.

"They'd always have a flatbed truck come in. A band would set up. They spread cottonseed hulls on Main Street to make people's feet slide on the asphalt. They got the hulls from George Black's hardware store. We'd sit there on the sidewalk and watch the grown-ups dance. Nobody around there knew how to dance, but they acted like they did."

His sister, Kathy Jantzen Webster — who lives in Oklahoma City — was Watermelon Queen one year.

Another big event was the annual Mennonite aid sale, which traditionally was held in Fairview, but now has outgrown that town and moved one county east to Enid. They sell quilts and crafts to raise money for missions.

They only went to Enid once a year, to buy school clothes, and they went to school in Ringwood. The days of the Turtle Races were, in their way, a far better time in which to grow up.

"Back then, nobody even knew what drugs were, at least at Ringwood," he says. "At Ringwood, the worst thing was smoking a cigarette ... that was the thing that everybody said was real bad.

"We've lost a lot of the values that we learned in a close-knit family growing up, which most of the families were. Sunday afternoons, we'd usually go to a friend's house. The parents would visit and kids would play. Even when we were sixteen and seventeen, we all had our own horse. About six or seven of us would pick a central location, we'd meet and ride around. We enjoyed doing that more than we did going in cars."

## Oklahoma County: Oklahoma City

CLYDE Hanks buzzes the back of Kevin Nichols' neck with his barber clippers. "He's lucky," he says, meaning me. "He's leaving here with all the blood he came in with."

All of the blood, but none of the stubble. That's because Clyde had just shaved me with a straight razor. My first time.

The idea for a barbershop shave came over me late last summer when I read about an Oklahoma state legislator who also is a barber. He mentioned the scarcity of straight razors in modern society.

While barbershop shaves are a thing of the past, they were a big part of the past, or at least a big part of cowboy movies. So I decided that my life would not be complete without one.

So as I have traveled Oklahoma's seventy-seven counties over the last months, a straight-razor shave became an elusive goal. On more than one occasion, I have asked a barber for a straight-razor shave, always to be denied.

Then, as I made my rounds in Oklahoma County, I found the man to make me a man.

IF you are traveling on Classen Boulevard and you see the gold-domed bank and the giant Braum's bottle on top of the little building, you are close to Hanks Barber Shop. Clyde Hanks is at North West 24th and Classen in Little Saigon.

So I found Clyde's shop, and as we talked, I noticed the leather strap for sharpening straight razors and made my request, fully expecting to be denied again.

But this was to be my day.

Clyde leans me back in his chair and props up my feet. He puts a hot towel on my face. Then he puts hot shaving cream on my face and another hot towel. Then he spreads on more hot shaving cream, shaves my face, finishes up with another hot towel, massages my face with lemon cream, applies another hot towel, and finishes off with an after-shave. Manhood at age forty-three.

Clyde only shaves about one face a week now, but in his early days as a barber in Shawnee, he would open shop at seven-thirty for merchants who would come in every morning for a shave.

One afternoon in Shawnee, a big fellow came in and Clyde noticed his boss pretended to be busy. So Clyde took the big guy and found out why the boss didn't want him.

The man, a blacksmith, had red hair, and men with red hair often have tough beards, Clyde says. This guy was one of them. Clyde had to sharpen his razor several times during the shave, but even a sharp blade wasn't enough. "By the time I finished with that ol' guy," Clyde says, "he looked like he'd been in an ax fight."

Clyde has been cutting hair for nearly fifty years. He has owned his own shop since 1972. He has, of course, seen styles come and go. "When the Beatles came over here, they messed things up real good," he says. "Everybody went for the long hair."

At seventy-three, Clyde has no plans to retire. "I'd

a heap rather they haul me away out of here than out of a
rest home."

𝕰𝕺𝕮𝕾    𝕰𝕺𝕮𝕾    𝕰𝕺𝕮𝕾

O<sup>N</sup> the chance that someone in Oklahoma hasn't
heard this particular story about Comanche war
Chief Quanah Parker, who had some wives but couldn't keep
'em, Don Akin is here to tell it one more time.

Don qualifies as an official teller of Quanah Parker
tales, since he heard the story from his Uncle Elmer
Houghton, who was a friend of Quanah's. So this is almost
as good as hearing it from the chief's own mouth.

Don himself is a treasure-trove of Oklahoma stories,
arriving by stork, as he did, only three years after
statehood. His family played a noteworthy role in the
early days of Oklahoma City.

His Uncle Elmer opened Oklahoma City's first
restaurant, the Saddle Rock, in 1889. Elmer came here for
the Land Run after a stint in the gold mines at Cripple
Creek, Colorado. Elmer's sister, who later became Don's
mother, came to Oklahoma City to handle Elmer's money when
she was eighteen.

Elmer's kid brother, Harry, came out, too, but his
first stay here ended abruptly. One day an inebriated
patron at the Saddle Rock refused to pay his tab, and
sixteen-year-old Harry pulled a forty-five on him. The man
paid, but vowed to come back and kill the kid.

Elmer put Harry on the first train back home to
Pennsylvania, but he later returned as a banker and
builder known as H.B. Houghton.

But back to Elmer's story about Quanah Parker, who
had many a wife, which became a problem.

According to Don, who heard it from Elmer, who
reportedly heard it directly from the chief, Quanah and
some of his many wives were in Washington, D.C., for a
treaty signing. The Secretary of the Interior mentioned to
Quanah that the United States allowed only one wife per
man.

"What am I going to do?" Quanah supposedly asked.

"Pick the one you want," the secretary advised, "and
tell the others they can't be your wife."

Quanah, the fearless chief who knew his wives better
than the secretary, replied: "You tell them."

𝕰𝕺𝕮𝕾    𝕰𝕺𝕮𝕾    𝕰𝕺𝕮𝕾

MAYBE a red rose will be the symbol of Cathy Keating's legacy in Oklahoma. I heard about her red roses from somebody else, which, I gather, is typical of Oklahoma's First Lady. She won't tell you what she's done. She works, and the work speaks for her.

I didn't live in Oklahoma on April 19, 1995, but I have been told that in a very literal way, Cathy Keating was part of Oklahoma's healing after the bombing. She was there with the others to rescue body and soul. In a bigger way, too, in the symbolic way we need after a tragedy, simply by her presence she lent a healing touch. She was there with them, I have heard Oklahomans say, and she came bearing red roses. Since she wouldn't volunteer the story, I asked her to tell me.

In the way that a small-town murder steals the innocence of a place, the Oklahoma City bombing stole what vestige of national innocence that remained.

Not that we expect it in the big cities, or think it less tragic, but we are less surprised at mass violence in those places. But Oklahoma City? *Of all places*, we say.

But they did it, they bombed the federal building, and they changed the nation. As one newspaper headline said the next day, all of us wondered: "Is Anyone Safe?"

The fancy-pants out-of-town reporters came to Oklahoma City expecting to see drunken cowboys looting stores along streets of dirt littered with tumbleweed. As any Oklahoman can tell you, at least one national television anchorwoman showed her ignorance and her bias when she expressed surprise that Oklahoma actually had running water, internal-combustion engines, people well trained for such emergencies and high-tech hospitals for the injured.

But Oklahomans would not be tagged with any of those negative labels. Nor would they lower themselves to respond in like spirit. Rather than allow itself to be defined by the violence of that awful day, Oklahoma City defined itself by its response to the murders.

The national memorial to the victims of the bombing is profound. The giant east gate reads 9:01, the minute before the explosion. The west gate reads 9:03. The long, silent, grassy expanse between the gates, the place where so many children, women and men died, represents the moment of the explosion. This silent expanse symbolizes the infinite minute — 9:02 — a silence that thunders into eternity.

On that day, Cathy Keating was at the Keating home in Tulsa putting the first family's furniture into storage for their term in the Governor's Mansion.

She learned about the bombing when a friend telephoned to tell her to turn on her television. Once she ascertained that Governor Keating was safe and helping to direct the state's response, she drove to Oklahoma City.

In the days that followed, Cathy was as busy as her husband in helping Oklahomans in their grief and anger.

As she was planning the prayer service for the Sunday after the bombing, a representative of the Oklahoma Florists Association called to say the group wanted to give roses to members of the victims' families.

She thought the idea appropriate, a symbol of love to be added to the hundreds of teddy bears that had been donated to the mourners as a symbol of hope.

Once the florists put out the word, roses arrived from all over the United States, at least 10,000, and maybe as many as 20,000.

After the Sunday night prayer service, thousands of roses were left over. About that time, one of the dozens of rescue workers who was sleeping in the temporary quarters at the Myriad asked a local volunteer where he could wash his clothes. She told him to leave his clothes on his cot, and she would take care of them.

Not only did she wash his laundry, she bought him new undergarments. When the man thanked her he said: "This is better than a four-star hotel. The only thing missing is a mint on the pillows."

With that, the volunteers began putting mints on pillows, which sparked the idea for the roses.

Cathy Keating arranged for a rose to be left on the pillows of the rescuers each night until they left town. A symbol of the state's love for the rescuers.

On the second Saturday after the bombing, after the search for bodies was finished and officials prepared to close the site, Cathy Keating helped to plan a closing ceremony. With hundreds of roses still in refrigeration, the volunteers handed them to people at that final service.

She recalls those final moments, with the skeleton of the Murrah in the background. Hundreds of people had gathered near the massive crater the bomb blew in the street beside the building.

After the last words were spoken, she says, something remarkable happened. "Spontaneously, everybody threw their roses into the pit."

Of the things I have heard about Cathy Keating, it is the story of the red roses I like the most. She

ministered to the victims and to their rescuers. She
ministered to the state.

That is part of Cathy Keating's Oklahoma legacy. The
face of Cathy and of Governor Keating became the faces of
courage many around the nation associated with the
aftermath. Cathy Keating's dignity, her compassion and her
strength in the face of the violence is the face of
Oklahoma. They blew up a building, and stole the state's
innocence, but not its heart or its resilience. Of that,
we have Cathy Keating's red roses to remind us.

# Babbs
# Switch
# Burning

# Prologue

O**N a fine autumn day in 1999, I mentioned to Judy Tracy that when I left her one-room school house, my next destination was a ranch outside of Hobart. Judy, who is in charge of the historic Roll school in Cheyenne, knows Oklahoma history. She told me about the fire at the Babbs Switch school, which was outside of Hobart. So that afternoon at Terry and Brenda Hawkins' Rainy Mountain Ranch, I asked about Babbs Switch and met my first witness to the fire, a man who remembered standing on the porch of his house and seeing the smoke to the southwest.

In the weeks that followed, I learned more about the fire. Seems everyone I asked remembered something about Babbs Switch. Although the fire had occurred seventy-five years before, clearly the impact had been significant.

The details I heard were tragic and gripping and mysterious. The Christmas Eve fire became a national story because of the day it occurred, because of the grim circumstances and because of the number of people who burned to death. The fire prompted state legislators to change laws in Oklahoma that required all one-room schools to have more than one door and that required all the doors to open to the outside.

But a mystery about Babbs Switch lingered, Bill Elix was the first to tell me about it. Bill, who grew up in the Hobart area and now works security at *The Daily Oklahoman*, told me that one child in the fire never was accounted for. That mystery, more than anything else about the fire, compelled me to pursue this story.

So in between my travels, I read old newspaper clippings and talked to a few people. Then I went to Hobart, holed up in the Hanna House bed and breakfast, which was once a funeral home, and finished my work. In the process, I discovered a survivor no one knew was still alive, and he happened to be the brother of the boy who started the fire. I combined the details from old newspapers with new recollections from people who had never granted an interview about the fire.

The most important interview, however, was with Joe Hancock, whose family has owned *The Democrat-Chief* in Hobart for fifty years.

**F**or nearly half a century, Joe has known the truth about Louis Edens' missing daughter and never reported it. For forty-two years, Joe Hancock has honored his father's request to keep the story a secret, to keep it out of the paper.

But in December 1999, with the approach of the seventy-fifth anniversary of the Babbs Switch school house fire, he told me the rest of the story.

Mary's parents are dead, Joe said, and her two surviving sisters know the truth, so the truth won't hurt anyone.

"I think it was a tough decision," Joe says of the choice his father, Ransom, made. "I know good and well he was right, and I don't know if I would have had the wisdom to do that or not. I don't see any reason to have hurt that family. ... Can you imagine how you'd feel years later, never having found a body?"

**A**LTHOUGH the mystery now has been laid to rest, this story won't ever really go away.

# Red tongue licking room

IN a little while, in a few short minutes, the night will indeed be still and very silent. But not before shrieks and screams echo off the low-hanging winter clouds that block the angels' view of this spot of Earth. Before the silence of death descends on Babbs Switch, fire will redden the sky.

Christmas Eve, 1924. Minnie and Leona Bolding sing *Silent Night* while one of their brothers, Dow, plays Santa and distributes presents.

The Christmas tree candles bode no ill for their two younger brothers, Gene and Edward. Too excited. Too young to consider that something bad might come from a Christmas tree. Their identical new leather shoes catch the light as their identical new wind-up tarantulas stagger over the desktop they share.

The brothers sit front row, head of the class, at the one-room schoolhouse in Babbs Switch. The rest of the Bolding family is spread throughout the room, anywhere each could find a place. Maggie, Roy, Claude. Mary Alice, their mother, and W.G., their dad.

Other families have come, too — like the Coffeys and the Curtises — arriving from every patch in the six miles between here and Hobart. The school's fifty desks are full, and every other available space is occupied. Later, after the fire, some would estimate that as many as 150 to 200 people had squeezed into the 26-by-36-foot room.

Those who drove the snow-slick dirt highway to the school parked their Model Ts close to the building and then, because the temperature was below freezing, drained the water from their radiators.

The program begins at eight o'clock, and by eight-thirty, the serious part of the Christmas Eve program is over. Six-year-old Gene and eight-year-old Edward aren't too impressed with Santa. The sixteen-year-old inside the red cotton suit, the face behind the white cotton beard, is their brother, Dow, after all. They are engrossed with their new mechanical tarantulas. They don't notice that every time Brother Santa bumps a limb, flames flicker perilously near the brittle needles of the Christmas tree.

At the start of the program, presents surrounded the base of the tree and a few were hanging from its limbs. Now that Santa, with the help of his mother, has

given all the presents from the floor, young Dow removes
sacks of candy from the tree limbs. In the crowd, Lillie
Biggers hugs her new doll, which is nearly as big as she
is. The Bolding brothers' spiders lurch across their desk.

Dow reaches high for a sack and bumps a limb. A
candle holder slips and flips, and the candle
hangs upside down. The cotton and tinsel wrapped around
the tree ignite. Santa tries to snuff the hungry flame,
first with a blanket, then with the sheet that doubles as
a curtain for the podium.

"Look out, Santa Claus," someone in the crowd jokes.
"You're going to catch fire."

Then Santa does.

The flame leaps from the tree to the combustible
suit. One of the Goforth men motions for Gene and Edward
Bolding to follow him. "Boys," he says, "why don't we get
out of here until this settles down?" Mary Alice, their
mother, goes with them.

About this time, eleven-year-old Joe Hebensperger
decides to leave, too. He walks casually to the door, the
only exit. That is the last time Joe will ever see his
nine-year-old brother, John.

At the front of the schoolhouse, the fire hisses and
crackles. The tree topples to the floor, knocking down a
kerosene lantern that hangs from the ceiling. Kerosene
fuels the fire.

'Stay calm," says fifty-five-year-old Tom Goforth.
"We're all going to get out all right."

Hattie Cizek, sitting in the front row with her
brother Mack, nudges him and says in their native Indian
language: "Let's get out of here." He pokes her back,
tells her to hush and sit still. She leaves anyway. At the
door, she stops and looks back. She can't see him.

The folks of Babbs Switch sense that this is about
to grow worse, and seemingly as one, they move toward the
single exit. Lillie Biggers' mother stands to leave, and
in the crush, she drops Lillie and can't find her. Lillie,
only four years old, crawls, following ankles and knees,
dragging her new doll with her. She makes it down the
steps, then realizes she has left her new coat. As Lillie
is about to go back inside the front door, her sister,
Bessie, intercepts her. Lillie discovers that, in her
escape, her new doll has lost an arm.

Inside, the fire spreads rapidly and picks its
victims. Dow Bolding, his suit ablaze, is losing his
fight. Alice Noah, severely burned, hugs her niece, Mary

Elizabeth Edens, close and pushes her way through the mass. Once outside, she hands Mary off to a person in the crowd.

The fire devours the building. Panic becomes hysteria. The door itself is a problem, because it opens to the inside. The crush of hysterical celebrants coming from the back side of the door has pushed it nearly closed. Men, women and children pile up against the door. Others trample them. The pile of people prevents rescuers from pushing the door open. A few break the glass out of windows, only to have their escape blocked by the heavy wire fastened to the windows to keep vandals and tramps out of the school.

When finally they swing the door open, W.G. Bolding, who watched his son, Dow, go down in flames, is pinned behind it. Mary Alice, his wife, lies in the doorway, feet stomping her head.

Roy Bolding, also W.G. Bolding's son, can't move through the throng, so when he spies the space between the heads and the top of the door, he dives for safety. Instead of sailing through, he hits the door frame, crashing into it with such force that it peels back his scalp. He rides out the door on the heads and shoulders of others.

Gene and Edward watch Louis Edens and Andrew Jackson grab people and pull them through the door. Edward realizes he has left his new spider inside the school, and somehow scrambles back through the door. Edward never comes out.

The heat intensifies. The cars parked next to the school catch fire, and soon gas tanks explode.

In the school yard, Hattie Cizek finally sees Mack escaping the building, but he is so badly burned, she hardly recognizes him. When she reaches for Mack's hand, he draws back. He places his burned hands under his armpits, and he and his sister start the two-mile walk home.

The air is cold, and they stumble through patches of snow, but they are too scared to feel it. Before he had left for the program, Mack had put on an extra pair of pants to fend off the cold. Three hundred yards from the burning school, near a railroad crossing, Mack asks his sister to take off the top pair of his pants, which were still burning on his hips. She helps him remove the pants, and they continue toward home at the Indian mission.

A quarter mile from home, Mack tells Hattie to run ahead and find their father. And to bring a quilt, because he is dying. She is afraid to leave him, but he says to hurry and run.

She bursts into the church where her parents are attending a Christmas Eve service, but she is crying so hard that no one can understand her. Finally, she blurts: "Mack wants a quilt! He is dying outside!"

Her father runs out of the church and falls down the steps. He finds Mack curled on the floorboard of a car.

JOE Hebensperger's sister, Helen, drives their car to Hobart with their mother and other passengers who are injured, including Lillie Biggers and her mother, whose flesh is falling off her hands. As they near Hobart, the engine overheats and the car stops because, in their rush, they had forgotten to put water back into the radiator.

In Hobart, switchboard operator Daisy Rogers has received a telephone call telling her about the fire and has alerted the town's doctors.

Gene Bolding and his mother arrive at the home of Dr. E.P. Miles, where rescuers are taking the overflow of patients. Somewhere in the house, a man is crying and screaming.

"Go find that man and find out what is wrong," Gene's mother tells him. "See if you can help him."

Gene finds the man, who is wrapped in a sheet. The man tells Gene that he can't find his family. "Ask him his name," Mrs. Bolding instructs Gene when he reports to her.

Gene goes back to him. The man's name is W.G. Bolding. The man is Gene's father.

Roy Bolding, Gene's brother, shows up at the drug store. No one knows how he made the trip, and Roy doesn't remember. He asks for a Coca-Cola. He constantly brushes his hair out of his face. What Roy doesn't realize is that the hair is his scalp, scraped off when he dove through the air and hit the door frame.

The druggist nearly faints.

IN less than twenty-four hours, newspapers all over the country are reporting the Christmas Eve tragedy in their Christmas Day editions. *The Daily Oklahoman* stretches a big, black headline across the top of its front page:

"32 DIE IN HOBART SCHOOL FIRE"

"Gay Christmas Crowd Turned Into Fear-Driven Mob as Tree Is Set Afire by Lighted Candle"

"HOBART, Dec. 24 — (AP) — More than thirty persons were burned to death in a fire which destroyed a country school, seven miles south of here during a Christmas entertainment Wednesday night.

"Thirty-two bodies had been taken out of the smoldering embers at midnight. ..."

On December 26, the coverage continues, with massive decks of headlines:

"BLACK ASHES ON DIRTY SNOW MARK SPOT WHERE 33 DIED"

"HOBART WILL BURY ITS DEAD TODAY"

"MASS WRITHED, CLAWED, CRIED, TO BREAK OUT"

"THEY LAUGHED AT FIRST, AS FLAME SPREAD"

"Flame Squirmed Like Reptile of Fire, Red Tongue Licking Room"

"HOBART, Dec. 25 — (Special) — "Still night, silent night."

"Cries of Christmas merriments as Babbs Switch folks came for miles to the country schoolhouse to celebrate His birth.

"Then the crescendo — flames pierce the blue-cold night. Harsh screams sobbed on the winds. Hands clawed at mesh-screened windows that would not give. Cries of anguish.

"A sob, a low curse and - 'God, this is awful....'

"It was the end. Sidewalls in the school house crumbled. The Red devil of the night sucked at the front door.

"The devil was full.

"Human cries dulled — slowly — then stopped.

"Tiny flames danced on the blackened wood — sputtered sometimes and then went out. A smoke veil mantled Babbs Switch's funeral pyre and in a spiral loop wound Heavenward for forgiveness from Him."

Graphic and overwrought as they are, the news reports only hint at the devastation. All told, thirty-six people die, although one included in the tally is Mary Elizabeth Edens, who many believe escaped with her Aunt Alice and was then picked up by a passing stranger.

Claude Bolding, badly burned himself, lost two brothers — Dow and Edward, his sister, Maggie, and his fiancee — Gladys Clements, whom he was supposed to have married on Christmas Day. Both of Claude's parents are severely burned.

W.T. Curtis, his wife and their two children died. T.C. Coffey died with his wife and four children huddled in his arms. Vesta Jackson was engaged to Aubrey Coffey. Both died. Brothers Cyril, Paul and Obil Peck perished.

Lillie Biggers' brothers, Walter and William, burned to death.

Rhoda Bradshaw. Juanita Clements Stephenson. Mary Juanita Stephenson. Mary Lois Clements. John Duke. J.T. Goforth. B. Goforth. Mattie Mae Bryan. John Hebensperger. Ernest Peterson. Alice Noah. Lillian Edna Revill. Lee Revill. Florence (Terry) Hill, the twenty-six-year-old schoolteacher at Babbs Switch.

Many of the bodies are so badly burned that identification is impossible. Volunteers dig a mass grave in the frozen ground at the Hobart Cemetery and bury the remains of twenty victims together.

In the Bolding family, the identification of their dead falls to fifteen-year-old Leona and six-year-old Gene. "Be brave," the grownups tell them.

Dow is easy. As he fought the flames, he fell on his back. His red Santa suit still clings to his back. But his head is gone. Next they see Edward. One leg is missing, but they identify him by the new shoe, just like Gene's, on his remaining foot.

At the body that is supposed to be Maggie's, their escort uses a stick to snag a piece of her petticoat, to see if it matches the fabric their mother used for all the girls. As a piece of burned fabric jerks free, the thirteen-year-old's body disintegrates before their eyes. The fabric matches. The body is Maggie's.

SEVERAL days after the fire, Alice Noah dies and her family buries her body next to her husband's, across the dirt road from the mass grave.

Before her death, Alice insisted that she carried her niece, Mary Elizabeth Edens, to safety, and then handed her to someone in the night. But no one ever found Mary, neither in the rubble of the school nor anywhere else.

Mary's grandfather searched the surrounding fields, hoping the three-year-old had wandered away. Occasionally, through the years the Edens would receive word that someone had found their daughter. The occasional newspaper story marking an anniversary would bring reports of sightings.

Then in 1957, thirty-three years after the fire at Babbs Switch school, Mary comes home.

# Long-lost Mary

THIRTY-three years, and the Edens have all but given up hope of ever finding Mary. Thirty-three years. Then the letter arrives.

Not that letters about Mary were anything new. Every year around Christmas, one or another of the Oklahoma newspapers would publish an account of the Babbs Switch fire, and the stories usually included an account of their missing daughter. Papers around the country would pick up the story, and someone would write to the Edens with information they think might be helpful.

But this letter is different.

In the fall of 1956, Elmont H. Place read a story about the fire in a California newspaper. Mr. Place, a district governor of the Lions Club in San Bernardino, was interested because Grace Reynolds, a friend of his, had confided to him that she never had felt at home with her family. She often wondered if she had another past. Mr. Place wondered if the Edens could be her parents.

Place wrote to Wayne Fite, a fellow Lion in Hobart, to ask for information about the Edens family. Fite contacted Betty Reynolds who was born to the Edens after Mary disappeared. (The married names of Mary's sister Betty and Grace were a coincidence.)

Fite wrote back, and his letter illustrates the hope and heartache of the Edens' search.

"Mrs. Reynolds asked me not to contact her parents, because they have only recently closed a similar case where another girl matched the description perfectly and their hopes were built up that the long search had ended, only to find by blood test that they were wrong again. Mr. and Mrs. Edens have carried on a constant search since the night of the tragedy.

"They have had detectives working on this case off and on since that date. They have turned up many finds that they thought were the real thing until some small detail dissolved the whole case."

Mary's sisters sent photographs. By February 2, 1957, they and Grace Reynolds had submitted blood for testing, which couldn't prove for certain that they were related but would show for certain if they weren't.

The clincher was a small scar on the arch of Grace's foot: Mary had a scar like that in the same place.

The reunion occurred February 9. The Edens were

convinced and overjoyed.

"We've been through this several times before when we thought we had found our girl," Ethel Edens told *The Democrat-Chief* for its February 10, 1957, edition. "We were afraid we'd be hurt some more. But this time, it's the real thing."

The story of the reunion made newspapers from California to North Dakota to Michigan. On March 27, 1957, the newly found Mary Edens and her parents appeared on Art Linkletter's television show, "House Party."

But while Grace Reynolds, using her new-found name and fame, was making the celebrity circuit in Hobart, someone in California who knew something of Grace's past was placing a telephone call to the local paper.

THE first hint that Grace Reynolds might not be the Edens' daughter came in a telegram sent to *Democrat-Chief* Editor Al Adams on February 19, 1957. The telegram was sent by Mel Bennet of the Stockton Record, the newspaper in Stockton, California. "CONFIDENTIAL. HAVE INFORMATION GRACE REYNOLDS REPRESENTING SELF AS DAUGHTER OF MR AND MRS L F EDENS YOUR CITY MAY BE IMPOSTER. BELIEVE HER TO BE DAUGHTER OF MRS GOLDIE THOMAS AND FORMER HUSBAND TOM GAITHER. PLS GIVE ADDITIONAL DETAILS MEANS OF IDENTIFICATION FINANCIAL CIRCUMSTANCES OF EDENS. WE WILL EXCHANGE OUR INFORMATION FOR ANYTHING MORE YOU CAN PROVIDE ON THIS CASE."

The Stockton newspaper had learned of the story from Dorothy Link, who telephoned after she saw an Associated Press photograph of Grace with the Edens. Link knew Grace Reynolds. In fact, she claimed to be Grace's sister.

Within weeks, *The Stockton Record* had obtain from Goldie Thomas a notarized statement, dated May 16, 1957, which made this claim: "I hereby certify that Grace Leona Reynolds (nee Gaither) is my lawful daughter. She was born July 11, 1923 on a farm near Cotton Plant (Woodruff County), Arkansas."

In a memorandum to Ransom Hancock, owner of *The Democrat-Chief*, reporter Eugene J. Kuhn summarized his investigation: Grace Reynolds was born in the farm home of an aunt in Arkansas. Grace's mother was attended at birth by Mary Manual, "a Negro midwife, who then was about 45 years old. The date and place of birth are certified by notarized statement."

Kuhn listed three younger sisters. Grace's younger sister, Dorothy, had been married to and divorced from Alfred R. Reynolds. Six years after that divorce, Grace married her sister's ex-husband, Kuhn reported and suggested that anger at Grace may have prompted Link to call the newspaper. Link also noted that Grace's claim made her mother appear to be a kidnapper.

To bolster her claim, Dorothy Link showed Kuhn a letter from her sister Inez Collins, which said in part: "What do you think of sister Grace now? New name, new family, money. She should be pretty well happy, don't you think? That's the most absurd thing I have ever heard of. I'd like to punch her in the nose."

About ten years before this reunion, Dorothy said, Grace had begun to tell people she had no family. When confronted about this, Grace replied that she would be less likely to land a job in a first-rate department store if people knew she came from a "poor people's family."

Kuhn confronted Grace Reynolds with his information and sent this telegram to *The Democrat-Chief*: "GRACE REYNOLDS REACH HER BARSTOW CALIF DRESS SHOP ADVISED OF NOTARIZED STATEMENT.   SAID PLANS CONSULT ATTORNEY BEFORE MAKING STATEMENT. 'I CAN'T MAKE ANY SORT OF STATEMENT AT THE PRESENT TIME,' SHE SAID. ASKED WHETHER SHE PERSISTS IN CLAIM SHES EDENS DAUGHTER, REPLIED 'I'M NOT CLAIMING NOTHING (SIC) AS YET.' HOLD STORY UNTIL WEDNESDAY.   MAY HEAR FROM HER TOMORROW."

The newspapers were close to publishing a story that would rock the town of Hobart, where the return of the long-lost Mary Edens had brought a measure of healing. In a letter to Ransom Hancock, reporter Kuhn concluded: "This letter also will serve to confirm our agreement to break the story simultaneously on Wednesday, May 22, 1957."

But *The Democrat-Chief* never published its story.

NOW that he had what he thought was irrefutable proof that Grace Reynolds was an impostor, Ransom Hancock was honor bound to show his evidence to Louis Edens. Joe Hancock, who took over the newspaper from his father, remembers the day.

"Dad ... went to Louis with this information before Mrs. Reynolds came back in June," Joe says. "Dad took all this information, met with Louis at his house, maybe in the yard. Dad was really shook up having to tell him, and Louis went through the trauma of finding out."

Then Louis Edens asked his friend for a consideration, a favor that kept the story about Grace Reynolds out of the newspaper until Christmas 1999.

Louis Edens said to Ransom Hancock: "Look, my wife believes this girl, she believes she's found her daughter."

Louis Edens asked Ransom to withhold the story until

his wife's death.

"Dad said, 'I just can't run that.' And he didn't," Joe says. "We had the information in the safe at the office in an envelope. Dad took it many years later to Delbert Braun. Delbert was the historian of the Babbs fire. Dad told Delbert, 'Here it is, and I hope you'll honor Louis' request that it be kept secret.'"

Like Ransom Hancock before him, Delbert Braun kept the secret. Then in December 1999, Joe Hancock shared the long-secret letters and telegrams with me even as he decided to publish it in his own newspaper.

"We decided that now is the time to tell it," Joe says. "Some of the people here through the years have questioned Grace's story and are suspicious of it. Every time there's been an anniversary, like the fiftieth, it comes up.

"It's time to get that missing baby deal put to rest; it's over. Now everybody will know for sure."

Joe Hancock concluded his revelation in *The Democrat-Chief* with these words: "Now, 75 years after the fire, with only two known survivors, it's time to set the record right. Mary Elizabeth Edens was not taken from the fire site that night but was in all probability burned with 35 other good Kiowa County folks."

He is proud of his father's decision, which, Joe says, reflects a humanity that's been lost in modern journalism.

"I hope we don't get away from having some feeling for the survivors," he says. "What good would have come from publishing the story? Mr. Edens knew she was a hoax. Mrs. Edens believed the story and accepted her for her daughter. I'm sure that gave her a peace that she never would have gotten."

GRACE Reynolds, who now goes by the name Mary Edens Grossnickle, politely rejects Joe Hancock's conclusion. Forty-two years after she first arrived in Hobart, she still claims she is the Edens' lost daughter.

After years of running restaurants in Idaho and Yellowstone Park, Grossnickle has settled in Colorado, where I reached her by telephone at her home.

The doubters don't bother her. "I really don't care what they think," she says. "It just bounces off of me. There was too many things that proved out before."

Of her younger sister Betty, Mary says Betty was jealous of the attention lavished on her when she returned to Hobart. "My younger sister, she just fully and totally

and completely accepted me too, until the new wore off,"
she said.                             •

Her childhood was rough, she said, and from the time
she was five or six years old, she was farmed out to any
family that needed a hand around the house. Of the
notarized statement by Goldie More, Mary, who is seventy-
eight, wasn't surprised she signed it.

"She was scared," Mary said. "If she wasn't my birth
mother, then she was a kidnapper."

Etta Henderson, who lives in Oklahoma City, is one
of the Edens' daughters. Like everyone else, she was
excited about "Mary's" return and believed they had found
their sister. But after their father learned what Ransom
Hancock had learned, the doubts began. Her parents
traveled to California and visited Grace's birth mother
and two sisters.

Grace and her son lived with the Edens for a while,
and then with Etta and her family. Mary's son Lee still
contacts Etta occasionally, and still calls her "aunt."
Which is fine with Etta; she likes Lee. She has no
illusions, however, about Grace.

"My daddy figured it out real quick, but we did not
want to hurt our mother," says Etta, who is seventy-six.
"I am not saying she is an impostor. I wouldn't. But I *am*
saying she is not my sister."

# Mama looked like a mummy

YOU could walk down the street in Hobart and tell who had been in the Babbs Switch fire. Claude Bolding, a barber in Hobart, wore a hat because the fire scorched his scalp and his hair never returned. The fire burned off both of Lewis Edens' ears. When you saw Margaret Biggers' hands and arms, you knew.

Now most of the survivors are gone. Only four remain, the last four standing: Gene Bolding, who was six. Lillie Biggers Braun, who was four. Joe Hebensperger, who was eleven. Mack Cizek.

Lillian, whose husband, Delbert Braun, is the town's official chronicler of the tragedy, became known as the girl who dragged her doll to safety and then tried to go back inside the one-room school.

As her mother Margaret attempted to leave the burning school with Lillie, she dropped her in the stampede. "I was crawling out, going one way, toward the door," Lillie says now. "I remember the screaming above me. It was the teacher, and she was going the other way.

"I had to crawl off of the porch. I laid the doll down on the step."

She had left her new coat in her desk and wanted to retrieve it. "We didn't get many coats. I was really proud of that — a new coat, new hat, new pair of shoes."

Bessie intercepted Lillie and rescued the doll. Then they piled into the Hebensperger's car, with Helen Hebensperger at the wheel. Both Helen's and Lillie's mothers were badly burned. "Mama was holding her hands up in the air, and the skin was hanging way down. Mother was burnt real, real bad — her head and hands. She had a great big bald spot on her head. She looked like a mummy when they bandaged her up."

Two of Lillie's brothers died in the fire.

EVERY time Gene Bolding talks about that night, which is rarely, he knows he'll pay in troubled sleep shot through with frightening dreams.

For the first forty years after Gene escaped the Christmas Eve fire at the Babbs Switch school, he hardly mentioned it. Then a doctor advised that talk would be therapeutic, that talk would shunt the built-up pain.

So he began to speak it aloud, and now, after thirty years of it, he can tell the story without tears.

Still the nightmares come.

Seventy-five years is a long time to harbor images, but what else can a six-year-old boy do? He was six years old when he saw his brother's Santa Claus suit catch fire, when he had to identify his three siblings.

He and his older sister Leona identified the bodies. Dow was the easiest: his Santa suit hadn't burned off his back. But, Gene remembers, Dow's head was gone.

Edward was missing a leg, but Gene and Leona identified him by the shoe on his other foot. Their sister Maggie was burned beyond recognition. Leona identified her through a swatch of fabric their mother used to make petticoats. Her body crumbled before their eyes.

Gene showed signs of emotional injury right away. He began to stutter, he says, and teachers would spank him because they thought he was putting on. During fire drills, he knocked down children in his haste to exit. Again, teachers thought he was acting out.

"I slept with mother for years. We never had another Christmas tree in our house. Mother would take an orange crate, decorate it with white paper."

His father, who was burned severely, never was right after losing three of his children in the fire. Often, his father would start for town and end up in Arkansas. Gene's parents eventually divorced.

During World War II, Gene was stationed in Brazil with the Army Air Corps when a plane crashed. He was part of the clean-up crew. As he picked up body parts and placed them in a bag, the smell of burned human flesh triggered the memories. "I vomited. I kept sacking and crying."

Gene is eighty-one, and still he fears crowds and unfamiliar places. When he goes somewhere new, he ascertains the location of all the exits. Gene, at the Forum in Los Angeles to see the Lakers play, spent much of the game counting and memorizing the number of paces to all the exits.

"Very seldom," he says, "do I get into a place that I haven't looked over pretty good, to see how to get out of it. I can't understand why it would stay so long with me."

THE Babbs Switch school that burned on December 24, 1924, was replaced in August 1925. When the district was annexed into Hobart and Roosevelt in 1943, Babbs Switch closed for good. Ben Newcomer bought the building at auction and salvaged the brick.

The site of the school is a rest stop now. The

monument there includes the names of the dead; the cornerstone from the brick building is part of the monument.

At the mass grave at the Hobart Cemetery, twenty coffins lie side by side. Here, too, a monument lists the dead. But the lists differ.

The roll on the monument at the grave site includes the name of Mary Edens. The one at the rest stop does not.

The stone monuments are here to stay. Other reminders, like those physically scarred, are disappearing. Etta Edens Henderson's father, who stood at the door pulling people out, lost all the skin on his face and hands and remained hospitalized for six months. He died in 1978.

Many families never again put up a Christmas tree. "We couldn't go to Christmas trees at schools," says Etta, seventy-six. "Their life changed. I was too young to know what it was doing to my mother. I know now. I know what it would have done to me if it had been my son. Life didn't really go on the same for them."

# Thanks

I did the driving, the interviewing and the writing. That was the fun part. A host of others did the real work. To thank the people who made the column and this book happen is to see behind the scenes at the newspaper and to understand how many people really are involved in delivering a newspaper to your front step. These are the people behind the by-lines whose names rarely appear in print but without whom there would be no newspaper.

At *The Daily Oklahoman*, former Executive Editor Stan Tiner gave me the green light for the tour of Oklahoma. Managing editors Mike Shannon and Joe Hight offered plenty of guidance, and Joe gave "Down the Road" its name. *The Daily Oklahoman* Executive Editor Sue Hale's enthusiasm for my project carried me through to the finish.

On the state desk, Mike Perry, Don Gammill, Tony Thornton, Mark Hutchison and Henry Dolive were the editors saddled with the first-run at the editing of my columns. On the city and copy desks, Don Mecoy, Wayne Singleterry, Joan Cuccio, Ed Sargent, John Perry, Graham Underwood and a legion of other nose-to-the-keyboard editors were the ones who gave the columns a second look and wrote headlines for them.

In the art department, Billy Sandlin, Todd Pendleton, Chris Schoelen and Mollie Erkenbrack made sure the map that was published with "Down the Road" was accurate. Billy Sandlin designed the "Down the Road" logo. Chris produced the cover for the book.

*The Daily Oklahoman*'s photography department, headed by Jim Argo, faithfully and without complaint (at least in my presence) processed my film, viewed my negatives and scanned my photographs into the computer system.

From the day I arrived in Oklahoma City, Jennie Herndon and Patti Shubert handled all my logistical needs, procuring with blinding speed all the equipment I needed and answering all my questions.

Sports columnist extraordinaire Barry Tramel taught me the ropes on my laptop and talked me through many a computer question in my first few weeks on the job.

With the guidance of *The Daily Oklahoman*'s Kirk Jewell and Harold Hawkins, who know all about automobiles, the newspaper purchased a 1953 Chevy pickup so that I would look the part as I traveled the state.

Harold Hawkins' crew at Oklahoma Publishing Company's downtown garage made the old pickup safe and comfortable. Ralph Webster's crew at the "Tower Garage" kept the truck clean and its oil fresh.

In our library, Carol Campbell, Billie Harry, Melissa Hayer and Mary Phillips always were quick on the computer when I needed help with research.

Dick Dugan, director of marketing services and promotion, spread the word about "Down the Road" with radio ads and billboards.

Of course, neither the column nor this book would have been possible without the generous support of The Oklahoma Publishing Company, *The Daily Oklahoman* and Edward L. Gaylord, Chairman, President and Publisher.

My job is a newspaper writer's dream come true, and to all of those who have made the new guy welcome at *The Daily Oklahoman*, thanks.

Plenty of people outside the newspaper helped, too. In writing about the Babbs Switch fire, I relied on the past work of Jeff Holladay, Lisa John, Shorty Shelburne, Clara Neal and Jim Jackson. RaDonna Churchwell, who was sixteen at the time, wrote an account for the fiftieth anniversary. In Hobart, Delbert Braun provided invaluable help, as did Joe and Todd Hancock of *The Democrat-Chief* in Hobart. KTOK talk show host Mike McCarville in Oklahoma City provided the expertise and equipment to dub a reel-to-reel tape of old interviews onto cassette.

Glen Zimmer — nom de plume Zen Glimmer — designed the Bigfoot Books logo and drew the illustration for the back of the book. Glen, his wife, Jill, and their daughters Raven and Addi live in downtown Perry, Oklahoma, in a 100-year-old, two-story rock building.

Sandra Busby of Noble gave the book a thorough

reading to transform the work from rough draft to literature (or as close as she could make it, given the raw material she was handed). Sandra and her husband David have taken my family in as their own.

Scott Busby, their son, took command of my computer at home and spent many late-night hours to prepare these pages for the printer. Scott and his family — his wife Glenda, his daughters Amber and Kara, his son David — have given generously of their friendship to the wayfaring strangers they found on their front steps.

Stephanie Buckley, our next-door fellow journalist, understood the importance of this project to my family and encouraged and pushed and prayed at all the right times, which means all the time.

**B**ut only God Himself has given more to my life, my career and this project than my wife Cindi and our daughters, Samantha and Rebekah, who spent many a night without Daddy while I roamed the state.

For twenty-one years, Cindi has walked beside me. She is the one who holds down the fort and cares for the children when I travel for stories. She has read nearly every word I ever have written, usually before my editors ever see the work. And our daughters, well, they are a gift from God. They think I am the best writer ever. With all that is in me, I want always to make them proud. That is a small thanks for the joy they bring to our lives.